Spiritual Barrenness That Leads to Spiritual Fruitfulness

Spiritual Barrenness That Leads to Spiritual Fruitfulness

HANNAH'S JOURNEY FROM BARRENNESS TO BLESSING

E. Truman Herring

WestBow
PRESS
A DIVISION OF THOMAS NELSON

Scripture quotations are from: The New King James Version
Copyright © 1979, 1980, 1982 by Thomas Nelson, Inc.
Used by permission. All rights reserved.

WestBow Press books may be ordered through booksellers or by contacting:

WestBow Press
A Division of Thomas Nelson
1663 Liberty Drive
Bloomington, IN 47403
www.westbowpress.com
1-(866) 928-1240

ISBN: 978-1-4497-7229-1 (sc)
ISBN: 978-1-4497-7228-4 (e)

Library of Congress Control Number: 2012919819

Printed in the United States of America

WestBow Press rev. date: 11/30/2012

Dedication

This book is dedicated to:

My godly mother who, like Hannah, gave me to the Lord from her womb.

And to my wife Connie who, like Hannah, was barren but God made her fruitful.

Contents

THE BURDEN OF THE MESSAGE: THE BLESSING OF BARRENNESS

God has blessed each of us with incredible memories. Every parent can tell you the details of the birth of their children. The date, weight, size, shape, and emotions are all permanently embedded in our minds. We can all remember significant events – both good and bad – that have happened to us.

I vividly remember the details surrounding my conversion. Gripping the pew of the third row of my church in April, 1956, the conviction and illumination of the Holy Spirit brought me to saving faith in the Lord Jesus Christ as I cried out, *"Lord, save me!"* I let go of the pew and took my first step of faith. That date is marked in my mind.

Twenty-nine years later, after serving as a senior pastor for twelve years, I agreed to join the staff of a church in Laurel, Mississippi. I committed to staying there for at least a year before seeking another pastoral position. I missed preaching on a regular basis, but no churches contacted me during that time about becoming their pastor.

In December 1985, I was studying my Bible over breakfast at Shoney's restaurant in Laurel. I was confused and did not understand why God had not opened the door to serve at another church. As I read in 1 Samuel 1 and 2 about Hannah's barrenness, her broken heart and her prayers, I began to identify with her. I read of how God opened her barren womb, and I identified with her faith and rejoicing.

At the same time, I overheard two local pastors in a nearby booth discussing the good news that one of the pastors had been called to a new church. His answered prayer only made me feel worse, that for some reason God had not answered my prayers.

I longed to experience spiritual strength, to be fruitful and to be fulfilled in the ministry – a fulfillment that came not from human recognition, but from divine blessing.

As I read the phrase in 1 Samuel 1:5 *But the Lord had shut up her womb*, I had one of those moments when the Scripture seemed to reach out and grab me. I knew this passage would have significant personal application to my own life. In that moment, I was deeply impressed that God was saying that no church has contacted me because He had "*shut up my womb.*" It was like God had closed the door and I could not open it, no matter how hard I tried. However, with the understanding that God was the One who had closed the door, I came to a point of submission: "*Lord, I will surrender to Your will and am willing to stay in a staff position as long as you desire.*" I reminded myself of a lesson that I had already learned, that my contentment was in the Lord first – and not in the ministry.

As I continued to read of the trial and prayer of Hannah as she struggled with her infertility, God seemed to impress me even stronger that, as He had opened the barren womb of Hannah, He had just answered my prayers, and had given me a new church to pastor. I was filled with such faith and assurance of this that I immediately closed my Bible and hurried home to tell my wife the good news. I rushed into the house to tell Connie, "*God has just given us a church to pastor!*"

She wanted to know if a church had contacted me and how I knew. I said, "*No! But I know God has just answered our prayer.*" I shared my encounter with God as I read how God had shut up Hannah's barren womb and then later how God supernaturally opened her womb. This was not just my emotions trying to make me think positively. This was not some name-it-and-claim-it blind leap of faith based upon my personal desires and bias. This was a moment when God had used the Scripture to make a personal application to my conversation with God that morning.

In about three hours God would confirm that He was the God who both "*shuts the womb and opens the womb.*" The chairman of the Pastor Search Committee of a church in Gulfport, Mississippi called me that afternoon. He began by saying they had been looking very hard for a pastor for nearly two years and had not found the right man. He told me that a lady in their church had a relative who lived in Laurel and had given them my name. Ken told me that, since it was the Christmas holidays, they had not planned on driving up to hear another preacher on Sunday. But, if I was preaching this Sunday, they were willing to drive up, hear me speak, and have lunch with my family. In God's providence, I was scheduled to preach that Sunday morning. Ken agreed that the committee would be there to hear me preach and that they wanted to meet my family and discuss their need of a new pastor.

While we talked on the phone that day, I already knew in my heart something that Ken did not know yet – that I would be his new pastor. I had a peace that did indeed pass all understanding. That Sunday I preached the message God had given me in the restaurant on *The Blessing of Barrenness*. Three weeks later, my family and I moved to Gulfport to pastor that church. God had kept the door closed until the timing was right for me to become their new pastor.

That message, born in my heart out of a burden in 1985, became the basis for this book. Since that time, I have had the privilege of sharing the principles of this message in nations where hearts were open to God. I've seen people move from spiritual weakness to strength, from spiritual unfruitfulness to fruitfulness, and from disappointment and a lack of fulfillment to a deep sense of divine fulfillment in their lives.

Perhaps you are in a season of waiting on God. You're trusting Him and you've poured out your heart to Him. And you are struggling as you wait for His answer. Be strong! Be faithful! God is at work! The rewards are worth it: strength, fruitfulness and fulfillment. Join me as we search God's Word and move from barrenness to blessing.

CHAPTER 1

Hannah: A Woman After God's Own Heart

THE BACK-STORY OF HANNAH'S LIFE

The books of 1 and 2 Samuel were originally one long book in the Hebrew Bible. Tradition tells us that the author was Samuel himself, the prophet God used to shape and establish the kingship in Israel. However, because his death is mentioned in 1 Samuel 25, he could not have written all the content of these books.

Though we are really not sure who wrote 1 and 2 Samuel, we know they are of divine origin, inspired and blessed by God. 2 Timothy 3:16-17 states, *All Scripture is given by inspiration of God, and is profitable for doctrine, for reproof, for correction, for instruction in righteousness, that the man of God may be complete, thoroughly equipped for every good work.*[1]

The book of 1 Samuel starts out, not with Samuel, but with his parents, a couple by the name of Elkanah and Hannah, who lived in the hill country of Ephraim. Their relationship was complicated by two factors: Hannah's inability to conceive children, and the presence of a second wife, Peninnah. The question of polygamy comes up often in studying the Old Testament. Polygamy was never God's intention. The LORD said in Genesis 2:24 that *a man shall leave his father and mother and be joined to his wife, and they shall become one flesh.* God's design was always for one man and one woman to be joined together in marriage: *the two* (not the three) *shall become one flesh.* It is likely that Elkanah married Peninnah because of Hannah's barrenness, so that she might provide him children. Polygamy, though tolerated by God, was never part of His design.

1   Unless indicated, all Scripture references are from The New King James Version of the Bible.

It was this very issue of barrenness that became the point of tension between Hannah and Elkanah – and between Hannah and Peninnah.

Hannah, whose name means "*grace*," was Elkanah's first wife. He loved her greatly, even though she was unable to bear any children. Imagine the shame and guilt she must have felt. She was a failure at her major responsibility as a wife. To make matters worse, Elkanah found someone else, Peninnah, whose name meant "*ruby*," who could give him children. Perhaps this red-head was outwardly even more attractive than Hannah. But certainly she was better at one thing: bearing children.

The biblical record doesn't tell us how many children she bore, but it is plural in number. So for several years Hannah lived under the same roof as this second wife and her children. And as women are prone to do, I'm certain that Peninnah reminded Hannah all the time of her infertility. In fact, verse six tell us, *And her rival also provoked her severely, to make her miserable.*

Did you catch that? *Provoked … severely … to make her miserable.* Hannah didn't ask for this. She didn't even deserve it, because the problem wasn't hers. Verse six ends with the phrase, *because the Lord had closed her womb.*

How could a loving God do such a thing? It was because He had a greater plan and purpose. Even a taunting Peninnah would not thwart God's purpose. Hannah trusted God. She prayed. And God responded.

Hannah eventually did conceive and bear a son, naming him Samuel, which means "*name of God.*" However, the Hebrew pronunciation sounds very similar to the words "*heard by God.*" God had heard Hannah's prayer. She gave Him the glory and herself a reminder by the name she gave to her first-born.

HANNAH'S TESTS OF FAITH AND GOD'S SUPERNATURAL WAY OF BLESSING HER

God is very interested in building the faith of His children. One of His consistent patterns in Scripture seems to be to reveal Himself and then make a promise that must be believed. Once that promise is believed, the answer comes in God's time and God's way. In the process, our faith is often tested to make it stronger and to bring greater glory to God.

This pattern is seen in the life of Abraham. God revealed Himself and gave an unconditional promise to be believed: God would bless Abraham and he would have many descendants. We are told in Romans 4:3 that *Abraham believed God and it was accounted to him for righteousness.* As one who was justified by faith alone, Abraham would continue to show his faith by his obedience in trusting God for the fulfillment of that promise (even into his 90s).

One of the promises that God gave Abraham was to go to the Promised Land. There, God would bless him and make him fruitful (Genesis 12:1-3). Abraham believed God and entered the land – but he was immediately met with a severe test: there was a famine in the land (Genesis 12:10). The natural responses of fear, self-preservation, and the temptation to rely on human wisdom loomed large. Abraham gave in to those temptations and headed toward Egypt where there was food. He was walking by sight and not by faith in God's promise. God soon corrected Abraham for his lack of faith and sent him back to the Land of Promise (Genesis 12:14-20; 13:1-4).

We will see this pattern of God testing and strengthening the faith of His children in the life of Hannah.

THE GREATER PURPOSES OF GOD

Before Hannah's birth and the supernatural birth of Samuel, God foresaw the coming corruption of His Tabernacle through the house of Eli and his wicked sons. God put His plan in motion long before the "*lamp of the Lord went out in the Tabernacle.*" It was God who purposed all things in Christ to raise up for Israel a godly deliverer who would do His will. That deliverer and prophet would be Samuel. Samuel, like Joseph, David, and so many others in the Old Testament, gives us a foreshadowing of Israel's true deliver and the Promised Seed of Abraham in the Lord Jesus Christ.

Thus when we read *the Lord had shut up her womb,* we have to understand that the Master Weaver was weaving the circumstances of Hannah's life into His greater tapestry that magnifies His grace to sinners and His purpose in Christ.

My approach in this study is to find spiritual lessons in Hannah's barrenness and subsequent fruitfulness that parallel God's work in our lives. He brings us to the acknowledgement that we too, like Hannah, are unable to bear lasting, spiritual fruit apart from Jesus Christ.

NOW IT'S YOUR TURN

I would like you to put this book down and to pick up your Bible and read Hannah's story for yourself. You will find it in 1 Samuel chapter 1, verses 1 - 28, and chapter 2, verses 1-11.

Read these verses thoughtfully, perhaps out loud, taking the time to feel the impact of this story. Take a pen and underline or circle anything in the story that stands out to you.

After reading these thirty-nine verses, take a pen and write down answers to these questions:

- What stood out to you in this story? What did you notice that perhaps you had never seen before?

- In what ways was Hannah weak? In what ways did she become strong?

- In what ways was Hannah fruitless? How did she become fruitful?

- In what ways was Hannah unfulfilled? How did she become fulfilled?

- What emotions did Hannah experience? In what ways did she struggle?

- What promises did God make to Hannah? In what ways did He meet the needs of her heart?

CHAPTER 2

The Path to Fruitfulness

We all long for spiritual strength, for fruitfulness and for a greater sense of fulfillment. But these qualities do not come naturally. They only come supernaturally.

We will journey together with Hannah through her tests of faith until she ultimately holds little Samuel in her arms. We will better understand Hannah by looking at her life from the perspective of God's purpose long before her birth. And by looking back at the circumstances of her life and her prayer of praise that magnifies the grace of God in dealing with her. We will see the workings of a Sovereign God who does all things well to bring us to strength, fruitfulness and fulfillment. To try to interpret the historical events of Hannah's life in 1 Samuel 1 without the eternal principles of her prayer of praise in 1 Samuel 2 is to miss many of the secrets of true fruitfulness that apply to our lives today.

The actual historical events around Hannah's life are not accidental, but are the very backdrop for us to compare and contrast the way of the flesh to the way of the Spirit; the law of works and grace, and the continual battle between Satan and our victory in Christ.

In this study, we will see the historical events of Hannah's story as eight tests of faith that believers of all ages pass through in their journey to true spiritual fruitfulness. Although not everyone passes through all of these tests, every believer does have to come to understand that God deals with us from the perspective of what Hannah learned through her test of faith and expressed in her prayer of praise, *for by strength shall no man prevail* (1 Samuel 2:9).

1. BARREN

The first test of faith that Hannah faced was how she would respond to God with her need.

But the LORD had shut up her womb (1Samuel 1:5). Hannah had four reasons to hope in God that He would open her barren womb:

- **The Purpose of the Womb.** God's purpose is birth and life, and not death.
- **The Promise of the Word.** Hannah was convinced that God did not want her to remain barren and unfruitful.
- **The Power of Biblical Examples.** Without God opening the barren womb of Sarah there is not Isaac and therefore no Hannah.
- **The Persistent Burden.** When it is God who *"shuts the womb,"* then only God can *"open the womb."* God had given Hannah a persistent burden that He placed in her heart – and He alone would fill that burden.

2. BENEFITED

The second test of Hannah's faith was to not accept a substitute but wait for God's best. Elkanah tried to satisfy Hannah by giving her a *double portion* (1 Samuel 1:5). Yet even his gifts of love were not enough for her.

It was this same test of faith that Abraham and Sarah failed when they tried to accomplish God's supernatural work by the works of the flesh. Sarah was also unable to conceive, and she suggested that Abraham impregnate her maidservant Hagar. The end result was Hagar gave birth to Ishmael.

The New Testament looks back on this event as an allegory of the contrast between the bondage of the law and our liberty in grace (Galatians 4:21-31). Every believer must pass this test of faith to know true spiritual fruitfulness in contrast to the children produced through religious effort (Galatians 4:26).

- **The Comparison.** There was a difference in the portion of the blessing that Elkanah gave Peninnah and Hannah.
- **The Consolation.** Someone will make up for what God has refused you.
- **The Comfort.** No one can give us comfort when it is God's will for us to suffer in order to bring us to the end of ourselves and make us dependent upon God.
- **The Contentment.** Beware of allowing others to get us to be content with a substitute.
- **The Counterfeit.** We are often tempted to rely on a counterfeit instead of waiting for God's best. In the story of Abraham and Sarah, it was at this time that Sarah would substitute Hagar for her barren womb.

3.   BATTERED

The third test that Hannah faced was a battering from Satan. The adversary will accuse you, condemn you and put you on a guilt trip. He will use other people to attack you, to discourage you, and to betray you.

And her adversary also provoked her (1:6,7). It is intriguing that the biblical record describes Peninnah as an *adversary*. This heightens our understanding of the rivalry and battle that was going on.

There are times we pray but our burdens become heavier, not lighter. Can you trust God and wait on God during these times? We are often burdened and in distress, to the point of wanting to give up and quit. That's exactly what our enemy wants. We will give up if we rely on our own strength. It is in these times that God often allows even greater pressures on the outside to bring us to absolute surrender and dependence upon Him (see 2 Corinthians 4:7-11; 1:8, 9).

- **We Are Battered and Face Accusations from Foes.** Peninnah was not a friend but a foe. Satan inspired her to accuse Hannah.
- **We Are Battered and Face Accusations from the Flesh.** Our own discouragement from the flesh is our greatest enemy to faith.
- **We Are Battered and Face Accusations from Family.** Hannah's husband did not help. Though he meant well, his words in verse eight only exacerbated the problem. Sometimes the advice from family members can hurt more than help. Do you remember the advice Job's wife gave him? She told him to *curse God and die.* That probably wasn't the gentile and quiet spirit that God encourages in wives (1 Peter 3:1).
- **We Are Battered and Face Accusations from Friends.** Friends will often give us sympathy rather than pointing us to God and encouraging us to trust Him. Friends sometimes misunderstand the work of God in our lives and turn from us. But those friends that have a walk of faith and can identify with you will encourage you, build you up, pray for you and keep you on the path God intends for you.

4.   BURDENED

The fourth test of faith was to not let discouragement lead to despair but to let your burden lead you to greater faith in God. *And as he did so year by year, when she went up to the house of the LORD, so she provoked her; therefore she wept, and did not eat* (1:7, 8).

- **The Burden and Patience.** Hannah was a follower of those who through faith and patience inherited the promises (Hebrews 6:12).
- **The Burden and Persecution.** Hannah was hurt over and over without relief. Peninnah's words were relentless. However, she endured. She held up under the pressure and trusted God. Can you tell the difference between your own discouragement and a burden from God? Can you distinguish between your suffering and the sufferings of Christ in you? (see Philippians 3:10).

- **The Burden and Perseverance.** Hannah fasted and would not let go of her burden from God. She would travail in soul before she travailed with a child.

When it is the Lord who has shut the womb, then it is only God who can open the womb. When it is God who has closed some door on you, it is only God who can open the door of fruitfulness. Will you continue to trust Him?

5.   BROKENNESS

The fifth test of faith was how tightly Hannah would hang on to God's blessing. She had to answer the question, who does my womb and the fruit of my womb belong to? Is it God's or mine? Through brokenness, Hannah learned that she had to relinquish her rights and give them back to God. Hannah prayed, *then I will give him unto the LORD all the days of his life* (1:10, 11).

In these chapters, we will look at seven principles of brokenness:

1. **The Purpose of Brokenness**
2. **The Proof of Brokenness**
3. **The Process of Brokenness**
4. **The Pattern of Brokenness**
5. **The Principle of Brokenness**
6. **The Pain of Brokenness**
7. **The Product of Brokenness**

Among the many lessons we will learn are:

- Without brokenness, God's glory is marred.
- Without brokenness, the blessings of God become a curse.
- Without brokenness, man is praised instead of God receiving glory.
- Without brokenness, God's gifts are abused.
- Without brokenness, we experience the fruits of the law and not the fruits of the Spirit.

8.   BLESSED

The sixth test of faith was to find God's will and receive the promise. *Then Eli answered and said, Go in peace: and the God of Israel grant your petition which you have asked of him* (1:17).

- **From Hope to Faith.** Hope precedes faith (Hebrews 11:1).
- **From Perseverance to Faith.** Patience works with faith (Hebrews 6:12).
- **From Faith to Faith:** Faith can grow to greater faith (Hebrews 11:33).

How do we know that we have heard from God regarding our need and prayer? The wise and mature follower of Christ understands that it is by faith.

9.   BELIEVING

The seventh test of faith says: Can we rejoice and thank God before the promise is fulfilled? Hannah did. *And she said, Let your maidservant find favor in thy sight. So the woman went her way, and ate, and her face was no longer sad. Then they rose early in the morning, and worshipped before the LORD, and returned* (1 Sam. 1:18-19).

- **True belief will believe before it can see** (John 20:29).
- **True belief will call that which is not as though it were** (Romans 4:17).
- **True belief will lift your burdens and enter into God's rest** (Hebrews 4:9).
- **True belief will change your behavior.**
- **True belief will hold the answer in its heart before it is actually received.**

Hannah was so sure of her son from the moment that God gave His Word that she did not have to wait for Samuel before she gave God thanks. Once a believer learns to hear from and obtain from God by faith, there is no limitation on what God can do through his or her life. They have learned the secret of fruitfulness.

10.   BETTERED

The eight test of faith: Will I walk with a new faith and dependence upon God in fruitfulness? (1 Samuel 2:1-10).

The paradox of faith and fruitfulness:

Hannah's prayer of praise in chapter two reveals the paradox of the walk of faith and the secret of fruitfulness with God. The paradox is that we cannot prevail with God by our own strength. John 15:5 says that *apart from Him we can do nothing.* In God's great work, the mighty are replaced by the stumbling, the full by the hungry, and the fruitful with the barren of God. It is God's way to bring down the proud and lift up the humble. Thus to bring us to fruitfulness, God often shuts up the womb of our strength to bring us to barrenness. It is when we recognize our barrenness to accomplish God's greater purpose in Christ and walk in dependence upon God, that He opens our barren womb and accomplishes His supernatural work of fruitfulness.

The blessing of barrenness brought Hannah:

- **To brokenness.**
- **To the end of herself.**
- **To faith and dependence upon God.**
- **To total commitment.**
- **To supernatural fruit that blessed her and others.**

Do you have any need in your life that has been met by God where you can say: this is my Samuel for whom I prayed?

Has God created in your heart a deep burden to see God work in such a way that you know that it was not accomplished by your own strength? Have you learned what it means to surrender?

Have you experienced the filling of the Holy Spirit and the abiding life in Christ that leads to fruitfulness?

Our challenge will be that we, like Hannah, may travail in spirit with such a burden to fulfill God's greater purpose in Christ that we will not be satisfied with anything less that God opening the womb that is shut. As we do, we will hold in our hands the thing for which we travailed in prayer.

Are you ready to trust Him?

DISCOVERING OUR BARRENNESS COMES BEFORE OUR GREATER FRUITFULNESS

For it is written: Rejoice, O barren, you who do not bear! Break forth and shout, you who are not in labor! For the desolate has many more children than she who has a husband. Now we, brethren, as Isaac was, are children of promise (Galatians 4:27-28).

If we are ever going to see fruitfulness in our lives, it is important that we identify with those in the Bible who were barren. There are great lessons for us to learn when we understand that in a spiritual sense, we are all barren in relationship to spiritual children and eternal fruit.

But do you know what the biggest trap is that we fall into? It is the trap of appearances.

There is much that we can do for God that gives the appearance of fruitfulness. We look so good, so busy, and so religious. But is it really eternal fruit? Or is it only temporal? Will it stand at the Judgment Seat of Christ or will it be like wood, hay and stubble that are burned up?

The Pharisees certainly gave the outward appearance of service to God only to have Jesus expose their works as to be seen of men and not God.

There is a difference between *"working for God"* and *"God working through us."* Moses was working for God when he first attempted to deliver Israel from Pharaoh with his sword. He failed in his fleshly effort, and ended up on the backside of the desert for forty years. But when Moses returned forty years later, he had learned dependence on God. This time he came with a simple shepherd's staff – but in the hands of a dependent one, it became the rod of God, and God worked through Moses mightily.

It's easy to get the two confused, however.

It is often the case that before salvation, we attempted to establish our own righteousness through our "works" only to discover later that they were "dead works" which could not justify us before God (see Hebrews 9:14). After we understand that, in our lost state we are incapable of good works that will please a holy God, we placed our faith in the perfect, complete and finished work of Christ. At salvation we discovered that we were powerless in relationship to God and eternal fruitfulness.

Abraham discovered that he was unable in his flesh to save himself and to produce a line of descendants. He had to die to his own self-effort and trust God by faith alone.

Before we discover our own spiritual barrenness, we work for righteousness, and we work to produce our best self-efforts to gain favor with God. But once we discover that we are barren to bring forth spiritual fruit, we *"do not work"* as in Romans 4:4-5, and we *"cease from our own works"* as in Hebrews 4:10. From such a position of spiritual barrenness and with no faith in ourselves, we are in a position to place our faith in God alone and have many children and bear much eternal fruit (see Hebrews 4:9, 10).

Romans 4:4 says, *Now to him who works, the wages are not counted as grace but as debt. But to him who does not work but believes on Him who justifies the ungodly, his faith is accounted for righteousness.* Righteousness is a gift from God that originated at Calvary. We receive God's righteousness, not as a result of our works, but by grace through faith … it is a gift of God by which no one can boast (Ephesians 2:8-9).

Hebrews 4:9-10 tells us that *there remains therefore a rest for the people of God. For he who has entered His rest has himself also ceased from his works as God did from His.*

Jesus taught His disciples that they were to *"abide in Him."* He reminds us in John 15:4-5, *Abide in me, and I in you. As the branch cannot bear fruit of itself, except it abide in the vine; no more can you, unless you abide in Me. I am the vine, you are the branches: He who abides in Me, and I in him, bears much fruit:* **for without Me you can do nothing** (emphasis mine).

By coming to an understanding that we are just as barren as Sarah was to produce God's Isaac, we are in a better position to believe God to supernaturally open our spiritual wombs.

God calls on us, as the barren of God, to rejoice in the promises of God and in our many children yet to come (Galatians 4:27). Remember, for the desolate (in our case the spiritually barren) has many more children than many of the religious who work so hard for God. The Church today gives birth to far too many *"Ishmaels"* who are the *"strange born"* fruit of the law. Carnal means of the flesh might seem to market or motivate people into the kingdom of God. But they are not of the work of the Holy Spirit convicting and illuminating men's hearts to produce regeneration, repentance and faith.

In this book we will glean principles and lessons from Hannah's barrenness and learn the destiny God has designed for His children.

God revealed Himself as the *"God of Abraham, Isaac, and Jacob."* It is interesting that barrenness was an issue with all three of these fathers. If God were not the God that opened the barren womb, then Isaac and Jacob would have never been born. All three were part of the promise that through their seed would come the chosen seed, which is Jesus Christ. Yet, all three were helpless to produce that promised son.

WHAT LESSON DOES THIS HAVE FOR US?

Abraham, Isaac, and Jacob were all tested by barrenness and brought to the place where they understood that only God could fulfill the promises and open the barren womb supernaturally.

We must admit that we too have a spiritually barren womb and trust God to open our lives to eternal fruitfulness by abiding in Christ. I am afraid that so many in religious circles have now turned to the methods of marketing, motivation, and human wisdom rather than the miracle of the supernatural to bring forth the children of God.

As I studied through the Bible and learned these lessons of strength, fruitfulness and fulfillment, I wrote the following poem a few years ago to express what I was learning.

Rejoice Thou Barren

From the barren womb, a baby is born
Preceded by a heart, broken and torn
A womb of hope, emptied of dreams
Brings forth God's prophets and kings

The barren of God will travail twice
Once to die to self, and once to His life
Not from Hagar's womb that is alive
But from Sarah's dead womb will Isaac arise

Sarah, Rebekah, and Rachael cries
Give me children, lest I die
Hannah, Elizabeth, and Manoah's wife
To the barren womb, God gave supernatural life.

Isaac, Jacob, and Joseph came
To barren wombs who knew great pain
Samuel, John, and Samson strong
From the barren womb, God did call

When God will visit with mercies to man
He fills the barren with His great plans
Broken, humbled, and brought to our end
Emptied of self, then His great work He begins

With God, is the secret of the barren soul
Greater fruit than you, could ever behold
The dying, the pruning, and the abiding, precedes
The greater harvest of souls that on Christ will believe

So rejoice thou barren and believe to see
More children of faith to come from thee
Like Abraham counted his seed like the stars
Many children of faith will be like you are. [2]

My dear friend, you may wonder what barrenness has to do with you. Perhaps you feel content in your walk with God. Perhaps you can point out a ministry that has blessed many, and you feel that your life is making a difference for Christ. But the lessons of fruitfulness are for us all. Our God, as with Hannah, often *"shuts the womb,"* before He *"opens the womb"* to fruitfulness that can only be explained as supernatural.

Each of us has a God-appointed purpose in Christ. Left to ourselves, what we do for God will fall short of that greater purpose in Christ. Thus, God often chooses some area of our life in which, like Hannah, He will purposely close the womb in order to bring us to greater fruitfulness.

In this sense, we all have many lessons to learn about strength, fruitfulness and fulfillment in God. My barren experiences have been many, but from them I have experienced the greatest fellowship with Jesus and have seen God do more through my barren womb than all my struggles to bring forth fruit for God.

My wife and I have identified with Hannah in a physical way as well, when we discovered that after nine years of marriage that we were physically barren and could not have children of our own. Later in this book, you will hear that our story, like Hannah's, has a God-blessed ending.

---

2   E. Truman Herring, © copyright 2006.

CHAPTER 3

How We See Life Affects How We Live Life

As you read through the first two chapters of 1 Samuel, I hope you noticed the comparison and contrast between the two women: barren Hannah with no children, and fruitful Peninnah with many children. But that was simply their outward appearance.

In this chapter we will see a very important principle that you must understand: *how we see life affects how we live life.* Do we see life from a human perspective? If so, our focus will be limited, short-termed and faulty. If we see life from God's perspective, we will realize that He is in control and we will see life through the lens of His sovereignty, grace and goodness.

And he had two wives; the name of the one was Hannah, and the name of the other Peninnah: and Peninnah had children, but Hannah had no children…. And when the time was that Elkanah offered, he gave to Peninnah his wife, and to all her sons and her daughters, portions: But unto Hannah he gave a worthy portion; for he loved Hannah: but the LORD had shut up her womb (1 Samuel 1:2, 4-5)

The bows of the mighty men are broken, and those who stumbled are girded with strength. Those who were full have hired themselves out for bread, and the hungry have ceased to hunger. Even the barren has borne seven, and she who has many children has become feeble (1 Samuel 2:4-5).

"Children Are a Blessing. Being Childless Is a Curse"

In Biblical times, it was thought that barrenness was a curse. Every young woman lived with the hope of having a husband and many children. To marry and then discover that you could not bear children had disastrous results:

- To fail to fulfill your husband's desire to carry on his family name and heritage could mean disappointment, hatred and even rejection from him.
- Barrenness could mean disappointment and anger from your own family and village.
- Other women might mock you and make it quite clear that you were somehow inferior, a freak of nature, and cursed by God.
- Personally, a barren woman could feel isolated, lonely and deserted. Her self-esteem and identity would be skewed by her infertility.
- A barren woman could even blame herself and feel guilt, social rejection and blame herself as a failure.
- Finally, she could even become angry with God and question, *"Why have you made me barren and shameful?"*

 ## How Do You Think Hannah Felt?

- Perhaps the whispers of the town's women followed Hannah wherever she went: *"There goes poor Hannah. I feel sorry for her husband. But at least he has one good wife that can give him as many children as he desires."*
- Perhaps she felt like an outsider. Rejected, alone, never included. Have you ever felt like that? Have you ever sensed rejection and suffered from the embarrassment and pain of failure? That was Hannah's lot ... at least from a human perspective.
- Can you image the dreams that Hannah had for children year after year and yet they remained unfulfilled? Can you identify with some area of your life in which you to have dreamed but your dream seems like it is only vain hopes?
- Maybe she got up every day believing Elkanah was disappointed in her. How would you feel if you believed your spouse was secretly disappointed with you because you could not fulfill his or her needs? Do you feel disappointment or rejection from a spouse, a friend, or a family member? Every day she was met with Peninnah's barbs and judgments. Maybe there is a person in your life that finds your weakest point of disappointment and exploits it and abuses you with it. Is there someone who finds pleasure by going out of their way to keep you down by exalting themselves at your expense? Can you identify with Hannah as you too have experienced one or more who seem to go out of their way to tear you down? Many Biblical characters went through such an experience. We will find that God used Saul in David's life, much like God used Peninnah in Hannah's life, to prepare David for God's greater fruitfulness.
- Did Hannah begin to blame herself for her miserable condition? Did she suffer from low self-esteem and depression? Did she question God's love for her? Did she ever wish that she weren't even born?

- Did she get angry at the silence of God month after month, year after year? There was no one else to blame for her infertility but God. Can you blame her? If an earthly, this-life-only perspective is our only alternative, Hannah would be right to be angry and justified at questioning God.

 ## MIRROR, MIRROR ON THE WALL

If we had Peninnah and Hannah stand side by side, most people in Israel in 1100 BC would have chosen Peninnah to be the fairest of them all. She was the blessed one, the favored one. Surely, there was something wrong with Hannah. She would not have had much of a chance in the beauty contest of outward blessings.

However, we must not evaluate our worth based on our circumstances. Our physical beauty, the size of our bank account, our standing in society, or our accomplishments and successes in this world, does not determine our worth. We have God's Word that tells us the truth about who we are and what is ultimate reality. God's Word has the ability to change us from an ugly and evil child of Adam to a transformed child of God in Christ.

AN ALTERNATIVE STANDARD

There is an incredible principle embedded in 2 Corinthians 3:18. That verse states, *But we all, with unveiled face, beholding as in a mirror the glory of the Lord, are being transformed into the same image from glory to glory, just as by the Spirit of the Lord.*

The idea is that we are progressively being changed into the image of Jesus Christ. It's a process that takes time, trust and cooperation with the Spirit of God. It is based on truth – because the truest thing about you is what God says about you.

For the one who believes and trusts in the Lord Jesus, what appears to be bad – a problem, a storm, a trial, or an attack – is really an opportunity to see God at work in your life in a greater way.

- Abraham failed to learn about trusting God in the midst of a famine. His son, Isaac, discovered that a hundredfold-harvest was possible with God in the time of famine.
- Jacob thought that the famine of his day was working against him. His son, Joseph, knew that God was taking everything in his life, including the impending famine, and was working it all together for his good (see Genesis 50:20).
- What you may feel is a closed door may be God's directing you to His greater open door of blessings.

One of the keys to understanding the secret of fruitfulness lies in Hannah's prayer of praise in 1 Samuel 2:4-9. This praise song from Hannah's lips underscores an unchangeable principle of God in His dealings with His children. The sooner we learn God's ways, the sooner we will discover that Jesus is not only our burden bearer but also our very Life. The more you struggle and resist God's process to move you to fruitfulness, the more you will crash into the doors God has sovereignly closed in your path.

Notice the words of Hannah's praise song:

> *The bows of the **mighty** men are broken,*
> *And those who <u>stumbled</u> are girded with strength.*
> *Those who were **full** have hired themselves out for bread,*
> *And the <u>hungry</u> have ceased to hunger.*
> *Even the <u>barren</u> has borne seven,*
> *And **she who has many children** has become feeble.*
> *The LORD **kills** and <u>makes alive</u>;*
> *He **brings down** to the grave and <u>brings up</u>.*
> *The LORD **makes poor** and <u>makes rich</u>;*
> *He **brings low** and <u>lifts up.</u>*
> *He <u>raises the poor</u> from the dust*
> *And <u>lifts the beggar</u> from the ash heap,*
> *To <u>set them among princes</u>*
> *And <u>make them inherit</u> the throne of glory.*
> *For the pillars of the earth are the LORD's,*
> *And He has set the world upon them.*
> *He will <u>guard the feet</u> of His saints,*
> *But the wicked shall be **silent in darkness**.*
> *For by strength no man shall prevail* (1 Samuel 2:4-9, emphasis mine).

In these six verses, I've highlighted in **bold** those who, from an earthly perspective, seem to have it all. They are mighty! They are full! But notice what happens: they are killed, made poor and brought low by God. Those who have many children become feeble. Their ultimate fate is silence in the darkness.

In contrast, I've <u>underlined</u> phrases that describe those who don't seem to be blessed with earthly things. They stumble and hunger. What happens to them? They trust in God. As a result, they are girded with strength; they have been made full and are no longer hungry. The barren becomes fruitful. God makes these people alive; they are made rich, lifted up, raised up from the dust, lifted from the ash heap, set among princes and made to inherit the throne of glory. God Himself guards their feet.

But it is the last phrase of verse nine that summarizes everything up to that point: *for by strength no man shall prevail*. What does that mean? God spoke directly to the prophet Zechariah and said, *Not by might nor by power, but by My Spirit, says the Lord of hosts* (Zechariah 4:6).

As we look closer into the mirror of God's Word, we will find that we identify with the men and women of faith and see ourselves in Jesus Christ. But we also must see our old sinful self in the illustration of the flesh to see ourselves as those who battle our flesh, our old identity in Adam. The old Adam in us works tirelessly to find something – anything – for which he can get some kind of credit. But there is nothing in our flesh that can please God.

Consider the following comparison of the two women. Sometimes we look like Peninnah and sometimes we look like Hannah:

- The Natural Way of Blessing: Peninnah. She was mighty, full, fruitful, alive, rich, and a princess.
- The Supernatural Way of God's Blessing: Hannah. She was stumbling, barren, hungry, dead, poor, and a peasant

One of the keys seems to be in the names of these two women. Remember, Peninnah's name means *"ruby."* Perhaps it described her physical beauty and attractiveness. But Hannah's name means *"grace."* Grace is never earned, never deserved. It is the free gift of God.

God ultimately blessed Hannah, not because she deserved it, not because she was better than Peninnah, or had done more religious activities than her rival. It was simply because she trusted God. She sought Him *by faith*. And God is always a rewarder of those who seek Him by faith (see Hebrews 11:1-6).

We see this same principle in effect at the birth of Jesus. The Holy Spirit would conceive in Mary's womb the Promised Seed who is our Lord and Savior, not because she was deserving … but because she was *graced by God*. And she sang,

> *My soul magnifies the Lord, and my spirit has rejoiced in God my Savior. For He has regarded the lowly state of His maidservant; for behold, henceforth all generations will call me blessed. For He who is mighty has done great things for me, and holy is His name.*
>
> *And His mercy is on those who fear Him from generation to generation. He has shown strength with His arm; He has scattered the proud in the imagination of their hearts.*
>
> *He has put down the mighty from their thrones, and exalted the lowly. He has filled the hungry with good things, and the rich He has sent away empty* (Luke 1:46-53).

As you read those verses, you may have noticed some familiar language. Read the last four lines again and notice the words *mighty, lowly, hungry, and rich*. Do those words sound familiar? Those are the very words Hannah used in her prayer to God.

How do you see life? Are you a *victim* or are you *blessed*? Are you *trying to please God* or do you trust *Him because of all that He has done for you?* Are you *disappointed in life* or have you recognized that *everything in your life is filtered through the lens of a loving, heavenly Father? Every good gift and every perfect gift is from above, and comes down from the Father of lights, with whom there is no variation or shadow of turning* (James 1:17).

 ## UNDERSTANDING GOD'S PRINCIPLES OF FRUITFULNESS

And he had two wives: the name of one was Hannah, and the name of the other Peninnah. Peninnah had children, but Hannah had no children…. But to Hannah he would give a double portion, for he loved Hannah, although the LORD had closed her womb (1 Samuel 1:2, 5).

Notice the phrase, *But the Lord had closed her womb.* The original King James translation says that God *shut up her womb.* That seems to emphasize the forcefulness and finality of it all. Her husband loved Hannah even more than Peninnah but *the Lord had shut up her womb.* Elkanah loved her but that did not solve her problem of barrenness. No matter what good things you might be able to say about Hannah, a giant neon light hung over her head flashing the words *"But she had no children."* She did not have what mattered most ... and she was grieved.

No matter how successful we might become, no matter what heights we may achieve, at the end of our life none of that matters. If the epitaph on our grave marker is "unfruitful," we will have misspent our lives. As a Christian, no matter what you may accomplish in life, if you are spiritually barren it means little in eternity.

PRINCIPLES OF INTERPRETATION

One of the ways that I like to study Scripture is to look at the big picture first and interpret all of Scripture through the lens of *God's Greater Purpose in Christ.* Life is not about us ... it is about Jesus Christ.

And though the story in 1 Samuel chapters 1 and 2 accurately records the events of Hannah's life, there is a greater story at work – the story of God's Greater Purpose in Christ. It is not about Hannah first; it is about Christ first. It is not about me first, and the problems that I am going through like Hannah but it is about how Hannah fits into God's bigger picture and God's Greater Purpose in Christ. The same is true of us. [3]

And before the lamp of God went out in the tabernacle of the LORD where the ark of God was, and while Samuel was lying down ... Then the LORD said to Samuel: Behold, I will do something in Israel at which both ears of everyone who hears it will tingle (1 Samuel 3:3, 11).

God had a greater purpose than Hannah. He wanted to correct the idolatry and disobedience in Israel and restore the nation back to Him. He also wanted to prepare David to sit on Israel's throne, ultimately laying the groundwork for the King of Kings who would come from the lineage of David.

To accomplish all of that, God used a simple, barren Hebrew wife who had been the victim of her rival's ridicule and scorn. God always gets His way ... and He uses the weak and dependent to accomplish His purposes.

A second way that we will study this theme of God preparing us for fruitfulness is to remember that the Word of God and the Old Testament in particular is written by God progressively revealing Himself until we have His full revelation in Jesus Christ and the completion of the New Testament. Therefore we look back on the barren like Hannah through the lens of the full New Testament revelation of God's Word and principles.

Beyond the normal rules of interpreting Scripture in its context, language, and culture, we also know that the Scripture is a commentary upon itself and its topics and characters are not isolated but woven together into God's tapestry of Truth. Thus we will seek to weave Hannah to all in

---

3   See *God's Greater Purpose in Christ*, E. Truman Herring.

Scripture who are struggling with fruitfulness to better understand the secrets of fruitfulness that God has for us.

Hannah, like most Jewish girls, dreamed of a happy marriage with many loving children. Before Connie and I were married, she was given a beautiful hope chest. It was made of cedar and just to open it sent out an aroma of cedar and hope. It was quite large, four feet long and two feet in depth and width. It was meant to hold many of Connie's dreams for our marriage. One of those dreams would be like Hannah's to have children of her own. To that dream Connie's hope chest would become more of a casket with a miscarriage but no child from her own womb. Connie and I continued to hope for nine years before we gave into the admission that we were barren.

We are not told how long Hannah was married before she realized that she was barren. It was obviously a period of many years. From month to month, year after year, she must have hoped, *"This could be the month I get pregnant."* Despite the shame from her culture and the pain in her heart, God was at work in her life. Her inability to conceive children was not a sign of God's displeasure. He was working out His greater plan and purpose in Jesus Christ.

God has made His children to hope. He identifies Himself as the *"God of all hope."* Without hope we cannot face tomorrow. Hannah had to keep opening the hope chest of the Word of God and be refreshed by the fragrance of God's love. She could not and would not let her hope chest become a casket to her God given dreams.

But God had shut up her womb. Let's examine this phrase from several perspectives.

How did Hannah interpret her circumstances? Obviously she knew that she had been unsuccessful at having children in contrast to her husband's other wife who had many children. She knew that her husband Elkanah was not sterile. Many would just see this as a health issue that perhaps time would heal. Others may have seen it as a chance issue and in one of the future months she would get lucky and get pregnant. It seems that no matter what her husband or Peninnah thought in their hopeless labeling of Hannah as barren, she still had a firm hope in God that would not let hope die.

She brought her case to God year after year. She pleaded her case, as did Abraham and Sarah, to God as a loving Father. She held on to hope when all hope was gone, like a mother who would die before she would let her child die. God Himself had impregnated her with hope and she would go through the labor pains until hope turned to the faith that obtains promises from God (Hebrews 11:33). She came to God as a daughter of Abraham and like him, *after he had patiently endured, he obtained the promise* (Hebrews 6:15). She yearly followed the footsteps of the faithful Abraham to worship God and prove herself a daughter of Abraham in her hope in God. Against the pain of her barrenness, she hoped in the God of fruitfulness. Even though Romans 4:18 describes Abraham's faith, it can equally be applied to Hannah's faith: *Who against hope believed in hope, that he might become the father of many nations, according to that which was spoken, so shall your seed be.*

One of the signs that you are maturing in grace is that you don't hope in hope. You hope in Jesus, so you hope well beyond what you can see. Is there a time in your life where you can say you "saw" with the eyes of faith and hoped against hope because your hope was in Jesus?

Certainly the words of Jesus should give us hope as well that we are not His unfruitful children but have been chosen to bear much fruit (John 15:16).

How do you interpret that area of your life where God may have shut up your womb? God will design an area of your life in which He will teach you that you are barren and that *without (Jesus), you can do nothing* (John 15:5). Have you given up hope that your prayers will ever be answered? Have you tried to knock down doors that God has shut? Have you like Jacob tried to manipulate God and man to accomplish what you think is God's will?

But God had shut up her womb.

From heaven's perspective, God had a blueprint for Hannah that was related to a much bigger picture than Hannah's calendar and personal agenda. God has purposed His will before time began and we are chosen to fit into God's purpose and timetable and not our own.

Hannah was deeply burdened by her inability to conceive. But what Hannah could not see was the future of the Priesthood was at stake through Eli's evil sons. She did not understand that God would not let the *lamp of the Lord go out in the Tabernacle of the Lord* (1 Samuel 3:3). She did not understand that God had planned before her birth that her son Samuel would be a prophet, a Judge and a leader of Israel. She did not understand how God had also chosen her son to be part of God's greater purpose in Christ and that God would promise Christ as His faithful anointed priest that would serve before Him forever.

Whatever problems you face in life remember that we see only today. But God's plan is much bigger and we must trust Him and remember *"all things work together for our good and His glory"* (see Romans 8:28).

CHAPTER 4

Barren

And he had two wives: the name of one was Hannah, and the name of the other Peninnah. Peninnah had children, but Hannah had no children…. But to Hannah he would give a double portion, for he loved Hannah, although the LORD had closed her womb (1 Samuel 1:2, 5).

 THE FIRST TEST OF FAITH

God takes Hannah through a series of eight tests of faith, designed to strengthen her, deepen her faith, and bring glory to God. The first test of faith is this:

How will she respond to God with her need?

AN OPPORTUNITY TO TRUST

God often creates a need in our lives to grow our faith. That need often comes from a disappointment we experience. For some, it is the loss of a job; for others it may be a health issue, while for others, perhaps a divorce or the death of a loved one. At other times, it may simply be a challenge we face.

Do you remember the story in the Gospels where the disciples encountered a fierce storm on the Sea of Galilee? The winds and waves were about to sink their boat – and Jesus was asleep on a cushion. The disciples quickly woke Him up and said, in what sounded like an accusation, *Do You not care that we are perishing?* (Mark 4:38). Jesus arose, rebuked the wind and waves – and there was a great calm on the sea. But then He turned to the disciples and said, *Why are you so fearful? How is it that you have no faith?* (4:40). That last phrase, *how is it that you have no faith,* is very powerful. The word *you* is emphatic. The idea is, *how is it that YOU, you who have followed Me day after day, have no faith?*

It's obvious from reading this story that what was uppermost in the purpose of Jesus was to increase the disciples' faith. Can you identify with that? Think back over the last few years of your life. What circumstance was there that challenged you? What fears did you face? What disappointments did you experience?

As you look back on those days, can you see the sovereign hand of God at work? Ask yourself these questions:

- Did my trial catch God by surprise? Was He even aware of what I was going through?
- What did I learn through that experience?
- Did my need or problem drive me closer to God, to live in greater dependence on Him – or did I allow it to drive me further from God? It is critical that our need not drive us *from* God but *to* God.

Hannah had such an opportunity to trust God. Through her inability to conceive, she was faced with a series of choices:

- Would she trust God – or would she lose heart and become discouraged?
- Would she obey God – or would she become rebellious against Him?
- Would she praise God no matter what – or would she become bitter?
- Would she allow her barrenness to define her – or would she make the right choices so that her faith would define her?
- Would she despair – or would she have hope?

Hannah had reason to hope that she would one day bear children. That hope was not based on her physical condition. Her womb had proven to be closed. But her hope was in God and His promises. Hope precedes faith and helps us seek God and His mercies. Hebrews 11:1, 6 says, *Now faith is the substance of things hoped for, the evidence of things not seen…. But without faith it is impossible to please Him, for he who comes to God must believe that He is, and that He is a rewarder of those who diligently seek Him.*

Hope is based on the person and character of God. We hope in God before we receive a specific promise from Him about our need.

REASONS TO HOPE

Hannah had four reasons to hope in God that He would open her womb:

1. THE PURPOSE OF THE WOMB

God created the womb for birth and placed a natural longing in women to have children. At Creation, God said *be fruitful and multiply* (Genesis 1:28). God has also spoken to every believer and said that His purpose for us is to be fruitful. Jesus said, *You did not choose Me, but I chose you and appointed you that you should go and bear fruit, and that your fruit should remain, that whatever you ask the Father in My name He may give you* (John 15:16).

WE WERE DESIGNED TO BE FRUITFUL

Spiritually, every believer has a God-given responsibility to bear fruit. Just as God created Hannah to give birth to the prophet Samuel, God's purpose is for us to also bear fruit and to be vessels through whom many of God's choice servants come to Christ. Our God is not only the God of hope. He is the God of purpose as well. Nothing God ever planned is without purpose. Look at the masterpiece of the stars. They declare the glory of God throughout the heavens and move in their orbits in orchestrated precision. There is a design and purpose to Creation.

Hannah knew that there was a design and purpose to her womb as well. That womb was not a tomb. To Hannah, barrenness did not fit into God's purpose for her life. In hope against hope, she believed. And that hope carried her through the days of discouragement and gave her strength in the face of the many discouraging voices she heard.

SETTLING FOR A LESSER DESTINY

One day I came face to face with a great American bald eagle. I stared in awe at his beauty and size. He looked so powerful. I imagined how with his great strength he could swoop down from the sky and capture his prey and carry it back with his powerful wings up to the mountains. God had equipped him with powerful talons and a beak able to rip apart his meal to share with his eaglets.

My interest in the eagle was piqued because I had recently preached a message entitled *"Carried on the wings of the eagle and our rest in God."* I remembered Isaiah 40:31 where God's promises His power to the weak and allows us to *mount up with wings like the eagle.* I thought of how such a large eagle could simply raise its mighty wings and let the power of the wind carry it without effort over the mountain heights.

But as I looked into the eagle's eyes, I saw something I had not expected. It was not the alert look of a mighty hunter that noticed every movement around him. It was the look of boredom and defeat. Why? I wasn't in one of our grand National Parks. I was at the zoo. I was staring into the eyes of a caged eagle – not one that was free in the wild.

How long had it taken that magnificent eagle to surrender its purpose and destiny for a cage? God the Creator had programmed into that eagle's DNA a purpose to fly to great heights. But this great bird had apparently given up hope that he would ever fly again.

In contrast to that caged eagle, an empty womb could not cage Hannah's hope. She had a firm confidence that God had a greater plan for her life – that her womb would one day carry His gift of a child.

My Story

I've learned these lessons the hard way. There was a day that I served Christ half-heartedly. Later I tried to serve him with zeal and grew weary with all my Christian commitments of service. In both attempts I failed to find fulfillment and rest. I was living and ministering in my flesh, attempting to please God with self-effort.

Then I discovered what Hannah knew, that *by strength shall no man prevail.* The eagle soars not by his own strength but by the lift of the unseen wind. I know when the Holy Spirit, like the eagle, carries me, and I know when I am struggling in my own strength. We do not live the Christian life in our own efforts. It is by His power and strength.

Paul writes about this truth in Galatians 2:20. *I have been crucified with Christ. It is no longer I who live, but Christ who lives in me. And the life I now live in the flesh I live by faith in the Son of God, who loved me and gave himself for me.*

Several years ago I wrote the following poem to express this idea of the exchanged life – that we are able to mount up on wings like eagles and soar, not because of our own strength and ability … but because of the grace and power of the Lord Jesus Christ who lives inside of us and empowers us daily.

Eagles Wings and the Cross

I walked but then fainted
With the cross I did bear
I ran to do God's will
But grew weary with my cares

I did not mount up like eagles
Carried by the Spirit's wind
I did not know the power
That begins where my life ends

But in my weakness I discovered
Two crosses made for me
One that I took and carried
And one cross that carried me

By faith we must discover
The two deaths of His cross
There Jesus died for my sins
And there I died with Him

Wait upon the Lord
And soar with eagle's wings
By faith exchange your life
For the Life His cross will bring [4]

---

4   *Eagles Wings and the Cross*, E. Truman Herring, © copyright 2005.

GOD'S DESIGN FOR YOUR LIFE

From the moment that you were born again, God put in you a spiritual DNA to produce spiritual fruit. We cannot be content to be caged in a man-made religion. God made us for better things – to soar with His Spirit and to be fruitful in our service for Him.

Unfortunately, so many settle for a lesser destiny. I have known thousands of Christians. In the eyes of most, you will see discouragement and defeat. They have accepted the status quo. They have settled into a religious routine of going to church once a week, reading the Bible occasionally, and serving in small ways in the ministry of the church. But the rest of their lives are their own to live as they please.

In the eyes of other Christians, there is a spark of faith to fulfill a God-given destiny. They know they have been called to bear fruit. They refuse to follow Jesus half-heartedly. They will not be caged by living lives equal to those around them. They expect God to show up and work in and through their lives every day. These eagle-like saints of God know it is God's purpose that their lives make a difference in the kingdom of God.

Stop here just for a moment. Take a spiritual inventory of your life. Have you been living a caged, defeated, fruitless life? Have you settled for a lesser destiny? Jesus has set you free to soar on eagle's wings. Are you ready to follow the One who has said *Follow Me and I will make you fishers of men?* When James and John heard those words 2,000 years ago, *they immediately left the boat and followed Him* (Matthew 4:19-20). That was their God-given destiny.

What's yours? Are you ready to experience it? Do you trust God as He guides you on the great adventure of discovering His purpose for your life?

2.   THE PROMISE OF THE WORD

There is a second reason Hannah could have hope in God. Not only was God's purpose for her to be fruitful – but she also had the promise of His Word.

PROMISES, PROMISES

God had given a covenant promise through Moses that if Israel was in a right relationship with Him, there would be no one in Israel who would miscarry or be barren. God Himself said in Exodus 23:26 that when Israel was obedient, *no one shall suffer miscarriage or be barren in your land; I will fulfill the number of your days.*

What a promise! God would supernaturally protect and bless Israel as she faithfully followed Him.

Not only had God destined Hannah for fruitfulness, she also had a promise she could hold on to. It was a pledge from The-One-Who-Cannot-Lie that promised fertility.

God's Word is such an encouragement to us:

- The Word of God produces faith in our lives. Romans 10:17 says, *Faith comes by hearing, and hearing by the Word of God.*

- The Word of God also tells us of the character of God. He is holy, loving and trustworthy. He will not withhold good gifts from us. When teaching on prayer, Jesus often referred back to the character of God. *If a son asks for bread from any father among you, will he give him a stone? Or if he asks for a fish, will he give him a serpent instead of a fish? Or if he asks for an egg, will he offer him a scorpion? If you then, being evil, know how to give good gifts to your children, how much more will your heavenly Father give the Holy Spirit to those who ask Him!* (Luke 11:11-13).

God spoke personally and directly to Abraham, giving him a very specific promise regarding Sarah in Genesis 17:21. He said that by that date next year, Sarah would bear a child. Abraham believed God – and it indeed did come to pass.

But Hannah did not have a clear, direct promise from God. However, she did have the principle and general promise that God had made to Israel in Exodus 23. And with that, she yearly went to the tabernacle to worship God in hope. I can imagine her praying, *"God, if I am in a right relationship with You, then I want to apply the promise that none of Israel faithful servants should be barren. I ask You to open my womb and give me children."*

And with the same confidence that Abraham had in Genesis 17, Hannah believed God. When the prophet Eli told her that her petition had been granted, she went on her way rejoicing. Her heart was no longer sad. And she was assured that, by the next year, she would have a child.

APPLICATION

We have already seen in John 15 that God has promised that none of His children should be spiritually unfruitful. Jesus said that *you will know them by their fruits* (Matthew 7:16).

As we walk in step with God's Spirit, we should expect the fruits of the Spirit to be produced in our lives (Galatians 5:16-25). In contrast to the works of the flesh, Paul writes that we will daily experience fruit of the Spirit, which is *love, joy, peace, longsuffering, kindness, goodness, faithfulness, gentleness, self-control* (5:22-23).

Are those qualities evident in your life? The Apostle Peter promises, *if these things are yours and abound, you will be neither barren nor unfruitful in the knowledge of our Lord Jesus Christ* (2 Peter 1:8).

As part of the laborers in God's harvest, we should expect the Word to bring forth thirty, sixty and one hundred-fold fruit (Matthew 13:23). Like Hannah, we should cry out to God until He makes us fruitful.

Would you take a moment and pray now: *God, I know Your will is that I be fruitful. Your Word has promised that. I desire to walk in step with Your Spirit. Produce fruit in my life. May the qualities of love, joy, peace, longsuffering, kindness, goodness, faithfulness, gentleness, and self-control be born in my life. May others come to know You through the words of my lips. And may You be glorified in my life as I seek to walk with You every day.*

3.   **THE POWER OF EXAMPLES**

GAINING STRENGTH THROUGH LIVES FROM THE PAST

The Bible is full of biographies. These stories of men and women of faith are meant to encourage us. They are the stories of people who trusted God in the face of insurmountable trials and problems. Hebrews 11 says that many of them never saw the answers to their prayers in their lifetimes. Yet they remained faithful … full of faith.

Think of Samuel growing up, hearing the story of how God answered his mother's prayers.

- How encouraging it must have been for Samuel to know that his name meant, *"asked of the Lord."*
- Knowing that his very conception and birth were miraculous must have given him a sense of destiny and purpose.
- His mother cried out to God to give her a son and God answered her prayer miraculously.
- He was raised in the house of Eli the priest because his mother had dedicated him to God. *Therefore I also have lent him to the LORD; as long as he lives he shall be lent to the LORD* (1 Samuel 1:28).

What an impact this knowledge must have made on Samuel! If Hannah remained barren and God did not answer her prayers, then there would have been no Samuel. Samuel had to feel like a child of purpose and destiny.

Hannah must have received similar encouragement as she looked back in her ancestral lineage.

- Abraham's wife, Sarah, was unable to conceive. Not only that, she was almost ninety years old and her husband Abraham was one hundred. Yet God performed a miracle and Isaac was conceived. If Sarah remained barren, then there would have been no ancestral line to Hannah.
- Later, Isaac and Rebekah had difficulty conceiving. But God also opened Rebekah's womb and she gave birth to Jacob.
- There were other examples, too, like Rachael giving birth to Joseph. And Joseph became the one through whom Israel was preserved through the famines in Egypt.

Hannah saw these examples and gained hope that God would do the same for her. Through the power of the examples of Scripture she had reason to hope.

 FROM MY PERSONAL DISCIPLESHIP DIARY

In a small way, I can identify with Samuel and how he felt when he understood his mother's prayer had been answered in relationship to his ministry. After God brought a revival to my life in my second year of marriage, I became sensitive enough to God to have the assurance that God had called me to preach. Though my godly mother influenced me by example to have a love relationship with Jesus, she never planted the thought in my mind to be a preacher. It was only after I made it public that I had surrendered to the ministry that she told me of her prayer. *"Son, when I was pregnant with you, I laid my hands on my belly and asked God to dedicate you to be a preacher of Christ. I dedicated you to God to be a preacher from my womb."*

Her story made a great impact on me because it confirmed a private moment that I had with the Lord as I struggled with God's call to preach. I was kneeling beside my bed and trying to explain to God that I was a poor choice to preach. I was not a good speaker and often stuttered when I was nervous and began to talk too fast. On many occasions I was publicly embarrassed by having someone stop me while I was speaking and tell me rudely, *"I cannot understand a word you are saying."*

Still on my knees, I was praying and reading my Bible. Immediately after pouring out my excuses to God, I read these words from Jeremiah:

> *Then the word of the LORD came to me, saying: "Before I formed you in the womb I knew you; before you were born I sanctified you; I ordained you a prophet to the nations." Then said I: "Ah, Lord GOD! Behold, I cannot speak, for I am a youth." But*

> *the LORD said to me: "Do not say, 'I am a youth,' For you shall go to all to whom I send you, and whatever I command you, you shall speak. Do not be afraid of their faces, for I am with you to deliver you," says the LORD* (Jeremiah 1:4-8).

In that moment I made the application of that passage to my personal prayer and felt another confirmation that God had indeed called me to be a preacher. From my perspective it was private – just between God and me. When my mom told me of her Hannah-like prayer, I had a deep sense that God's call on my life began long before I even knew about it.

Nearly fifty-two years after my mother dedicated me to God to preach His Gospel, she was on her deathbed. I was torn between staying with her and leading our mission team to India. Part of my assignment was to lead a pastor's conference and to preach two of the three nights of a mass crusade of 55,000. My mom had given me to the Lord before birth and she now gave me to the Lord at death. She knew I had to decide between staying at her bedside or preaching the Lord Jesus in India. She pulled me close and prayed that God's Spirit would be on me and then in her weakness she whispered in my ear, *"Win many souls to Jesus, win many souls to Jesus."* Like Hannah released Samuel, mom again released me to preach.

Those would be the last words I would hear from my saintly mom's lips as her ninety years on earth ended and her eternity in heaven began. They echoed in my ears during my time in India. Over 12,000 decisions cards were turned in at the crusade, indicating people's commitments to the Lord Jesus. Again my mother's prayer had been answered, *"Win many souls to Jesus, win many souls to Jesus."* Those words still echo in my ears. My mother's example and her prayers have truly made an impact on my life and ministry.

The examples from the lives of godly men and women in the past give us great encouragement. God placed every Bible character in Scripture for us as an example to build our faith and to believe that God can meet our needs as well (1 Corinthians 10:11).

🌿 Let's Look at the Lives Around Us

The examples of Scripture are for us as well. As we look at them, God can start a fire of hope in us: *what He did for others, He can do for us.*

Why should we be unfruitful when we have powerful examples of God answering the prayers of His children? Why would any of us want to face the giants of our Promised Land and not follow the example of Joshua and Caleb and boldly say that we are well able to take what God has promised us rather than draw back in fear like the ten spies who choose fear over faith? (See Numbers 13).

God also puts living examples around us to challenge our faith. Paul told the Philippians to follow his example (Philippians 3:17). Paul praised the church at Thessalonica because they had become examples of faith to the believers at Macedonia and Achaia (1 Thessalonians 1:7). Pastors are to walk with God as examples for the flock of God to follow (1 Peter 5:3).

Despite the encouraging examples around us, many of us continue in our unfruitful condition. It's easy to ignore our lack of fruitfulness. We rationalize that our lives are not that different from most Christians. Unfortunately, that may be true … but it does not excuse us. God has called us to be fruitful. How can we be satisfied with little or no fruit when Jesus said, *Abide in Me, and I in you. As the branch cannot bear fruit of itself, unless it abides in the vine, neither can you, unless you abide in Me. I am the vine, you are the branches. He who abides in Me, and I in him, bears much fruit; for without Me you can do nothing* (John 15:4-5).

Some believers envy the examples of faith in our generation that God has raised up in His vineyard. Others mock or condemn these powerful examples of faith. What we should do is to find out what unbelief, what sin, what fear, or what apathy is present in our lives that have left us with little fruit … and then deal with that issue before God.

I have only been fishing a few times in my life, but I've learned that some people can catch fish out of the same boat on the same river while others do not. If someone in your boat is catching fish and you are not, you need to ask yourself why.

- Perhaps there is sin in your life. God will not use an unclean vessel. Repent from it. Confess it to God and ask Him to cleanse you from it.
- Perhaps your problem is simply one of not knowing what to do. Don't be so stubborn that you won't follow the example of those who are winning people to Jesus. Find out what bait they are using and where they are casting their bait. Have them point out the mistakes you are making in your casting technique. But do not excuse your lack of catching fish on the sovereignty of God. Don't try to explain it away by saying that evangelism is not your gift. If somebody in your boat is always catching fish while you are not, then be motivated by them.

If others are winning the lost to Christ and you are not, something must change. Why remain unfruitful in that area of your Christian life? Listen to the instructions of Jesus and *Cast your net on the other side and you will catch men.* Remember Jesus said, *Follow me and I will make you fishers of men.*

If someone is following Jesus and becoming a fisher of men, then it just may be God challenging you to follow them like they follow Christ.

My faith has grown in these last years as I've been challenged by the example of others. Do not use the excuse that God is working through their life because they are smarter, more talented, better communicators or more gifted than you. God still works through the weak, the foolish and the base to accomplish great things (1 Corinthians 1:27-28). Fruitfulness is always a heart-and-faith issue, never an issue of talent and ability.

For the eyes of the LORD run to and fro throughout the whole earth, to show Himself strong on behalf of those whose heart is loyal to Him (2 Chronicles 16:9). I'm convinced that God wants to demonstrate His strength and power throughout the earth. All He needs is one of His children to have a heart that is completely devoted to Him.

Are you ready to do that? Are you ready to trust Him, to be inspired by the examples of those in Scripture and those around you? Don't lose hope – rather, be inspired by the hope that you see in others.

4.   THE PERSISTENT BURDEN

There is one final reason that gave Hannah hope. It was her persistent burden. There was something deep within Hannah's heart that would not allow her to give up the dream of fruitfulness.

Sometimes it is hard to determine if what we are praying for is from God – or if it is based on our own fleshly desires and motives. Did our burden originate in the heart of God, or did we simply invent it and wish it were true on our own? How can you determine the source?

- **The Test of Perseverance**

  A prayer based on selfish desires fades away after a period of time and is forgotten. However, when the burden is from heaven, persistent prayer that does not lose heart follows it. If the burden is not self-motivated out of personal bias, and it will not subside, then it is probably God's burden from heaven for you. If so, persevere. Don't quit.

  Remember God was just as much involved in shutting Hannah's womb as in opening her womb. God was just as much involved in sending a famine as He was in sending Joseph to provide during the famine (Psalm 105:16-22). The same God who shut up the heavens for Elijah also opened the windows of heaven at His Word and purpose (James 5:16-18).

  Do you have a persistent burden that you believe God has given you? Then you must wait on God and be persistent in prayer.

- **The Test of Motive**

  What's your motive in praying for that, which is on your heart? Is it to give … or to get? Is it selfishly driven or Gospel-driven? Is your motive to be generous or to keep for yourself?

  Admittedly it is hard to understand and trust our own hearts. Jeremiah 17:9 states that *The heart is deceitful above all things, and desperately wicked; who can know it?* But there is hope in the very next verse: *I, the Lord, search the heart, I test the mind, even to give every man according to his ways, according to the fruit of his doings.*

God knows our true motives. Ask Him to reveal them to you. He tests the heart. Ask Him to test yours.

- **The Test of Glory**

Ultimately we are called to do all things for the glory of Jesus Christ (1 Corinthians 10:31). As you pray, will your prayer glorify God? Will Jesus Christ be lifted up through the answer to your prayer?

Hannah knew her burden was from God. She also knew that the answer to her prayer would glorify God. That's why her words of praise in 1 Samuel 2:1-10 ring so true. They express the true joy found when God answers a deep burden of the heart.

Christian history gives us many examples of God placing the burden of His heart in heaven in the soul of one of His children on earth. One example was the burden God gave John Knox for the country of Scotland.

Knox was a leader in the Protestant Reformation in the 1500s. He faithfully fought for the truths of the Gospel, but was persecuted throughout his ministry, ending up in prison and later in exile. However, his passion for his countrymen never wavered. His famous prayer was born out of that burden: *"God, give me Scotland or I'll die."* One account states,

> *During these troublesome times of Scotland, when Rome was using all her power to suppress the Reformation, the cause of Protestant Christianity was in great danger. John Knox was seen to leave his study and proceed to the rear of his home. He was followed by a friend who, through the silent darkness, heard Knox as if in prayer. After a few moments of silence his voice became clear, and the earnest petition went up from his struggling soul to heaven: "O Lord, give me Scotland, or I die!" Then a pause of silent calmness, then again the appeal broke forth: "O Lord give me Scotland, or I die!" Once again all was silent, when, with a yet intense poignancy, the thrice repeated intercession struggled forth: "O Lord give me Scotland, or I die!" God gave him Scotland despite Mary. Knox's prayer was heard and largely answered.* [5]

HAS YOUR BURDEN "PASSED THE TEST"?

Has God created a persistent burden in your soul that will not go away? Are your motives pure? Will He receive the glory when the answer comes? If so, take heart. Persevere. And look expectantly for His long-awaited answer.

---

5   Taken from a web site article entitled *"Revolution and the Battle of the Boyne and a Prayer for Scotland,"* http://www.tranenttrueblues228.50megs.com/custom3.html

CHAPTER 5

Benefited – Part 1

But to Hannah he would give a double portion, for he loved Hannah (1 Samuel 1:5).

 THE SECOND TEST OF FAITH

Elkanah tried to satisfy Hannah by giving her *a double portion*. The second test of faith that Hannah experiences is:

> *What does it take to satisfy you? Will you accept*
> *a substitute – or will you wait for God's best?*

1.   THE COMPARISON: PENINNAH'S PORTION AND HANNAH'S PORTION

As a husband, Elkanah was helpless to give Hannah a child. However, he tried to encourage Hannah by giving her more than he gave Peninnah. But *more* is not always *better*, especially when it is God who has created the need in our life that only He can fulfill.

You may think that Hannah should have been content that she was loved more and given more than her rival Peninnah. But those who God has chosen for His purpose cannot compare themselves to others, but only to the will and purpose of God for their lives (2 Cor. 10:12). The special favors she received would never fully satisfy Hannah. Her struggle was not against Peninnah, and her fulfillment would never come from being more loved than Peninnah. The issue for Hannah was knowing and doing the will of God. And so it is for us.

When God wants to draw us deeper into His fellowship and love, we begin to lose interest in the bigger and better things that this world offers. More money, newer cars, or fancier toys will never satisfy us. God has created deeper desires in our lives to bring us to the greater fruitfulness that He has for us.

I am afraid that we often compare ourselves to below-average Christians and then think that we are above-average Christians. Such comparisons are never accurate. Nor are they healthy. How can we prevent this?

As a young married man, I was considered a committed Christian and a young leader at my home church. I never missed church. I taught Sunday school. I was a good steward in giving both tithes and offerings. I had a consistent quiet time in the Word. I even evangelized at times. Quite a spiritual resume! But I was comparing myself to a lower standard of Christianity around me that made me feel satisfied. I was eventually reunited with an old schoolmate, Sammy Tippit, who was so on fire for Jesus that it made me thirst for an even closer walk with Christ. God created that desire in my life to be more of a disciple of Christ with greater faith and then showed me a living example of it through Sammy's life. I would never be satisfied with "business as usual" again in my relationship with God.

WHERE DO WE FIND EXAMPLES LIKE THAT?

How can we be sure that we do not settle for temporal blessings? You may be in a church where you do not know of an example of a Christian who challenges you to have greater faith and fruitfulness. Then I would suggest that you began a search for a better Biblical standard of Christians! Where should you look?

- Look to the Scriptures. Let the men and women of faith in Scripture challenge you.
- Read biographies of great Christians. History is replete with the stories of men and women in every generation who were filled with the Spirit and driven by great faith. They were the pace setters for their generation of Christianity. Learn from their lives!
- Watch Christians who are making an impact on the world today. There are those today who will challenge you to not be content with less than God supernaturally working through your life to experience great fruitfulness.

Have you ever been around another Christian who makes you want to be closer to Jesus? Praise God for people like that. Jesus said they are the *salt of the earth,* making you thirsty for all that God has for you. God will often create a "holy discontent" in your life to bring you to the place that you can only be content with God's greater purpose in Christ for your life.

Do not be surprised if others try to tell you that you are a fine Christian just as you are. They may even encourage you to enjoy the blessing of a double portion of prosperity. But when you see that God is the One you really need, you will understand that He is the only One who can satisfy you.

EVEN GREATER FRUITFULNESS

In 2004 I first caught a bigger vision of world missions on a mission trip to India. I carried that burden home to our church and we became involved with a direct partnership with an association of about 400 churches in India. From 2005 to 2008, we saw God do incredible things in that ministry. In partnership with three other American churches and a Christian businessman, we sent teams to India to evangelize, preach in churches, hold pastor conferences, and conduct mass evangelism crusades. We built medical camps, an orphanage that could house up to 200 children, a few church buildings, and a Bible conference center that could seat 700. We created two ongoing and fully equipped evangelism film teams and a six week new believers discipleship follow up program. We dug fresh water wells in 120 villages. Finally, we introduced a few other ministry networks to our mission partner in India. In those three years our partnering director in India, Sushil Kumar, sent us reports telling of over 50,000 decisions for Christ during that time.

I was experiencing a great contentment and fruitfulness in ministry. But it is in times like that where it is easy to compare the fruitfulness you are experiencing to what others are doing. If you do that, it is possible to miss an even greater harvest and effectiveness in the future. It is possible for us to become content and miss even greater things that are on the heart of God for this world. And I was slipping into that contented state. However, my contentment with our past fruitfulness was to change dramatically when I had lunch with a local pastor in our area.

I heard of Dr. David Nelms and his ministry in India. I called and asked if we could meet and discuss what God was doing in India through their church. When we got together, I shared the great things God was doing in India through our mission ministry. David politely listened to my zealous descriptions of our mission fruitfulness in India. Then he shared his vision and mission strategy, not only in India but in many nations of the world. I listened to David tell how he had founded *The Timothy Initiative* (TTI) [6] with a mission strategy to plant 500,000 churches by training national pastors through church planting schools in many nations. TTI would train national directors who trained regional directors who trained local church planning school directors who trained twenty-five pastors in each church planting school. Each pastor was given the ten-book training curriculum free of charge to complete his church-planting diploma. In order to graduate, each pastor had to plant a new church. Through this mission methodology, TTI had already planted over 6,000 churches in a little over 2 years. As I heard more of what God was doing and the wisdom of this approach and the incredible fruitfulness and the little expense involved, I was more than challenged. I was convicted and burdened. [7]

I was hearing a vision so big that only God could bring it to pass. This was a God-sized vision. I was no longer content to continue our same approach of missions in India. I had heard God at work in a much bigger way than I was experiencing and I immediately wanted to be part of it. Sometimes when you hear that God is at work, you can be passive, indifferent, envious, or

---

6   *The Timothy Initiative* is based in West Palm Beach, FL, and is founded on the multiplication principle from 2 Timothy 2:2, *And the things that you have heard from me among many witnesses, commit these to faithful men who will be able to teach others also.* For more information, visit their web site, ttionline.org.

7   Updated TTI numbers from 2009 to 2011 indicate over 15,000 new church plants and over 150,000 baptisms.

jealous. Or you can choose to be part of it. I wanted our church to partner with TTI in India. Our mission committee met with David where he shared TTI's vision. We were ready to partner with them in India.

It is hard to describe how quickly God moved. Once we contacted our partners in India and Sushil shared the vision of church planting schools through TTI, they felt that God had answered one of their long term prayers to bring training and church planting centers to their personal villages. In less than four months, one of TTI's regional directors had trained ten leading pastors that we had been working with to be the individual directors of ten schools of 25 pastors each.

For an investment of $150 per pastor, it is amazing how much they are able to accomplish for the Kingdom of God. Each pastor is given a little transportation money to arrive and stay at the school for one week out of the month for ten months. This also includes simple meals and the 10 training books. The curriculum includes courses on Church Planting, Preaching, Old Testament Survey, New Testament Survey, Systematic Theology, Evangelism, etc. These church-planting schools may meet in an existing church, a home, or even under a tree. By the end of the first year, Sushil sent me the report of our 10 schools. 250 pastors received diplomas, and 260 new churches were planted. There were 7,700 conversions, and 3,500 baptisms with many more awaiting baptism. The pastors sent us wonderful testimonies of conversions and how their ministries were strengthened.

Our first mission approach was certainly blessed of God with much fruit. However, we could not compare the effectiveness of our past mission dollars to what $150 through our TTI partnership could do long-term with our mission partners in India. In addition, we knew that true Biblical multiplication was occurring. We were training men who were reaching others who would reach others also. It became the best mission delivery system for our direct international mission partnerships.

Do you think God may want to do greater things through your life or the life of your church? Are you content with the fruit you are now seeing? Could that contentment keep you from missing something much greater?

Take a moment and ask God what He has for you. Don't settle simply for what you can see at this moment. Ask Him to open heaven's doors of blessing and fruitfulness in your life.

2. THE CONSOLATION

When God gives the burden, then He can give the consolation. Nothing else will satisfy (see 2 Corinthians 1:3-7).

When I was six years old, we moved to a new town. My mom took me to a new church where I did not know anyone. I was uncomfortable and wanted to stay with my mom, but she was trying to get me into my own Sunday School class so she could attend her women's class. She tried to comfort my fears with her words, but I used one of my best weapons in my young arsenal to get my way. I began to cry and cling to her. It was my hope that this would publicly embarrass her and she would take me home. What I really needed was a good spanking but since we were in a public place, she resorted to a bribe. Reaching into her purse, she pulled out a silver half dollar and said, *"Truman, if you will be a good boy and go to your own Sunday school class without crying, then I will give you this half dollar."* I reached out and immediately took the money, turned off the tears and walked into my class. I had succeeded in getting my way and was rewarded for it. However, when I got home my mom made it very clear that I was never to act that way again. That was the last time I was paid to go to Sunday School.

Nothing could stop Hannah from crying every time they went to the house of the Lord. Elkanah did not give her a shiny half dollar, but he did try to stop her from crying by a spiritual bribe. Elkanah loved Hannah but he could not give Hannah that which God had in His greater purpose withheld. As the family went up to worship, he seemed to try to console Hannah by giving her a worthy portion, more honor, or twice as much as he gave Peninnah.

HANNAH'S TEST

The test of faith for Hannah was, "What would it take to satisfy her?" Would she simply accept Elkanah's special love and favor as a substitute for what God wanted to do in her life? Or would she wait in faith, knowing that God had a greater purpose? We must be careful that we do not want relief more than we want God's refinement in our trial of faith.

Many of us act just as I did when God begins to wean us from clinging to God in our emotions when we face a test of faith. God must teach us to walk by faith. The absence of physical blessings is not a sign of His displeasure. We're simply in the middle of a test. We must learn that Jesus is just as much with us when He is in the boat in our storms as He is when He is on the mountain watching from a distance as we go through the storms in our lives.

In Mark 4:35-41, Jesus was in the boat with them. In Mark 6:46-51, He was on the mountaintop praying for them. But in both cases, His eye was on them. Jesus expected the disciples to apply what He had taught them in their first storm and exercise faith in their second storm. In the same way, as we grow through the storms of life, the life of Jesus will be manifested through us. [8]

God touched Hannah's life, making her unable to bear children. But with His same touch He added His consolation. The trials that God sends us are not to ruin us but to refine us. If the Great Physician allows trials to bruise us, then He will bind up our wound. God does not give us a burden for us to become the burden bearer. With the burden comes more grace that is sufficient for us. The burden is only to help us identify better with Christ and His people. We are to enter His rest and discover that Jesus is the One who will console us as we come to Him. He promised, *My yoke is easy and my burden light* (Matthew 11: 28-30). If we have to be bribed by blessings or consoled by a double portion to be satisfied, then we will never discover our unlimited potential to bear fruit as a child of God.

Paul certainly understood this when he asked God three times to remove his thorn in the flesh. Instead, God said, *My grace is sufficient for you, for My strength is made perfect in weakness.* As a result, Paul concluded, *Therefore, most gladly I will rather boast in my infirmities, that the power of Christ may rest upon me* (2 Corinthians 12:9). Paul gladly chose God's consolation over the

---

8   See the author's book, *Growing Through the Storms of Life.*

removal of his thorn. If you had to choose between a problem and the power of God, which would choose?

It is the God of all comfort *who comforts us in all our tribulation, that we may be able to comfort those who are in any trouble, with the comfort with which we ourselves are comforted by God. For as the sufferings of Christ abounded in us, so our consolation also abounds through Christ.... And our hope for you is steadfast, because we know that as you are partakers of the sufferings, so also you will partake of the consolation* (2 Corinthians 1:4, 5, 7).

The word *consolation* is made up of two Greek words: *para*, meaning beside, and *kaleo*, to call. [9] The word means *"comfort, solace; that which affords comfort or refreshment."* [10]

Jesus promised, *And I will pray the Father, and He will give you another Helper, that He may abide with you forever— the Spirit of truth, whom the world cannot receive, because it neither sees Him nor knows Him; but you know Him, for He dwells with you and will be in you. I will not leave you orphans; I will come to you* (John 14:16-18). The word translated *helper* in that passage is from the same Greek word – *parakaleo*. The Holy Spirit is our divine helper, dwelling in our lives, called alongside to comfort, encourage, empower and refresh us.

God assures us that if we are partakers of Christ's sufferings, He will also be the One to give us His consolation. Don't short-circuit the process. Do not accept a substitute until you have heard from God in His Word and have learned what He is trying to teach you.

LESSONS FROM THE BUTTERFLY

We must not interfere with God's purpose in the lives of others. He is working in their lives. As a young Christian, I read the story of a woman who was watching a cocoon outside of her kitchen window. [11] As she watched with interest, the cocoon began to vibrate as the caterpillar emerged from its place of transformation into a butterfly. She could see the great struggle that the butterfly was having, trying to escape from its prison of the past. She became impatient with the long process and wanted to help the butterfly. She noticed what the problem was. It was the silk threads that kept the opening of the cocoon too tight for a quick and easy release to its new destiny to fly. She tried to help by picking up her scissors and cutting the silk threads. She saw immediate success, as the butterfly was free – but it could not fly. Instead of wings on its back, there were only two little bumps where the wings should have been.

Then she noticed another cocoon began to vibrate as another butterfly went through the same process of struggle. However, this time she watched and resisted the temptation to help. This butterfly came to the same point where its body seemed too large to squeeze through such a small opening. Again she noticed the silk treads that kept the opening small. As she watched the second butterfly finally squeeze its body through the opening, she realized that the Creator had

---

9   Vine, W. E. ; Unger, Merrill F. ; White, William: *Vine's Complete Expository Dictionary of Old and New Testament Words*. Nashville : T. Nelson, 1996, S. 2:110

10   Strong, James: *The Exhaustive Concordance of the Bible*. Electronic ed. Ontario: Woodside Bible Fellowship., 1996, S. G3874

11   I believe I first read this story from Hannah Whitall Smith.

designed the struggle to force body fluids into its wings to develop and strengthen them. Now free from its cocoon and struggle, the caterpillar was transformed into a beautiful butterfly and used its colorful wings to take flight and enjoy its freedom.

The question we must consider as we go through our trials is simply: is the cocoon a tomb, or is it a hiding place where true transformation occurs?

Hannah was placed in the cocoon of trial and pain – but for her it became God's place of hiding and strengthening. God intended Hannah to fly and the struggle of barrenness was designed by Him to fill her wings with the beautiful character of His empowering Spirit. Through her total submission to God's will, she became strong, fruitful and fulfilled.

God also has His silk threads that seem to delay our freedom as we struggle through some trial. Consider the wisdom of James:

> *My brethren, count it all joy when you fall into various trials, knowing that the testing of your faith produces patience. But let patience have its perfect work, that you may be perfect and complete, lacking nothing* (James 1:2-4).

How are you doing in your trials? Are you patiently letting God do His work in your life? Are you growing toward maturity? [12]If you're still struggling with trusting God in your trials, you need wisdom to see things from His perspective. Read the next verse as James writes, *If any of you lacks wisdom, let him ask of God, who gives to all liberally and without reproach, and it will be given to him* (James 1:5).

Far too often, we ask *"Why?"* when we are in a trial. Instead, we must learn to ask *"What?"* What is it that God wants us to learn?

Stop right now and pray. Ask God for wisdom. Submit to Him as you struggle in the cocoon of trial. Ask Him to teach you what you need to learn.

LESSONS IN OBEDIENCE

It was the coldest spot in the United States on the day that I helped my friend and his young family move into a trailer only a few miles from the Canadian border in Washington State. I was planting a church in Spokane, and my friend from my home church in Louisiana had accepted the position as pastor of a small church near the Canadian border.

Another couple from our home church in Baton Rouge had also arrived to pastor in northern Idaho. As they were coming over one of the mountains they had a head on collision with another car. They were rushed to a hospital in Spokane and after their release from the hospital we opened our home to them until her broken bones could heal. During this time of helping our friends we had a great time of fellowship in the word, prayer, and ministry together. We had been a source of consolation and comfort to them.

---

12   James' words are *perfect and complete,* but they imply mean *"fully developed and spiritually mature."*

Only a couple months after I had helped my other preacher friend unload his U-Haul on his new church field, he and his family pulled into my driveway with another U-Haul trailer. He told me that God had told him to leave that church because the people did not want to hear the Word of God. I was surprised because only two months earlier, he said God had sent him there. They asked if we could take them in and Connie and I opened our home to them as well.

However, instead of peace in our house, we experienced confusion and stress. I sensed that something was not just right about us giving our friends relief and consolation. My wife and I prayed about it and we felt like we had to help our friends out when they were going through such a difficult time. Yet I became so burdened that I went off alone to seek God about it. I received a clear answer as I reread the book of Jonah. Jonah was sent to Nineveh and he ran from God. It was God who sent out a storm to get Jonah's attention. All of those on the ship who were giving Jonah passage were shaken until they put Jonah back into the sea. As they threw Jonah into the waves of God, they had immediate calm.

I met with my friend and told him that I had prayed and read Jonah. I then asked him, *"Did God release you from that church or did you run from your assignment like Jonah?"* He told me that the ministry was difficult and that he just quit and ran from his assignment. I told him that I could not get in the way of what God was trying to teach him by giving him aid. He told me that he would leave in the morning and return to Baton Rouge.

In the one case Connie and I had been used of God to be a source of God's comfort and help to one family. In the other case we had picked up the scissors and interfered with God's chastening of one of His children.

TIME FOR REFLECTION

- Is it possible for us to get in the way of what God is doing in the life of someone? Like Hannah, has God shut up their womb for some reason and season?

- Can we really have a ministry to others if our only solution is to give them physical relief? Rather, we must ask God to give us spiritual insight into their lives and problems. Only then can we truly minister to them in their deepest needs.

- How can we develop the perceptive wisdom to know when to offer encouragement and comfort, and when to challenge them to go deeper with God?

CHAPTER 6

Benefited – Part 2

But to Hannah he would give a double portion, for he loved Hannah (1 Samuel 1:5).

 ## THE SECOND TEST OF FAITH

Elkanah tried to satisfy Hannah by giving her *a double portion*. The second test of faith that Hannah experiences is:

> *What does it take to satisfy you? Will you accept*
> *a substitute – or will you wait for God's best?*

We're continuing our study of *Benefited* that we began in chapter 5.

3.   THE COMFORT

No one but God can give us comfort when it is God's burden to bring us to the end of ourselves and make us more dependent upon Him.

Elkanah probably thought that his love for Hannah and his special attention to her sorrow would be enough to comfort his dear wife. It's right for Christian husbands to seek to comfort their wives when they are hurting. Perhaps he held Hannah, comforted her and spoke tenderly to her. Maybe he tried to get her to focus on the blessings that she already had. Perhaps he tried to point out others whose circumstances were much worst. If he had been alive in the 21st century, perhaps he would have bought her a new car or given her a new piece of expensive jewelry to make her happy. Elkanah could have done everything right – but it still would not have eased Hannah's troubled heart. We may be able to comfort others temporarily on the emotional or physical level. But in our hearts where the Holy Spirit abides, He alone can be our Comforter. Elkanah probably did not see God's greater purpose for his wife and therefore could not understand that her tears were not simply the expression of emotional disappointment or weakness but the God-given burden of her spirit.

LESSONS FROM LASSIE

Wally, my neighbor and best friend growing up, had a wonderful collie dog. I envied him and wished I could have a dog like his. I was in the first grade and movies like "Lassie" made it seem that a dog was a boy's best friend.

I was over at Wally's house looking out his upstairs bedroom window when I saw a little cocker spaniel puppy lost and alone across the street. I raced Wally to be the first one to claim her. I hoped there was no owner to be found and pleaded with my parents to let me take care of her. They agreed but warned me not to get too attached to her just in case the owner was found. I did get attached to the puppy and finally the waiting period was over. My parents officially told me that the puppy was mine. I named her Spotty because of the brown spots on her white coat of hair. We became inseparable. I had never experienced such loyalty and devotion from any friend. I could not wait to get home from school to run and play with Spotty. Spotty would grow and soon have her own puppies that we gave to other children to experience the same kind of joy I had. Then Spotty had another litter of puppies and my dad began to feel that Spotty was too much of a burden.

One day I came home and ran to the shed to let Spotty out and she was gone. I called for Spotty but she did not come to me. I went into the house to tell mom that I could not find Spotty and could tell by mom's teary eyes that something was wrong. She told me that dad had taken Spotty away. I never experienced a broken heart like I did in that moment. I was so hurt and lonely. Tears began to flow. How could dad take my best friend away without asking me? I went looking everywhere for Spotty but to no avail. I considered running away from home to get back at my dad. I told mom that I was going to fail every exam to get back at them for what they had done. I felt injustice and betrayal. My precious dog was gone.

My mom had tried to stop my dad from getting rid of Spotty but was not able to do so. She tried daily to comfort me but I would not be comforted. I grieved for weeks at my loss. No one could comfort me. I reluctantly submitted to my dad's decision but I was not in agreement. After several weeks, I finally stopped grieving and my mind was not constantly focused on finding Spotty. However, even up until the 6th grade when I saw a dog that looked like Spotty, I would run to it and call Spotty's name. A boy never forgets his first or best dog.

We all have similar loses…some lesser, some greater. The question is how can we be comforted in the midst of those losses?

HANNAH'S COMFORT AND TEARS

Hannah's burden was great. Hers was a burden from heaven that only God could comfort. Her tears were not from depression, or from emotional instability, or from selfishness to gain the attention of her husband and others. Her tears were from the burden of God to cleanse her soul in preparation for God's great work in her life and in Israel. Her tears were the oil that kept her prayer machine in constant motion. Hannah was not looking for relief from her husband – only from God.

God has His Hannah's in many churches around the world that are misunderstood by well-meaning believers. Those like Peninnah have never received from God's heart a God-given vision that burdens them. They do not understand that God works His great work around the world by ministering to people before He can minister through people.

Here's the principle: *God cannot use you greatly until He works in you deeply.*

As a result, there are often tears. But these are not the tears that come because of a broken necklace or lost watch. They are the tears that come over a God-given burden that will impact God's kingdom.

The Bible has much to say about tears. At times it gives us a reproof for selfish tears. But there is also a ministry of tears that God has given to those that intercede before Him.

When my mom saw my tears, it always moved her heart with compassion toward me. It would always lead to a hug and her comfort. When my dad saw my tears it normally lead to a reproof. *"Son, don't be a baby. Quit crying – you need to grow up and be a man."*

Elkanah may have not given Hannah a strong rebuke for her tears, but he certainly did not understand her weeping. *Then Elkanah her husband said to her, Hannah, why do you weep? Why do you not eat? And why is your heart grieved? Am I not better to you than ten sons?* (1 Samuel 1:8). He tried his best to comfort her, but he did not understand the great work that God had chosen to do in Hannah's life and only God could dry away her tears.

Consider Hannah's tears as we look together at a few verses on tears: *Hear my prayer, O LORD, and give ear to my cry; do not be silent at my tears* (Psalm 39:12). Hannah was not crying tears of self-pity. Her tears were inseparable from her deep supplication to God.

> *As the deer pants for the water brooks, so pants my soul for You, O God. My soul thirsts for God, for the living God. When shall I come and appear before God? My tears have been my food day and night, while they continually say to me, "Where is your God?" When I remember these things, I pour out my soul within me. For I used to go with the multitude; I went with them to the house of God, with the voice of joy and praise, with a multitude that kept a pilgrim feast. Why are you cast down, O my soul? And why are you disquieted within me? Hope in God, for I shall yet praise Him for the help of His countenance* (Psalm 42:1-5).

Hannah was thirsting for God and came each year to appear before God with prayer and tears.

The culture of the Jews had tear bottles to catch their tears when they cried. Perhaps Hannah had a tear bottle, but if not, God did catch every one of Hannah's tears. *You number my wanderings; put my tears into Your bottle; are they not in Your book?* (Psalm 56:8).

Those who sow in tears shall reap in joy (Psalms 126:5). Hannah would indeed reap in joy, but not until her tears had brought her closer to God.

Consider how Jesus responded to tears:

Immediately the father of the child cried out and said with tears, "Lord, I believe; help my unbelief!" (Mark 9:24). Jesus would answer this broken hearted Father just as God answered Hannah. *Then He turned to the woman and said to Simon, "Do you see this woman? I entered your house; you gave Me no water for My feet, but she has washed My feet with her tears and wiped them with the hair of her head…. Therefore I say to you, her sins, which are many, are forgiven, for she loved much. But to whom little is forgiven, the same loves little* (Luke 7:44, 47). This woman washed the feet of Jesus with her tears. Jesus responded to her faith and love for Him.

Blessed are you who hunger now, for you shall be filled. Blessed are you who weep now, for you shall laugh (Luke 6:21). These words are similar to the prayer of praise of Hannah in 1 Samuel 2. Hannah was hungry, but God fed and filled her with His Spirit. She wept in sorrow to God, but she also laughed in praise to God. She would indeed be lifted up from the garbage heap to be set among princes. Despite her infertility, she would bear many children.[13]

The shortest verse in the Bible, *Jesus wept* (John 11:35), is long on understanding the tender heart of our Lord. When He saw those He loved like Mary and Martha weeping for their dead brother Lazarus, He identified with them and wept with them. Even the Jews who were there remarked how much Jesus loved Lazarus (11:46). Jesus wept over Jerusalem.[14] As He wept in prayer, *His sweat became like great drops of blood (fell) down to the ground* (Luke 24:44).

The apostle Paul prayed with tears as well, *serving the Lord with all humility of mind, and with many tears… Therefore be on the alert, remembering that night and day for a period of three years I did not cease to admonish each one with tears* (Acts 20:19).

If the tears you have are from the heart of God, then only He can dry them away. Seek your comfort from Him who alone understands the depth of His burden and work in you.

MY BURDEN FOR CONNIE THAT LED TO TEARS

My wife, Connie, was experiencing the beginning of many health problems. It began over ten years ago when she developed diabetes. A few years later her liver was damaged and began to fail. As a result of the diabetes she also had nerve damage in both her stomach and intestines. In 2005 before she received a liver transplant, her stomach paresis was so bad that she would begin to throw up and could not stop. This would be followed by unbearable pain. I rushed her to the emergency room about every month where she would require additional treatment to stop the vomiting and gagging.

13   There is a phrase in 1 Samuel 2:5 that states, *Even the barren gives birth to seven.* In the Bible, seven is the number for completeness. Here, Hannah was not predicting the number of children she would have. In fact, 1 Samuel 2:21 tells us that after Samuel was born, she had five other children, for a total of six. However, through her words she was saying that her life would be filled and complete with the children she bore.

14   Matthew 23:37-39

One evening I again rushed Connie to the emergency room. While the medical staff worked on her, I walked around the hospital that night weeping with many tears before God. Then I began to sing as I wrote this song. I sang it back to God through tear stained eyes.

"The Tear Bottle of God"

Verse 1:
God keeps my tears in His bottle; He counts them one at a time
Not one tear is every forgotten, His heart is touched like mine
Weeping may last for the nighttime, Sharing God's burden of soul
But once the burden is lifted, Joy like rivers will flow

Chorus:
Oh Joy comes when the Son doth rise, Joy comes when the Son doth rise
And Jesus, who wept for us, Will wipe all the tears from our eyes
Yes, Joy comes when the Son doth rise, Joy comes when the Son doth rise
And Jesus, who now prays for us, Will wipe all the tears from our eyes

Verse 2:
God gives both joy and burdens, Mountains make valleys below
Stars are not seen in daytime, its darkness that lets them glow
Washing His feet with your tear drops, Toucheth the heart of Christ
Sowing in tears reaps a harvest, Souls redeemed in life

Chorus:
Oh Joy comes when the Son doth rise, Joy comes when the Son doth rise
And Jesus, who wept for us, Will wipe all the tears from our eyes
Yes, Joy comes when the Son doth rise, Joy comes when the Son doth rise
And Jesus, who now prays for us, Will wipe all the tears from our eyes [15]

As I walked the hospital grounds and sang my song to Jesus, I experienced the comfort of the Holy Spirit. In just a few months Connie's liver transplant helped change the constant vomiting and trips to the emergency room. I knew that my burden was from God, my tears were to God, and no one could dry them away but God. It was in that secret hiding place of fellowship with Jesus that I not only received peace and assurance but I also obtained the answer to my prayer and, like Hannah, would say, "*for this thing I prayed.*"

POINTING PEOPLE BACK TO THE TRUTH

I was in my sixth or seventh year of ministry and was becoming drained by those who were coming to me for comfort. I began to see a pattern among some who kept coming with similar problems. God had taught me that every believer is indwelt with the Holy Spirit and every believer

---

15   E. Truman Herring, © copyright 2005.

can hear from God for himself in the Word. I had also learned that God uses our problems to get us into the Scripture for God to be our greatest counsel and comfort.

One day a person who had come many times to me came again to tell me about their problems all over again. This time rather than sit and listen to them I gave them an assignment. Based upon what I knew about them and their problems, I assigned them a book of the Bible to read. I told them to take notes and be ready to explain what verses they marked and what they meant to them. To one I assigned them to read the entire book of Job and take notes on it. To another I told them to read the life of Joseph from Genesis 37-50. To another I assigned many Psalms and asked that they personalize them and pray them back to God, inserting their own needs.

After several weeks no one had come back to see me. I was a little concerned that I had offended them and pushed them away. I asked why they had not called me back. Their response was just what I needed to hear: *"Oh, pastor I did not need to call you back because as I read the Scripture, God began to speak to me and comfort me."*

I learned a great lesson that day. We must mature believers to the point where they learn to be comforted by the Scripture. Once they learn this lesson, then they will be able to go to the Word of God for themselves, to seek wisdom and answers from Him.

Consider how God used His Word to comfort the Psalmist in his afflictions:

> Before I was **afflicted** I went astray, but now I keep **Your word**…. It is good for me that I have been **afflicted**, that I may learn **Your statutes**. The law of Your mouth is better to me than thousands of coins of gold and silver…. I know, O Lord, that **Your judgments are right**, and that in faithfulness You have **afflicted me** (Psalm 119:67, 71, 72, 75; emphasis mine).

Did you see David's emphasis? Three times in four verses he uses the word *afflicted*. But in his affliction, he learned to *keep (God's) word* (v. 67). He was pointed toward God's statutes and judgments, and he said *they became better to me than thousands of coins of gold and silver* (v. 72).

Think about that! How much money do we pay to find inner peace, fulfillment and the strength to face the challenges of our lives? David got all that – and more – from God's Word.

This was God's plan for the nation of Israel. God purposely led them through tests to humble and test them in order that they might learn to depend upon Him through their knowledge and application of His Word.

> He humbled you, allowed you to hunger, and fed you with manna which you did not know nor did your fathers know, that He might make you know that man shall not live by bread alone; but man lives by every word that proceeds from the mouth of the Lord (Deuteronomy 8:3).

God must mature us by His Word. Once we learn to hear from God in His Word about His will and our problems, then there is nothing that can keep us from fellowship and comfort from God.

Once we have learned to be comforted by God from His Word, then God will be able to use us in a ministry inspired by the Holy Spirit to comfort others: *Blessed be the God and Father of our Lord Jesus Christ, the Father of mercies and God of all comfort, who comforts us in all our tribulation, that we may be able to comfort those who are in any trouble, with the comfort with which we ourselves are comforted by God* (2 Corinthians 1:3-4).

I have seen a pattern among young Christians and immature believers – they want to talk about their problems with others. This seems to be especially true among women. They often want to talk a problem to death only to have it resurrect itself with two other problems. Support groups have met a need – but they must go to the root problem. God is the one who must ultimately mature, chasten, refine, and use the storms of life to grow us and make us fruitful.

Hannah did not need a group of barren women trying to support her by baking cookies and taking her shopping with them and telling one another that not having children is not the worst thing in the world. She did not need to hear that she could look on the positive side and realize that she did not have to change diapers and be tied down by the constant needs of a child. No! Hannah would become a woman of faith who would base that faith on Scripture.

Where do you first go when you need help or comfort?

It is our natural tendency to go to a husband or wife, a mother or father, a close friend. And God may use that as part of His comfort. Titus comforted Paul when he was struggling (2 Corinthians 7:6). Just be careful that those that you go to for comfort are pointing you to Scripture and encouraging you to endure the test of faith in an obedient walk with God. I have seen non-believers and carnal believers give false sympathy to a troubled believer that weakens their faith and resolve to obey God and do what the Scripture said. I have talked to believers who told me that they were going to get in the Scripture, obey God, and grow through their problem, only to have others give them false sympathy and therefore they missed God completing His work to make them mature and fruitful.

I have also known other Christians who get together in a men's or women's Bible study. They support each other with the truths and principles of Scripture. Their lives become a testimony to God's faithfulness in their lives.

WHAT ABOUT YOU?

We must come to the point of maturity that the Holy Spirit in the Word can comfort us. Until then we will not fulfill our greater purpose in Christ.

- Where do you first seek comfort from in your trials? Do you go to friends? Do you withdrawal in despair? Do you escape through alcohol or drugs? Do you eat "comfort food"? Do you go on a spending spree? Or do you go to God and His Word?

- Do you get upset with others if they do not see your burden and offer you immediate comfort and resolution?

- Is God really the source of your sufficiency? Are you satisfied with a human answer to the problem when God is still waiting for you to come to Him?

- Do you know how to get into His Word and seek His answers in the truths of Scripture? [16]

4.   THE CONTENTMENT

Be careful not to allow the world to get you to be content with their answers and solutions, rather than seeking God for His intentions for us.

Hannah's husband expected her to be content with his gifts and himself. *Hannah, why do you weep? Why do you not eat? And why is your heart grieved? Am I not better to you than ten sons?* (1 Samuel 1:8). He was trying everything he could to cheer her up, but he did not understand the burden of God in her heart. It was not about ten sons. It was about Hannah's unique purpose before God. If Hannah did not find her contentment in the purpose of God, then even ten sons would not satisfy her.

It is amazing that God can work so deeply and intimately in our lives that other believers do not understand. Those who set their affections on the things of this earth will have a hard time understanding those who set their affections on Christ and building His kingdom now. Even the disciples who loved and forsook all to follow Jesus did not fully understand what God was doing in Christ.

OTHERS WILL NOT ALWAYS UNDERSTAND

The disciples had walked with Jesus for three years. But their mindset was that the Messiah would restore the kingdom to Israel and defeat the oppressing Romans. As a result, they misunderstood the cross, the sufferings of Jesus, and the mystery of the Church.

- When Jesus spoke of going to Jerusalem to be crucified and rising the third day, Peter reproved Him. He could not understand or identify with the burden that Jesus was carrying. *From that time Jesus began to show to His disciples that He must go to Jerusalem, and suffer many things from the elders and chief priests and scribes, and be killed, and be raised the third day. Then Peter took Him aside and began to rebuke Him, saying, "Far be it from You, Lord; this shall not happen to You!" But He turned and said to Peter, Get*

---

16   For additional help in this area, please see the author's book, *God's Greater Purpose in Christ*.

behind Me, Satan! You are an offense to Me, for you are not mindful of the things of God, but the things of men (Matthew 16:21-23).

- When Jesus spoke of going back to the Father after finishing His mission, Philip became confused. Jesus told him, *If you had known Me, you would have known My Father also; and from now on you know Him and have seen Him. Philip said to Him, "Lord, show us the Father, and it is sufficient for us." Jesus said to him, "Have I been with you so long, and yet you have not known Me, Philip? He who has seen Me has seen the Father; so how can you say, 'Show us the Father'?"* (John 14:7-9).

- When Jesus took the disciples to the Garden of Gethsemane to pray with Him before His death, they did not understand His great agony as He prayed. *When He came and found them sleeping, and said to Peter, "Simon, are you sleeping? Could you not watch one hour?"* (Mark 14:37).

Moses found that those to whom he was sent did not understand the burden God gave him. As Moses followed God through the wilderness, he was on a different level of understanding of God and His ways than the people he led. This can create a loneliness of soul that only God can satisfy.

Contentment is a Learned Quality of Maturity

Hannah was on a different page than Elkanah and her rival Peninnah. Peninnah was not even reading the same book and sought to discourage Hannah. When it is God who has engineered the trial in our lives, no one but God can give us contentment. Paul found his contentment in Christ. *Not that I speak in regard to need, for I have learned in whatever state I am, to be content* (Philippians 4:11). Paul could be content with little or much, in a palace or prison, in eating or fasting, because his contentment was in Christ.

One of the tests of faith that we must pass through in our maturity is to answer the question, *"Is Jesus enough to make you contented and filled with purpose and joy?"*

If we cannot be content until the world gives us more things, then we will find out that those things enslave us. We will have wasted our lives on ourselves. When God sees that your chief love is Jesus, then He can entrust greater things to you. When God has seen that you have been faithful with money, then He can entrust you with His true riches (Luke 16:11).

Would you give your unlimited credit card to a son who was addicted to crack cocaine? Of course not! However, if you had a child that had demonstrated faithfulness and maturity in his life, then you could entrust everything to him.

If Elkanah had given his Visa card to Hannah, she would have resisted going on a spending binge because she desired God's best. But if he had given his Visa card to Peninnah, she might have maxed out the card – but still not be content in her life.

When God puts in your heart His will, other things seem to fade in significance. If it is God's will for one to remain single, then God gives the grace to be content. But if God's will is for you to marry, you will persevere in faithfulness to Him – and be joyful in the process.

BURDENED FOR THE NATIONS

I have marveled at some of great missionaries to whom God gave them His burden for a pagan nation. With that burden came a holy discontent with their comfortable lifestyle at home. Family and friends did not understand why they could not be happy with their life in their own country.

Hudson Taylor became so burdened for China that wealth at home could no longer bring contentment to his life. Hudson tells of how he felt that God came to Him and said, *"I am going to evangelize inland China. If you will walk with me, I will do it through you."* There are some things that God is going to do with or without us. It is an incredible blessing when God finds a faithful person whom He can trust.

The great missionary Adoniram Judson left America in the early 1800s to become a missionary to Burma. How does one understand the burden that motivates a man to go to a nation that is hostile to him? It took him three years of daily study to learn Burmese language. He faced the death of children and his wife in a foreign land that God had put on his heart. He was imprisoned and tormented for nearly two years. Yet he continued to faithfully fulfill God's purpose for his life.

> *By 1823, ten years after his arrival, membership of the little church had grown to 18, and Judson had finally finished the first draft of his translation of the entire text of the Burmese New Testament. When Judson began his mission in Burma, he set a goal of translating the Bible and founding a church of 100 members before his death. When he died, he left the Bible, 100 churches, and over 8,000 believers.* [17]

The world will never understand why he could not be content until he had forsaken all to follow Christ to Burma. It is through the burden of God and call of God upon our lives, that God accomplishes his purpose around the world.

MISUNDERSTANDING THE BURDEN AND CALL OF GOD

I was in my third year of college and my dream was to have a career where I could make a good income. Yet, when God burdened my heart to preach, I found that I could not find contentment unless I followed God's will for my life. I lost all interest in my former dreams and found my greatest joy in doing the will of God for my life.

This is how God accomplishes His great work around the world. He finds a faithful man or woman and entrusts His heavenly vision to them. As a result, they will never be content unless they are in the center of God's will.

---

17   http://en.wikipedia.org/wiki/Adoniram_Judson

Connie and I were content in our home church where we had family and friends. We had such sweet fellowship with young Christian couples that filled our lives with great satisfaction. Yet I began to feel a restlessness of soul. I could no longer be content to simply sit and hear others preach. I knew I was called to preach. I knew I must preach. A call came to start a mission church 2,600 miles away from our families. I knew my mom and dad would understand and be supportive of our move. My mother had known from my birth that this day of releasing me to the will of God would come and she had the grace to *"lend me to the Lord."*

However, we dreaded breaking the news to Connie's parents. It proved to be one of the most difficult days of our young marriage. Connie was willing to follow me even though it meant leaving her family. I had a man-to-man talk with my father-in-law on the patio of his back yard. He did not want me to take his daughter away from home. He did not understand why I could not minister in a church locally and be happy. He offered alternate suggestions. He questioned if I could know God's will and feel called to a small town in the state of Washington. His view of ministry was much like a normal job in which you could choose where you wanted to work. I was at the point in my life where I knew I had to follow the great burden of my heart. Otherwise, I would be disobedient to God.

Then things became even more difficult. My father-in-law began to attack me personally. He told me that I was stealing his daughter from him and that he had no respect for me at all. About that time a stray dog was crossing through the backyard and he said words that hurt me deeply: *"I have more respect for that dog than for you."* My wife was in a vice between the pressure of pleasing her parents and following her husband.

We had left my parent's home with prayers, blessings, and hugs and kisses. We left Connie's parents with harsh words and broken hearts. Connie cried for fifty miles. I have a vivid image of pulling a little four foot by six foot U-Haul behind our little four cylinder car over the Mississippi River Bridge as my dear wife sobbed deeply. We were in our fourth year of marriage and Connie had left her family and a good job to follow me. I was sorry for the agony I was putting her through and was tempted to try to compromise to keep everyone happy. But I knew I had to be faithful to the vision and call God had given me.

The good news is that there was a happy ending to this story. Connie's father would later give us his blessing and our fellowship would be restored. They visited us in the Northwest and saw firsthand God's blessing s on our ministry.

Doing the will of God is often hard on the outside, but as we follow Him, there is the deep peace of God on the inside … a peace that passes all understanding.

HARD QUESTIONS

The issue of contentment produces some very hard questions that we must answer honestly and repeatedly.

- Where is your contentment? Is it in possessions? Is it in relationships? Is it in social standing or other's opinion of you? Or is it solely in God?

- Could you be content with less material things? What are you willing to sacrifice?

- Have you ever misunderstood the burden God gave someone else? What were the circumstances? How did that person respond? What did you learn from that experience?

- Has God ever changed your heart to the point where you could not be content unless you did the will of God?

- Can you pass the test of misunderstanding?

- Can you pass the test of loneliness of soul?

5.   THE COUNTERFEIT

It's easy to settle for a counterfeit. Counterfeits cost far less than the real thing. They are easier to obtain … and a lot less trouble … initially.

THE BEGINNING OF THE MIDDLE EAST CRISIS

Hannah would have remembered when Sarah's faith wavered. She settled for a counterfeit and substituted Hagar for her barren womb. But we must not use natural means to do supernatural work. Though the choice seemed easy at the time, the nation of Israel is still suffering the consequences of Abraham and Sarah's bad choice four thousand years later. It is the children of promise we seek, in whom the Promised Seed will be called, and not the children of the flesh, the Ishmaels of our own making.

Hannah had to resist the temptation of transferring her hope from God to anything else. She had a wonderful husband who loved her. Many men in that day would divorce their infertile wives. But Elkanah loved her too much to reject her. He didn't beat her – he blessed her. He did not rebuke her – he rewarded her. He did not humiliate her – he honored her. And those were all good and godly things. But sometimes even the good things can keep us from receiving God's best.

Most women would have accepted the blessings of a husband who loved them that much and missed the supernatural working of God in their lives. Hannah learned that God's work in her life left her dependent on God and no one else. We must discern when someone offers us a *"worthy portion"* if it is a diversion from God's greater purpose in our life.

Certainly God can use others to be the means by which He answers our prayers. God uses natural means to accomplish his work through the ministry of His people. We are God's hands to minister to others. However, in the church we must not confuse activity for Holy Spirit power, numbers for holiness, and man's approval for the approval of God. Hannah's husband may have tried to encourage her many times by telling her of the many other benefits that she had, but thank God she would not be comforted, content, or compromised to receive a counterfeit, but would wait for God to answer her prayers.

DISCERNING THE COUNTERFEIT

Some counterfeits are easy to discern while others are not. We are warned that not everything that comes in the name of God or even Christ is always from God. Paul warned the Church that Satan could come as an angel of light and that some would preach a false Jesus (2 Corinthians 11:1-4; 13-14).

The altar that Jeroboam built at Bethel was similar in design and purpose to the true altar of the Lord at Jerusalem. The multitudes that would substitute the altar of Bethel for the true altar at Jerusalem found the words of Jeroboam convenient, *It is too much for you to go up to Jerusalem* (1 Kings 12:28). However, God sent a prophet to rebuke Jeroboam for his counterfeit religion. It was a trap, a deception that was designed to ensnare God's people and take them away from true worship.

Hannah was tempted to be satisfied with something less that God's best for her life. We have all heard the warning, *"Do not let something good have you miss God's best for you."* You may be the only one who knows the vision that God has placed in your heart. We need to be *followers of those who through faith and patience inherit the promises* (Hebrews 6:12). It may be hard to wait on God to bring to pass His plan for our lives, but we must not accept a substitute.

- It's easy for pastors to experience the counterfeit. They feel called to "preach" but not to shepherd, love and care for God's people. They grow weary with church people and their problems. One pastor told me when an offer came for better money in a secular job, *"I believe I can be more effective as a Christian witness with a secular job."* Time would prove him wrong.

- Sometimes it is not a secular job but another ministry position that gives a pastor relief from his current difficult situation. What appeared to be an attractive blessing becomes less than what God had planned.

Many singles grow weary in waiting for a godly Christian mate and settle for what is immediately in front of them. They ultimately find themselves in an unequally yoked relationship and miss God's best for their lives.

TIME FOR AN INNER-AUDIT

Audits are always difficult experiences. In business audits, an outside agency comes in to analyze the financial records of a company to see what discrepancies may exist.

A spiritual audit is one where you allow the Holy Spirit to shine the light of His Word and truth on the motives of your heart and the choices you have made. It's difficult to ask the "hard questions," but it is so rewarding to come clean before God and live honestly in His presence. Ask yourself ...

- Are you tempted to invent a man-made alternative rather than wait on God? Sarah did that and wound up with Hagar and Ishmael.

- Have you transferred your hope away from the one true God and on to anything else? If so, how did that happen? Were there warning signs you ignored in your decision-making process?

- Is spiritual duplicity going on in your life? In what areas are you "pretending" rather than living authentically before God?

- What compromises have you made in the past? Are there patterns of compromise that you can identify? How can you keep that from happening in the future?

- What lies do you believe? Where do you allow your mind to wander? What do you do when you are alone that you would never want anyone to know about? How negative and critical are you of others?

Take some time and pray about each of these areas. Confess any sin that the Spirit of God brings to your mind. Claim God's promise from 1 John 1:9 that *if we confess our sins, He is faithful and righteous to forgive our sin and cleanse us from all unrighteousness.*

CHAPTER 7

Battered

And her rival also provoked her severely, to make her miserable, because the LORD had closed her womb. So it was, year by year, when she went up to the house of the LORD, that she provoked her; therefore she wept and did not eat (1 Samuel 1:5).

 ## THE THIRD TEST OF FAITH

The third test that Hannah faced, and one that each of us will face, is:

> *Can you trust and wait on God even when you are battered by the enemy?*

A PROMISE FROM GOD AS TRUE AS JOHN 3:16

The Apostle Paul wrote in 2 Timothy 3:12, *All who desire to live godly in Christ Jesus will suffer persecution.* This promise is just as true as John 3:16 or any of the other great promises in the Bible. If you choose to walk with Jesus and seek to glorify Him with your life, you will be persecuted. That persecution may come from unbelievers, friends, neighbors, those inside the church, and those outside the church. But ultimately the source of all that persecution is Satan himself, the enemy of our souls.

Satan will batter and accuse us. He employs several unique strategies in his accusations against us:

- His goal is to cause you to doubt God and His promises.

- He will bring people in your life that will criticize you, put you down, hurt you, remind you of your failures, and make you feel worthless.
- He wants to discourage you.
- He will put you on a guilt trip because of your sins and will tell you that God could not possibly forgive your sin over and over again.
- He will bring accusations against God – that God has abandoned you, failed you, or ceased to love you.
- He seeks to have you accuse and condemn yourself.

 ## ACCUSATIONS 101

Peninnah mistreated Hannah day after day. The inspired record of Scripture says she *provoked her severely.* Why? *Peninnah wanted to make Hannah miserable!* Have you recognized that there are people out there who take great delight in bringing misery to others? Peninnah found Hannah's weak spot. She couldn't say that Elkanah loved her less. It was obvious that Hannah was his favorite. She didn't attack Hannah's physical appearance. But she found the one thing that could really get to Hannah: her infertility.

Satan does exactly the same thing to us. He studies us. He knows our weak spots. And he brings along an attack tailor-made to get to us. When under attack, we often try to hold on as long as we can … but because we do it in our own strength, we fail. God wants us to come to the point where we completely surrender to Him. Many will hold on as long as they can in their own strength, trying to be strong for God. God will often allow even greater pressures on the outside to bring us to the place of absolute surrender He desires so that the life of Jesus will be manifest through us (2 Corinthians 4:7-11; 1:8, 9).

 ## TWO PRINCIPLES: RESTING AND EXCHANGING

In the midst of our struggle, we must come to the place of resting in the sovereignty of God. Hebrews 4:9-10 tells us that *there remains a rest for the people of God.* This principle of trust isn't a *resignation,* where we *give up,* but a *rest,* where we *give over* control to our heavenly Father.

When we rest and give our struggles over to Him, we will experience the principle of exchange, where we exchange our human insufficiencies and weaknesses for the manifest power of God. Read these words carefully:

He gives power to the weak, and to those who have no might He increases strength. Even the youths shall faint and be weary, and the young men shall utterly fall, but those who wait on the LORD shall renew their strength; they shall mount up with wings like eagles, they shall run and not be weary, they shall walk and not faint (Isaiah 40:29-31).

God *gives power to the weak.* He *increases strength to those who have no might.* Where does this strength come from? Not from our own abilities, but from the Holy Spirit who lives inside of us.

God did not give Hannah relief from her burden until she reached a point where she let it go. It is at that point she discovered that God was there to carry both her and her burden all the time. Remember the story of the woman who prematurely interfered with the transformation process of the caterpillar to a butterfly? God will not preempt the process of sanctification and fulfillment of His specific purpose for our lives. God must bring us all the way through the refinement process. For Hannah the battering of her adversary made her turn to God even more.

 ## I Needed a New Dad

As I shared earlier, my mom's prayers about me were answered – and I became a pastor. But she faced incredible challenges as she prayed for God to change the heart of my dad. She knew that my dad needed God to work in his life. If dad had been a better husband, perhaps she would not have been so burdened to pray for him. But the battering she endured became a catalyst to make her even more determined to have God hear her prayers.

I was seven years old as my dad and I walked by a local bar. He took me inside and we sat on bar stools as he drank beer with other men. I remember thinking, *"This is what real men do. One day I will be big enough to come here and drink with my friends like my dad."*

One day I found my mom on the kitchen floor crying. My dad, in a drunken state, had knocked her to the floor. It was not the first time as a seven-year-old that I had witnessed the damaging effects of alcohol in my father's life.

Many women would let this battering make them bitter. Not my mom. She knew that what dad really needed was for Jesus to control his life. Satan may have tried to discourage mom from her Christian faith, but these episodes only moved her to turn her tears into intercession and prayer that got God's compassionate attention. She began praying and trusting God to work miraculously in my father's life.

Mom found bottles of whiskey that dad had hidden in the house. I watched as she boldly poured them down the drain. She even let me help, as a teaching tool to warm me of its dangers. I remember walking through my dad's bedroom on Sundays as he slept off a hangover. Mom faithfully took my three sisters, along with me, to church each week. Satan's battering had released a sleeping giant as my mom faithfully continued praying.

Then overnight, like the caterpillar turning into the butterfly, God changed my dad. His victory in Christ sprouted wings and took flight. He was a new man, a new husband, and a new dad. Alcohol never entered our house again. Now at every meal my dad would lead us in prayer. A Bible reading, short devotion and prayer before evening meals became a family tradition. Every Saturday mom and dad would make a drive to minister at a prison. It was seeing this transformation in dad that made me begin to think that I needed to be a Christian like mom and dad.

HAVE YOU BEEN BATTERED?

What do you do when you are burdened and your trial of faith seems too heavy and too long? Do what Hannah did: persevere in prayer! Most of us want God to end the trial of faith. When an adversary batters us and beats us down, we want to run away and hide. It's easy to become passive and depressed at this point.

Martial arts teachers tell their students to use the force of their opponent's blows against them. Satan used Peninnah to provoke Hannah – but that backfired because it made Hannah even more desperate, dependent, and determined to trust God to deliver her. She would later express her victory in praise: *The bows of the mighty men are broken, and those who stumbled are girded with strength* (1 Samuel 2:4). Like a soldier on the battlefield, Satan had battered her and knocked her down. But against his natural attacks, God did the supernatural, giving her His strength in weakness and she prevailed over her enemy.

In this chapter we are going to look at four places accusations come from and learn how to fight them from a spiritual perspective.

1. BATTERED AND ACCUSED BY FOES

The first place accusations come from is from our enemies. Peninnah was not a friend, but a foe, and Satan inspired her to accuse Hannah. *And her rival also provoked her severely, to make her miserable, because the LORD had closed her womb* (1:6).

When Elkanah put his two wives under the same roof, it was a recipe for disaster. I'm sure he wanted them to get along with each other – but that was never going to happen. In fact, the relationship intensified into a *rivalry*, where Peninnah *provoked her severely*, day after day.

Peninnah was able to take advantage of Hannah's barren condition to provoke her and make her fret. She found the crack in her rival's armor. She found the point where Hannah was most vulnerable and she battered her there over and over again. Her home, the place that should have been a place of safety, became a battleground every day.

That same thing can happen in the church. You probably won't find it shocking to learn that the place where you should be the most loved, understood and accepted can also be the place where you are the most hurt, misunderstood and rejected. Unfortunately, not everyone in the church is walking with God. Not everyone exercises wisdom in what they say and how they relate to others. There are those who will not understand what God is doing in your life as you carry God's burden. There are those who are carnal, fleshly, self-seeking, and envious of what God is doing in your life.

Behind Peninnah's provocations was Satan himself. Remember he is called *the accuser of the brethren* and is constantly *accusing us before God day and night* (Revelation 12:10). Is it any wonder that he also motivates others to participate in the same strategy?

HANNAH'S GREATER ADVERSARY AND THE GREATER CONFLICT IN HEAVEN

Remember we are not simply looking at the historical setting of the conflict on earth between Peninnah and Hannah. We must also look from heaven's viewpoint and interpret these events from Hannah's prophetic prayer of praise as well. Hannah fits into God's greater purpose in Christ as one puzzle piece that is part of the whole. Notice Hannah's prophecy of the coming of the Anointed King who is the Lord Jesus Christ. *The adversaries of the LORD shall be broken in pieces; from heaven He will thunder against them. The LORD will judge the ends of the earth.* **He will give strength to His king, and exalt the horn of His anointed** (1 Samuel 2:10; emphasis mine).

Many commentaries acknowledge that this is a reference to the coming Messiah. What began in Genesis in the Garden as a battle between Satan and Christ continues until the end of the book of Revelation where Christ will cast Satan into the eternal Lake of Fire forever. God promised Adam and Eve that there would come the *seed of the woman* who would crush the head of Satan while Satan would only bruise the heel of Christ (Genesis 3:15). [18] Throughout Scripture we see evidences of Satan's hatred of Christ and his attacks upon God's people like the unseen hand behind Peninnah attacks upon Hannah.

The Holy Spirit picks up the Messianic theme in Hannah's prayer when Mary is told that God will bring forth Christ from her virgin womb. Notice how similar the words of Mary's praise are to Hannah's: *He has put down the mighty from their thrones, and exalted the lowly. He has filled the hungry with good things, and the rich He has sent away empty* (Luke 1:52, 53). Hannah calls God her *rock* and in reference to her enemies she says, *my horn is exalted in the Lord* (1 Samuel 2:1, 2).

One commentary helps us understand the use of the word *horn*:

> *The predictive element in Hannah's song is most apparent in this word, and it is obvious from Luke's quotation of this verse (Luke 1:69) that he regards the song as predictive prophecy finding its ultimate fulfillment in Jesus Christ, God's King in the line of David, God's Servant who finally accomplishes salvation for His people.* [19]

Regarding Hannah's use of the word *anointed*, we learn *"The word 'anointed' is a translation of the Hebrew mashiah, 'messiah.' This is its first occurrence in the Old Testament; it is singularly appropriate for Mary's song of exultation."* [20]

In Hannah's prophetic prayer regarding God's anointed king we see a battle that goes beyond her and Peninnah. It is a battle that involves Satan's hatred of all who love Christ. Notice the big picture of this battle in Psalm 2.

> *Why do the nations rage,*
> *And the people plot a vain thing?*

18 Every other reference about bearing children in the Old Testament refers to *the seed of the man*. But here in Genesis, God refers to the coming One as born *of the seed of the woman*. Though veiled in incompleteness, this was the first reference to the virgin birth that was fulfilled in the life of Mary.

19 *KJV Bible Commentary*. Nashville: Thomas Nelson, 1997, p. 536.

20 *Believer's Study Bible*. electronic ed. Nashville : Thomas Nelson, 1997, 1 Samuel 2:10.

> *The kings of the earth set themselves,*
> *And the rulers take counsel together,*
> *Against the LORD and against **His Anointed**, saying,*
>   *"Let us break Their bonds in pieces*
> *And cast away Their cords from us."*
>   *He who sits in the heavens shall laugh;*
> *The LORD shall hold them in derision* (Psalm 2:1-4; emphasis mine).

If we think our conflict is only with our earthly adversaries, we will never discover the secret of fruitfulness that God has for us. Sometimes our greater enemy, Satan, indirectly inspires the attacks from people. *Put on the whole armor of God, that you may be able to stand against the wiles of the devil. For **we do not wrestle against flesh and blood,** but against principalities, against powers, against the rulers of the darkness of this age, against spiritual hosts of wickedness in the heavenly places* (Ephesians 6:11, 12; emphasis mine). We must heed the words of Peter, *Be sober, be vigilant; because your adversary the devil walks about like a roaring lion, seeking whom he may devour* (1 Peter 5:8).

If we are to experience the greater fruitfulness that God has for us, we must know that our victory over Satan is grounded in Christ's victory on the cross. We must not fight the flesh with the flesh, thinking that if we can somehow be free from our adversary, the conflict will be over. No! We must learn to run to Christ, rest in Christ, submit ourselves to God and resist the Devil. It is then that we will discover that the fiery darts from our foe's sharp tongue will be quenched with the shield of faith.

Have you noticed that when God calls you to do His will, that Satan always stirs up an adversary to discourage you? In the Bible, those adversaries were named Peninnah, Saul, Absalom, Sanballat, Haman, and even Judas. If we are chosen by God to carry His burden, then if we become rid of Peninnah, we will face a Saul. If we are rid of Saul, we will face an Absalom. If we are rid of Absalom, we will face a Sanballat. If we are free of Sanballat, we will face a Haman. We will never be free of adversaries and accusers as we walk with God. If you were of the world, the world would love you. Because you are no longer of the world you are a threat to Satan's kingdom. Satan is a roaring lion seeking to defeat and discourage you. Therefore you must learn to become a skilled soldier who uses the enemy's mighty bow against him as God breaks it. As you are battered, knocked down, humbled, and stumbling in the battle, you are now in the best position to, by faith, be girded with God's strength.

There is a common thread in Scripture that we must understand: the closer we get to God and doing God's will, the more it angers Satan. As a result, he launches a spiritual attack against us. If he can find one that will be an unknowing ally, he will prompt them to provoke us to give up on God's vision for our lives. Pray for your adversaries. Do not become bitter toward them. Leave them in God's hands – and it will be God who removes them from you. From the Bible's pages we learn:

- Continue to build God's wall and do not be distracted by Sanballat. The wall will be completed (Nehemiah 4).

- Be like Mordecai and seek God. Rather than fighting your foe, trust God to fight the battle. And the gallows that Haman built against you will be used against him (Esther 7).
- Be like Jesus who taught us, *But I say to you, Love your enemies, bless those who curse you, do good to those who hate you, and pray for those who spitefully use you and persecute you* (Matthew 5:44).
- Learn from the early church that prayed for their greatest persecutor, Saul of Tarsus. He was miraculously converted by God and became the Apostle Paul, the greatest leader of the New Testament church (Acts 9).

On your journey to greater fruitfulness with God, do not be surprised if God allows someone to batter you so that you become even more dependent upon God in your greater troubles.

APPLICATION TIME

- Have you ever been battered when you began to do the will of God? How did you handle it? Were you tempted to first fight the flesh with the flesh?

- In what ways have you learned to run to God and resist the devil?

- What keeps you from praying for your enemies as Jesus taught us to do?

2. BATTERED AND ACCUSED BY THE FLESH

There is a second source of attacks and accusations. Besides coming from our foes, we also fight against our flesh. There is a battle that goes on inside each believer, as our flesh (also referred to as our old nature) attacks and batters us. It wages war with our new life in Christ.

The secret to fruitfulness is to reach a point that we see our flesh as a greater adversary than Satan. We must reach a point that we are so disgusted with our flesh that we seek to die to our self-life daily. We must be so provoked that we cannot coexist with this adversary. We must reach the point that Paul described in Romans 7 in which we discover that our flesh is our worst enemy.

Notice again what happened in Hannah's life:

*And her rival also **provoked her severely**, to make her **miserable**, because the LORD had closed her womb. So it was, year by year, when she went up to the house of the LORD, that* *she provoked her; therefore she* **wept** *and did not eat. Then Elkanah her husband said to her, "Hannah, why do you weep? Why do you not eat? And why is your heart* **grieved**? *Am I not better to you than ten sons?"* (1 Samuel 1:6-8; emphasis mine).

She was *provoked severely;* she felt *miserable;* she *wept* every time she went to worship God; her heart was *grieved.* That doesn't sound like "the abundant Christian life," does it? However, God used the continual provoking of her adversary to bring Hannah to absolute surrender to God. Peninnah certainly reminds me of my own flesh that is unrelenting in provoking me daily.

YOUR FLESH IS NOT YOUR FRIEND – IT IS YOUR FOE

The Lord saved me as a third grade boy. It would be years later that I would discover that I was spiritually barren to bring forth fruit unto God. I was a young married man when my heart was stirred to get more serious with my walk with Jesus. I began to discover that the harder I tried to serve God, the harder my adversaries resisted me. I knew little of Satan and spiritual warfare. I had known for years that Satan could tempt me to sin. However, I was so ignorant of his strategies that I did not recognize his disguises as he tempted me with what appeared to be good things.

My greatest shock came as I discovered what Paul declared that *in my flesh dwells no good thing* (Romans 7:18). I was shocked to learn that I could attempt to serve God in the flesh. And when I did attempt to defeat my flesh by discipline, Satan provoked me even more. Even when I made a greater commitment to the law of God, I was defeated and unfruitful. The desire to bear fruit and please God was His burden, but I was reduced to Paul's cry, *O wretched man that I am! Who will deliver me from this body of death?* (Romans 7:24). Our failure and barrenness can be a great teacher to humble us and make us realize that without abiding in Christ daily, *we can do nothing* (John 15:5).

The Apostle Paul had to come to the point where he realized that his flesh was unable to do anything of spiritual value:

> *For we know that the law is spiritual, but I am carnal, sold under sin. For what I am doing, I do not understand. For what I will to do, that I do not practice; but what I hate, that I do. If, then, I do what I will not to do, I agree with the law that it is good. But now, it is no longer I who do it, but sin that dwells in me. For I know that in me (that is, in my flesh) nothing good dwells; for to will is present with me, but how to perform what is good I do not find. For the good that I will to do, I do not do; but the evil I will not to do, that I practice. Now if I do what I will not to do, it is no longer I who do it, but sin that dwells in me.*

> *I find then a law, that evil is present with me, the one who wills to do good. For I delight in the law of God according to the inward man. But I see another law in my members, warring against the law of my mind, and bringing me into captivity to the law of sin which is in my members. O wretched man that I am! Who will deliver me from this body of death? I thank God—through Jesus Christ our Lord! So then, with the mind I myself serve the law of God, but with the flesh the law of sin* (Romans: 14-25).

A chapter earlier, Paul spoke of dying daily to his flesh and allowing the life of Jesus in him to bring forth fruit unto God (Romans 6:1-14). Our flesh cannot be reformed, trained, educated or improved. Even when we dedicate ourselves to serve God and try to reform our flesh by baptizing it with the law or strong commitment to God, we come up empty, frustrated and unfruitful.

My greatest enemy in serving God is my flesh. That's why there is so much biblical truth in this principle: *when I try, I fail. When I trust, He succeeds.*

 ## WHY DON'T YOU DROP DEAD?

While in college, my pastor shocked me as he began his Sunday message with the words, *"Drop dead! Why don't you just drop dead?"* It sure got my attention for what was to become a milestone in my understanding of how to deal with my greatest enemy.

I already knew that ministry was not all about what you wanted. It made sense to mature to the point that we were not so self-centered in ministry. However, the Biblical concept of death to self was a hard pill to swallow.

I remember my pastor's imaginary illustration of a dead man in a casket. He began to mock him and insult him. The dead man made no response. He then pointed out that dead men do not get their feelings hurt. They do not wear their feelings on their sleeves. Every time I am tempted to have my feelings hurt I can hear the echo of his words, *"Drop dead! Dead men do not get their feelings hurt!"*

Perhaps you are coming to realize that Hannah's greatest problem was not her barrenness. Neither was it Peninnah. Hannah's greatest problem was … Hannah!

And so it is with us. The greatest hindrance to our fruitfulness is our flesh. And God's answer to the flesh is death and resurrection. Paul writes, *I have been crucified with Christ; it is no longer I who live, but Christ lives in me; and the life which I now live in the flesh I live by faith in the Son of God, who loved me and gave Himself for me* (Galatians 2:20).

The flesh is self-centered. It wants attention. Until we learn that life is not about us, but about God and His glory, we will never be ready for God to use us to bear fruit for Him.

Read the following verse slowly, carefully. Meditate on it. Pray it back to God, asking Him to make its message a reality in your life:

> *Not unto us, O LORD, not unto us, but to Your name give glory, because of Your mercy, because of Your truth* (Psalm 115:1).

APPLICATION TIME

- How have selfish desires and fleshly motives sidetracked you in your walk with God?

- How often do you get your feelings hurt in ministry? How many times have you let your feelings be a stumbling block to God's great assignment for you?

- Can you identify with Paul's cry, *O wretched man that I am, who shall deliver me from the body of this death?* Have you reached a point where you are so disgusted with your self-efforts that you cry out to God for spiritual power and victory?

- Can you truly say that you have been crucified with Christ, that it is no longer you who lives, but that Christ lives in you? Are you living for His glory and honor?

3. BATTERED AND ACCUSED BY FAMILY

There's a third source of attack. We must deal with accusations from our family. These attacks may hurt the most because they come from the people who are supposed to love us. Elkanah's attempt to encourage Hannah could have hindered her faith and short-circuited God's process of making her fruitful. He loved Hannah – and it was only natural for him to comfort her. This battering was not just from her rival. It was indirectly from her husband.

It would have been easy for Satan to twist Elkanah words, *Am I not better to you than ten sons?* into an accusation or condemnation.

EAVESDROPPING ON A CONVERSATION

Let's imagine a dialogue between Hannah and her husband …

> *"Hannah, can't you just be happy? Look at all the ways I've tried to show you I love you! I'm getting tired of all this crying. You don't have to have a child to be happy. Why can't you just accept the fact that you cannot have children? I have children through Peninnah and am satisfied – so it is not necessary that you give me children. Just accept the way things are. You are barren – so learn to live with it."*

We have already seen that it was the Lord who shut up Hannah's womb, yet He created the deep desire for a child that would not be denied. Why would God give her the burden for a child if it were not His desire to open her womb? If God has given you His burden from heaven for a purpose, a mission, a person, or a ministry, then you must not allow even your family to accuse you with false comfort. Remember, there is a difference between the comfort God offers through His Word and the Holy Spirit who is our promised Comforter, and false comfort (John 14:16, 26; 15:26).

It is common when we are going through a trial of faith for a family member to sympathize with us and offer encouragement. Perhaps one of Hannah's family members said, "*I am so sorry that you have to go through this problem. It just isn't fair the way Peninnah is treating you. You have every right to stand up to her and give her a taste of her own medicine. If your husband cared about you, then he would have more understanding of your special circumstances and be more protective of you.*"

When a daughter is having marital problems she will often seek comfort from her mother, and, in an attempt to sympathize with her daughter, that mother sometimes may interfere with God's process of humbling both the husband and the wife.

God does choose many means to comfort us – and it is often that a family member confirms and supports us in our trial of faith. However, the comfort a family member offers must not contradict the comfort that God gives through His unchangeable Scriptures.

 ## EXAMPLES FROM THE BIBLE

- Did you ever notice that Jesus' family did not understand His burden and mission from God (John 7:4-8)? Jesus calls us to forsake all to follow him (Mark 10:28-30). Even our family's misunderstanding of our call can be part of God's process to test and strengthen our faith.
- The patriarch Joseph had his brothers misunderstand his God-given dreams.
- Job's wife could not understand God's bigger purpose with her husband. Satan used her to say to her husband, *Curse God and die* (Job 2:9).

Let me offer a word of caution at this point. There are some who think they have a mission from God and become fanatical. They are deceived by their pride and they put on the garment of super-spirituality. They claim that their sufferings are because they are following Christ, when in reality they suffer from being outside of the will of God. You must make sure you are doing what He has called you to do – and not what is self-motivated.

APPLICATION TIME

- Have you ever had a spouse or family member misunderstand the burden that God put in your heart? What happened? How did you react?

- Have you ever had their comfort sidetrack you from the will of God?

- Have you ever had a family member encourage you not to give up on the burden that God had placed upon your heart? In what ways did that inspire you toward greater fruitfulness?

4.   BATTERED AND ACCUSED BY FRIENDS

It seems Hannah was misunderstood wherever she went. Elkanah didn't know what to say. Peninnah attacked her. And even Eli misunderstood the burden that God had placed upon her heart.

> So Hannah arose after they had finished eating and drinking in Shiloh. Now Eli the priest was sitting on the seat by the doorpost of the tabernacle of the LORD. And she was in bitterness of soul, and prayed to the LORD and wept in anguish. Then she made a vow and said, "O LORD of hosts, if You will indeed look on the affliction of Your maidservant and remember me, and not forget Your maidservant, but will give Your maidservant a male child, then I will give him to the LORD all the days of his life, and no razor shall come upon his head."
>
> And it happened, as she continued praying before the LORD, that Eli watched her mouth. Now Hannah spoke in her heart; only her lips moved, but her voice was not heard. Therefore Eli thought she was drunk. So Eli said to her, "How long will you be drunk? Put your wine away from you!"
>
> But Hannah answered and said, "No, my lord, I am a woman of sorrowful spirit. I have drunk neither wine nor intoxicating drink, but have poured out my soul before the LORD. Do not consider your maidservant a wicked woman, for out of the abundance of my complaint and grief I have spoken until now."
>
> Then Eli answered and said, "Go in peace, and the God of Israel grant your petition which you have asked of Him."
>
> And she said, "Let your maidservant find favor in your sight." So the woman went her way and ate, and her face was no longer sad (1 Samuel 1:9-18).

 SHUT UP TO GOD

Those who are "shut up to God" must learn to stand-alone with God. There will be times when friends misunderstand the burden of our soul and test our faithfulness to God. There will be other times when God brings along those who share in the common walk of faith with God. They will encourage us, lift us up, and keep us pointed in the right direction.

It is only natural when we are burdened to seek for someone to stand with us. However, we should desire someone who understands what God is doing in us; not just someone who stands beside us, but cannot grasp the depth of our burden. Hannah's husband certainly did not understand the depth of what she was going through. She was all alone; shut up to the will of God. Often in the process of the trial of faith, we learn to stand-alone with God. Once this lesson is learned we are never alone.

The principle that Hannah discovered is that *when God is all you have, God is all you need.*

ABRAHAM

Hannah descended from a long line of Abraham's children. By faith, he had learned to walk alone with God.

Abraham was called of God to leave his family and go to the Land of Promise. It took him years before he left his father and later Lot. He had many solitary walks with God in which God revealed more of Himself and His purpose to Abraham. One of the great lonely moments with God came as he took Isaac, his promised son, up Mt. Moriah to offer him unto the Lord. No one but God could understand what Abraham was going through. He was alone with God. Even Abraham could not fully understand how his offering up of his only son fit into God's greater purpose for his life. But he knew God. God was all he had at that point – but God was also all that he needed.

MOSES

Though Aaron, Joshua and the entire nation of Israel surrounded him, Moses experienced being alone with God. From the burning bush to receiving the Law of God on Mt. Sinai, Moses had learned that the burden of God brought with it the presence of God.

Moses was often alone in his leadership of Israel because the people did not understand the strange way of God leading His people from one test of faith to the next. They murmured at the Red Sea at the sight of Pharaoh's army and rejoiced only when they saw his army drown. They murmured only three days later at Marah when they thirsted for water. They murmured with their desire for meat and food and God gave them daily manna. They were tested again by thirst and again murmured until God gave them water from the Rock, which Moses struck with the Rod of God. Moses understood what it meant to walk with God by faith. The people he led only wanted to walk by sight. The result was a lifetime of being alone.

But that aloneness drove Moses deeper into his relationship with God. He learned to depend on Him fully … because God was all he had.

DAVID

Later David would receive the burden of God and his brothers did not understand what God was doing in his heart. Saul called himself David's friend, but later became a foe, making him even more dependent upon God. David experienced the loneliness of leadership as he became responsible for the lives and welfare of the band of 600 faithful outcast followers and their families.

However, David found solace in the presence of God to encourage him in some of his most difficult trials of faith. He had to learn to stand-alone with God as many of his psalms reveal.

Notice David's confidence in spite of opposition in this psalm. That confidence came from the very presence of God in his life during times of loneliness.

> *Truly my soul silently waits for God; from Him comes my salvation. He only is my rock and my salvation; He is my defense; I shall not be greatly moved.*

> *How long will you attack a man? You shall be slain, all of you, like a leaning wall and a tottering fence. They only consult to cast him down from his high position; they delight in lies; they bless with their mouth, but they curse inwardly. Selah*

> *My soul, wait silently for God alone, for my expectation is from Him. He only is my rock and my salvation; He is my defense; I shall not be moved. In God is my salvation and my glory; the rock of my strength, and my refuge, is in God* (Psalm 62:1-7).

Those words of wisdom were forged in a faithful heart during times where God was the only one David had.

SAMUEL AND JONATHAN

Samuel, the son of Hannah, learned from his mother that when God gives you His burden, He also gives you His presence and as a result, you are never alone. Samuel did not find anyone in the house of Eli who understood the burden that God places on the souls of His children. But his mother's example must have encouraged him. Through her he learned that when God is all you have, God is all you need. Samuel would do the same for David. David was comforted by the times he spent with Samuel because they both understood the walk of faith and the ways of God.

God also gave David a friend in Jonathan who, like David, had a heart after God. The Scripture sets Jonathan's faith in direct contrast to his father Saul's unbelief. Jonathan was a comfort to David, not because they were buddies, but because they both understood the walk of faith with God. Therefore their hearts were knit together. Perhaps when David was pursued by Saul and questioned the call of God and the suffering that came with doing the will of God, he took comfort in knowing that somewhere were two godly men who understood what he was going through to do the will of God.

JESUS

Jesus had many who loved and followed Him.

- Multitudes followed Him wherever He went, hanging on His words, listening to His teaching.
- There were the seventy that He sent out with the power of God to minister two by two.
- He had the twelve disciples who were with Him every day. They had a better understanding of His burden and mission. But even one of them proved to be a traitor.

- Jesus had three who were invited to be with Him on the Mount of Transfiguration and see His glory and hear the audible voice of God confirming His Son.

But despite the crowds and the intimacy of those who followed most closely, there were things He endured alone. From the Garden of Gethsemane to the Cross Jesus stood alone with God in a level of burden that no one could understand except His Father.

JOB

Job had to learn to stand alone in the will of God when he faced a trial of faith like few have ever faced. He lost his fortune, his health, and the lives of all his family except his wife, who had the gall to say that he should *"curse God and die."* He had three friends come and sit silent to comfort him. But they had never carried the burden that God gave Job to carry and they misunderstood what God was doing in Job's life. They proved to be a hindrance and not help. Job was left alone. But he was not alone, for God had shut him up to Himself, and he could only find relief in God alone.

As a pastor I often feel alone and shut up to the will of God. There is the discipline of waiting before God for a specific message to preach to God's people. Who can understand God putting the burden of His people on a heart and the unbearable load to carry, until God carries both you and His people? Who can understand the spiritual warfare and attacks that come as you try to lead God's sheep? I have found that God often gives someone who has walked in the same shoes to encourage me.

LESSONS LEARNED

These biblical characters remind of us several truths:

- We do not produce fruit in our own strength. Spirit-filled people who live out of God's strength produce spiritual fruit.
- God is ever-present with us. In contrast to the wicked who will be alone and silent in darkness, we will walk in the light of His presence.
- We are secure in Him. Even if the enemies are many and strong, even if we feel deserted and alone, even if we no longer have enough strength to hold on to God, God will hold on to us. He will not let us go. Our feet will stand firm and we will prevail.

Remember that all that happened to the faithful in Scripture are to help us in our personal and similar walk with God. To better understand the depths of being shut up alone to God, consider the following passages that reveal the great travail of soul that both Job and David endured:

My friends scorn me;
My eyes pour out tears to God.
Oh, that one might plead for a man with God,

As a man pleads for his neighbor! (Job 16:20).

All my close friends abhor me,
And those whom I love have turned against me.
My bone clings to my skin and to my flesh,
And I have escaped by the skin of my teeth.
Have pity on me, have pity on me, O you my friends,
For the hand of God has struck me! (Job 19:19-21).

For it is not an enemy who reproaches me; then I could bear it.
Nor is it one who hates me who has exalted himself against me;
Then I could hide from him.
But it was you, a man my equal,
My companion and my acquaintance.
We took sweet counsel together,
And walked to the house of God in the throng (Psalm 55:12-14).
My heart pants, my strength fails me;
As for the light of my eyes, it also has gone from me.
My loved ones and my friends stand aloof from my plague,
And my relatives stand afar off.
Those also who seek my life lay snares for me;
Those who seek my hurt speak of destruction,
And plan deception all the day long (Psalm 38:10-12)

Even my own familiar friend in whom I trusted,
Who ate my bread,
Has lifted up his heel against me (Psalm 41:9).

Those passages teach us that it is common for those who walk with God to sense their great loneliness and be drawn deeper into their dependent-relationship with God. How was it possible for Hannah not to grow bitter at Peninnah or to accept the comfort of Elkanah? How was it possible for Hannah to be carried deeper into the refiner's fire until she came forth as God's chosen vessel to carry in her womb the prophet Samuel? It was only because God was the source of her sufficiency.

Paul learned this lesson well and experienced a deepened relationship with Jesus. He wrote, *That I may know him, and the power of his resurrection, and the fellowship of his sufferings, being conformed to His death* (Philippians 3:10).

Once we have learned to be comforted by God and identify with Christ as He conforms us to His image, we will sing with Hannah, *He raises the poor from the dust, and lifts the beggar from the ash heap, to set them among princes, and to make them inherit the throne of glory* (1 Samuel 1:8).

As we close this section, let me give you two cautions and one blessing about friendships:

- Friends can give you sympathy and you may be tempted to go to them rather than go through the refiner's fire. Don't do it. God is at work in your life.

- Friends can stand with you one day and turn against you another day. Enjoy the friendships God has given you – but don't put your trust in them.

- Friends can give you Scripture and understanding to build your faith.

APPLICATIONS

- Have you had a friend like Peninnah who provoked you? Did you grow bitter through that experience? What have you done with your bitterness? Have you given it to God? Have you allowed God to replace your tears of bitterness with His joy?

- Have you ever had a friend who became your enemy like Saul? How did you respond? Were you able to leave him in God's hands?

- Have you ever had a friend like Samuel and Jonathan that understood the burden and trail of faith that you were going through? How did they encourage you? Were you tempted to depend on them too much?

- Do you feel that you have reached the point in your walk with God that you identify with David in the Psalms as he puts in trust in God alone?

CHAPTER 8

Burdened – Part 1

So it was, year by year, when she went up to the house of the LORD, that she provoked her; therefore she wept and did not eat (1 Samuel 1:7).

 ## THE FOURTH TEST OF FAITH

When God chooses to work His will on earth, He shares the burden of His heart from heaven to a receptive heart on earth. Hannah was given God's burden because He had chosen to bless her and through her, to raise up Samuel as God's prophet.

> *The test of faith was not to let discouragement or*
> *her own private burden distract from the burden of God.*

When it is the Lord who has shut the womb then it is only God who can open the womb. When it is God who has closed some door in your life, it is only God who can open the door of fruitfulness through you. Do not allow discouragement to lead you to despair. Let your burden lead you to greater faith in God.

To understand the burdens God places on our hearts, let's consider a series of questions.

1.   WHAT IS THE DIFFERENCE BETWEEN GOD'S BURDEN AND OUR BURDEN?

OUR BURDENS ON EARTH ARE SELF-GENERATED

I love to ask children questions. They are so open and honest! One of the ladies in our church was pregnant and I asked her daughter, *"Do you want a brother or sister?"* Deflecting my question, she said, *"Momma wants a girl and daddy wants a boy."* *"But what do you want?,"* I asked again. Now she was emphatic: *"I do not want a brother. I want a sister!"* Most of us are like that little girl. We have a strong preference of what we want God to do for us. But however strong they may be, that's all they are: *personal preferences.* Our burden and preferences must be conformed to what God in His wisdom has planned for us.

Hannah began with a natural burden or desire for a child. But before God opened her womb, she would have God's specific burden from heaven. God humbled her before He exalted her. He emptied her before He filled her:

- He emptied Hannah of her hopes and dreams.
- He emptied her of the physical ability to have children.
- He emptied her of the comfort from her husband.
- He emptied her of her ability to seek revenge on Peninnah.
- He emptied her of her confidence in herself.
- He emptied her of her own burden for children and gave her God's burden for a son who would have a specific purpose before God.

And so it is with us. johnGod humbles us before He exalts us. He empties us before He fills us. He teaches us dependency and faith. We must go through the process of abandonment of our own desires and absolute surrender to His purposes.

To a barren woman, any child would have been fine. At first Hannah's burden and desire may have been to just be a mother and have the opportunity to lead her child to adulthood. Perhaps she was also burdened to have the shame of barrenness removed. To that end, any child would do. However, God's burden for Hannah was not for any child. It was for a specific child – for Samuel.

I conclude this from looking at the big picture of how God dealt with other childless women in Scripture. They found themselves in humanly impossible situations, but God supernaturally opened their wombs to produce his chosen prophets, servants, and kings.

Elizabeth was barren, old, and beyond the child bearing years. None of those things were problems to God. At His time, he sent an angel to appear to Elizabeth's husband. Notice that this child would not be any ordinary son. He was chosen and appointed by God for a specific and high calling:

> *But the angel said to him, "Do not be afraid, Zacharias, for your prayer is heard; and your wife Elizabeth will bear you a son, and you shall call his name John. And you will have joy and gladness, and many will rejoice at his birth. For he will be great in the sight of the Lord,*

and shall drink neither wine nor strong drink. He will also be filled with the Holy Spirit, even from his mother's womb. And he will turn many of the children of Israel to the Lord their God. He will also go before Him in the spirit and power of Elijah, 'to turn the hearts of the fathers to the children,' and the disobedient to the wisdom of the just, to make ready a people prepared for the Lord" (Luke 1:13-17).

Elizabeth's barrenness was not related to her burden or desire to simply have a child. God had a greater purpose … to send John the Baptist as the forerunner of Christ. God set His clock around His eternal purpose in Christ, and not around Elizabeth's desire for a child early in her marriage to Zacharias. Hundreds of years before Elizabeth was born, God had already included prophecies of how John would be born and how his ministry would relate to Christ (see Isaiah 40:3-5; Malachi 3:1). God not only ordained the forerunner, but his parents as well. God gave specific instructions to Zacharias and Elizabeth about how John was to be raised: he was to be a Nazarene from his birth.

We also see the specifics of God's choosing a son before birth with Samson as God gave specific instructions to his mother that he was to be a Nazarene from his birth and he was chosen to be a Judge and deliverer for Israel (Judges 13:3-6).

I conclude that God specifically chose Hannah to give birth to Samuel in a way similar to His choosing of Elizabeth and Mary to be the mothers of John the Baptist and Jesus. To prepare her for this role, Hannah went through a refining process that brought her to the place of absolute surrender where she was able to dedicate him to the work of the Lord as long as he lived.

Many of us have not worked through the process that Hannah did. We run to God with a great need in our lives that occupies us at that moment. We only see the need from our temporal perspective of how it affects us at that moment. We may not be ready to see God's big picture of how it affects others, and how it fits into God's greater purpose in Christ beyond our time frame and geographic world. Hannah's process of coming to understand God's plan and surrendering to it took time. Her faith was forged in the trials of disappointment year after year.

It is a difficult process to die to dreams, needs and desires. It is hard to be willing to submit wholeheartedly to God. But it is possible – and well worth it. Notice the words of Hannah's vow to God:

> *Then she made a vow and said, "O LORD of hosts, if You will indeed look on the affliction of Your maidservant and remember me, and not forget Your maidservant, but will give Your maidservant a male child, then I will give him to the LORD all the days of his life, and no razor shall come upon his head"* (1 Samuel 1:11).

Three times in that one verse she refers to herself as *God's maidservant*. Though she uses a common Hebrew word to describe a female servant, it speaks loudly of Hannah's submission to the will of God. She had reached the point where she did not desire *her child*, but *God's child*. Hannah was fully surrendered to God as *His maidservant*. God's burden for a son to be dedicated to Him from birth had been realized. Hannah had reached the point that the burden of God's heart was her burden as well.

Many Christians want the blessings of God on their own terms.

- Rather than submitting to *God's dreams and plans,* many want God to bless *their dreams and plans.* They want to be fruitful on their terms and in their timing.
- Many churches are confidant God is blessing their programs and methods because they see increased numbers and fruit, no matter how that fruit was obtained. Remember Peninnah could produce children naturally any time she desired and appeared outwardly fruitful. Religion produces a lot of activity, and our best efforts in the flesh can produce results. But only the Holy Spirit can bring forth spiritual fruit to the glory of God.

 ## A TIME FOR SELF-EVALUATION

- What are you burdened for? Are you burdened and broken to the point of believing God for the impossible? Or are you simply living for your own desires and fulfillment?

- Is your dream self-initiated – or is it something that God has chosen for you in His eternal purposes?

- Have you come to the point where you declare yourself to be under the Lordship of Christ? Are you ready to surrender back to God that which He gives you?

- Have you reached the point in your life where you would rejoice in God using another and not receiving recognition yourself?

During my forty years of ministry, I have had many Christians tell me that God had burdened them in a certain area. However, time reveals that most of these are still chasing their own dreams and looking for God to rubber stamp His approval on them. The strength, fruitfulness and fulfillment that are found in God are never the work of the flesh. Fruit that abides and multiplies is always the work of the Holy Spirit.

 ## GOD'S BURDENS FROM HEAVEN ARE SPIRIT-GENERATED

As you read the pages of the Bible, you see the unfolding theme of the plan and purposes of God. History is *His Story.* It is futile to try to understand history's overarching theme and direction without Jesus.

The burden from heaven for the will of God for our lives is much like the burden of our salvation. It doesn't begin with us. We were not first burdened for our soul and our lost state. God first began to draw us to Himself by the Holy Spirit and then began to burden us to see our need for Jesus. We did not initiate our salvation. God did.

The same principle is true in sanctification [21] and discovering the specific will of God for our lives. We are not asked by God to come up with great plans and then plead with Him to accept our ideas for building His kingdom. We are to enter into a close, loving relationship with Jesus, and in our daily walk with Him through Scripture, prayer, and obedience, God allows us to discover His will for our lives. God is the One who has a greater purpose in Christ and He allows us to discover how we fit in.

Hannah was burdened for far more than a baby. She was a chosen vessel for a specific purpose. Her baby was to be given back to God for a special calling. Paul describes God's incredible purpose for our lives in Christ when he writes, *For we are His workmanship, created in Christ Jesus for good works,* **which God prepared beforehand** *that we should walk in them* (Ephesians 2:10; emphasis mine). God's plans for your life started long before you were born.

As a young girl, Hannah had her share of personal dreams, desires, and hopes. She probably wanted a husband that loved her. She wanted children that she could love and nurture. But her dream for children became a nightmare with the words, *But the Lord had shut up her womb.* Hannah went through various trials of faith that refined her and brought her to the point where her personal burden was surrendered to God. She submitted to His specific burden from heaven.

> *And she was in bitterness of soul, and prayed to the LORD and wept in anguish. Then she made a vow and said, "O LORD of hosts, if You will indeed look on the affliction of Your maidservant and remember me, and not forget Your maidservant, but will give Your maidservant a male child, then I will give him to the LORD all the days of his life, and no razor shall come upon his head* (1 Samuel 1:10-11).

She gave up her dream of raising a child at home and exchanged it in full surrender to God's pre-ordained purpose for Samuel.

It is important that we understand that our dreams, desires, burdens, and hopes must be given to God. We should desire to discover what is on God's heart in heaven for us. God is the initiator and we should respond to His will. When we have a close love relationship and a walk of faith with God, He changes our desires so that the desire of our heart is first His desire.

Many have told me, *"But God wants to give us the desires of our heart."* My response is that many have conveniently forgotten the first half of that verse: *Delight yourself also in the LORD, and He shall give you the desires of your heart* (Psalm 37:4). That verse is not suggesting that God will give us what we want. It is telling us that God will give us *the desire* to want what He wants. If we first *Delight ourselves in the Lord,* then He changes our desires to be in tune with His desires. When we reach that point that we desire what is on God's heart, then we will have that truth fulfilled in our life. Too many Christians are asking God to give them the desires of their flesh and not God's heart.

How does the desire or burden of God in heaven become ours on earth?

---

21   Sanctification is a theological term that describes the process where God grows and matures His children into the image of Jesus Christ.

I am using the term "God's burden" in a broader sense for the individual believer discovering the specific will of God for his life. In the Old Testament many prophets had the *"Word of the Lord,"* come to them as direct revelation from heaven. Prophets like Isaiah, Jeremiah, Habakkuk, Malachi, and others received God's word and proclaimed it even when it came as a burden or weight of God's coming judgment.

Consider the burden on the heart of Zechariah the prophet: *The burden of the word of the LORD against Israel. Thus says the LORD, who stretches out the heavens, lays the foundation of the earth, and forms the spirit of man within him* (Zechariah 12:1). I am not suggesting that the burden God places on our hearts is the same as the direct revelation that the prophets received and became part of the eternal Scriptures. However, I am saying that God still speaks, leads, guides and reveals His will for men and women today.

It is the will of God for all believers to grow in grace, to read and study God's Word, to serve in His church, to proclaim the Gospel to the lost, to walk in faith and holiness, etc. However, in our study of Hannah I am using the phrase the *"burden of God"* more in the sense of God sharing His specific burden or calling for a specific believer for a specific assignment. The application for our study is to try to understand how God also desires to shares His specific will or burden to the receptive hearts of His children to transform their lives from barrenness to fruitfulness.

How do we know when God has shared His specific will or burden with one of His children? In reading the biographies of great men and women of God, you will find a common thread of how many came to a point where they felt a specific calling of God for a specific purpose.

Many pastors and missionaries can point to a time when God seemed to share His burden or call to ministry and missions. I myself felt a specific call upon my life for full time ministry as a young man. But this is not something reserved just for pastors and missionaries. Every believer who walks in a love relationship with Jesus will have the Lord share His specific call upon his or her life.

Let's Personalize This

- It was in seeing the Lord high and lifted up that Isaiah shared God's burden and cried, *"Here am I send me"* (Isaiah 6:8). Have you ever sensed a time when God spoke to you and revealed His will for your life? How did you respond? Were you afraid? (Isaiah was!) Did you obey? (Isaiah did!)
- It's easy to make excuses or to explain away times when God speaks to us. In what ways have you done that?
- There is only one acceptable response when God speaks to us: *Obey immediately!* If you have not done that, it's time to go back to square one with God and begin to obey what He has called you to do.

2. Does God Still Share His Burdens in Heaven with His Children on Earth?

The simple answer is, *YES!* I believe that God shares His burden and will for our lives with us. I've read the accounts from other men and women of God where God has spoken and led them.

I've talked with many Christian friends who have received God's burden about a specific person, calling, ministry, etc.

Because I believe it is helpful to hear how God has spoken and worked in the lives of others, I am going to share four personal stories of receiving God's specific burdens.

GOD'S BURDEN FOR ONE PERSON

When I experienced revival as a college student, no one had to train me in evangelism to motivate me to share Jesus. [22] I had walked across the campus hundreds of times, passing thousands of students, but had never been deeply burdened for them to know Jesus. That all changed when I experienced brokenness and surrender to the will of God. One day, as I walked by a student sitting alone, I was impressed to share Jesus with him. As I sat in class, I felt called to talk to a classmate about Jesus. Later I developed a biblical conviction that all believers were called to be witnesses of Christ. I would set aside one day out of the week to devote to evangelism. I would describe this, as the general will of God for my life.

Then in my first pastorate, I had an unusual experience that I would describe as a specific burden from God. I was starting a church in a small town in Washington and had been systematically going from house to house trying to share Christ with people in the community. In the process, I meet a couple that began coming to our church. The wife had responded to Christ, but the husband had not. He would attend church regularly with her. I had already witnessed to him personally, and he had not trusted Christ for salvation.

One morning I was praying in general for people I had witnessed to. I prayed for this man as well and decided to visit his house again. I went to my car to make that personal visit and my car would not start. I prayed a simple prayer: *"Lord, I am trying to witness to this man and my car will not start. I need your help."* I was no mechanic, but I checked what I could and cleaned the battery cables and tried again, but still the car would not start. I finally gave up and thought to myself, *"Well as a last resort, at least I can pray for him."* I got on my knees next to my bed and, as I began to pray, it was like a heavy weight or burden for his salvation came upon me. As I prayed, my heart began to break for him and I wept and pleaded with the Lord for his salvation like I had never experienced before. It seemed that the indwelling Holy Spirit was intensely making intercession for that situation (Romans 8:26). Then as quickly as the burden fell on me, it lifted. It was as though God had answered my prayer. I felt in my heart that God had just done a work in that man's life.

I went to my car with confidence that it would start and he would be home. My car started immediately and, when I arrived at his home, I discovered that God had worked in his heart at the exact time that God's burden for him came upon me. He told me that he was at his office when, suddenly a great burden for his soul fell on him. He was convicted of his need of salvation in Christ. And even though he was at work, he could not stop crying. The Holy Spirit was

---

22   One of the fruits of the filling of the Holy Spirit is seen in the promise of the Holy Spirit, *But when the Helper comes, whom I shall send to you from the Father, the Spirit of truth who proceeds from the Father, He will testify of Me. And you also will bear witness, because you have been with Me from the beginning* (John 15:26-27).

dealing with him so strongly that he felt compelled to go home. I arrived just after he did. He now knew that he was lost and Jesus alone could save him. That Sunday in church he made his public profession of faith.

That day I learned that prayer is not our last resort in evangelism and ministry. Rather, it is essential for the release of the Holy Spirit going before us. I learned that there are times that the Holy Spirit burdens our hearts with the will of God and gives us the faith to believe to see God work.

GOING TO SCHOOL IN SOUTH KOREA

My first mission trip was to South Korea in 1987. I was asked to recruit a team of four that would be part of a larger team arranged by the Southern Baptist Convention. As we prayed and prepared, our team heard how God was working in a great way in South Korea. We were expecting to see God at work during our time there. Our team faced a disappointment on the first day as we were assigned to a small storefront mission. We evangelized in the day and preached at night. Our first night we had only 30-40 in attendance. We tried to resist discouragement, and asked the pastor how we could have more evangelistic opportunities for the week. I asked him if we could preach in the local schools. He said that would not be possible because the students were preparing for their college entrance exams.

That night at the hotel, our team of four knelt around a bed and began to pray. While in prayer, I again experienced what seemed to be God's burden and initiation. Then we all began to pray with a burden specifically that God would open the doors for us to minister in the schools that were closed to us.

When the pastor came to pick us up the next morning, he said that we had an open door to preach in every class of an all-boy's school of high school seniors. We arrived to find each class of around 60-80 students had given us one hour to preach Christ to them. One of our team members gave his testimony and I shared the gospel and gave an invitation for them to trust Christ. God was at work, and in six hours we presented the Gospel to more than 400 students. That day 150 indicated that they wanted to receive Christ. The next day we were invited back by the principal because his students asked for us to return! We were able to speak to the other classes we could not get to the first day.

The following day the pastor picked us up and we were taken to a girl's school where 1,700 high school girls allowed us to share Jesus with them in an open assembly. Again, about 150 made decisions for Christ.

I learned afresh that when God opens doors for His Word, there would be a fruitful response. He had already been at work in the lives of these students, preparing them to receive the message we would proclaim to them.

STOPPING THE RAIN

Years later we took a team of 30 to India. We were in over 130 churches and conducted a mass evangelism crusade. The three-night attendance was around 55,000. God showed up in a great way with thousands coming to Christ. However, we faced a great trial of faith one night as our open-air crusade was being drenched with rain. Our team, partners and churches all prayed for God to demonstrate Himself powerfully and stop the rain. Honestly, I did not have the faith to ask God to stop the rain. It was easier for me to pray for God to change our attitudes and help us to accept and adjust to the rain. But it seemed that it was God's burden for us to pray specifically for God to stop the rain.

Our prayers went up to heaven as the rain kept coming down. The churches in the far villages sent word, asking if they should come into the city because it was raining in their villages. Our partners told them to come. The attendance was down that night because it was raining all over the region – except for the small area surrounding our crusade.

The next day word spread among the Hindus that the Christian God had stopped the rains over their meeting place. The next night, thousands came to the crusade, heard the Gospel, and responded in saving faith.

DEAD MAN'S HILL

We led a mission team to Brazil in the Rio region. A pastor who ministered in a small church in an area controlled by gangs had pleaded with me to come preach at his church. Just behind his church, the road ended at the top of a vacant hill. The pastor led me up the hill to tell me the story of that oppressive place. He said nearly every morning a dead body of a gang member was dumped on the hill. I could not imagine living in that environment.

As we came down from the hill at sunset, God's burden of prayer fell on my heart. I said to the three pastors with me that I must go back up to what I called *"Dead Man's Hill"* and pray again. As we stood there looking out over the lights of the city of Rio, I felt led to pray a specific prayer, *"Lord, break Satan's hold on this hill and stop the dumping of dead bodies here behind the church."* Though most of my prayers are what I would call "normal praying," this time I again felt that this was God's burden to pray.

The next day the pastor told me that there was no dead body on the hill for the first time in a long time. The second and third day as well, he reported that there was no dead body on the hill. This amazed him. When our mission team left for home, there had been no dead bodies since the burdened prayer.

This past year I was back in Rio to preach at the national convention of the pastors and deacon congress. I saw that pastor and asked him about *"Dead Man's Hill."* He reported that since that prayer, dead bodies have no longer been dumped there. I do not know what may happen there tomorrow, but I share this to say that sometimes we pray with a broken heart that is expressing not our own burden, but the burden of heaven. When we do, God opens the doors of heaven and we experience strength, fruitfulness and fulfillment.

3.   WHAT IS THE RELATIONSHIP BETWEEN GOD'S BURDEN AND PRAYER?

The purpose of prayer is not to change God's heart – but to put us in a position where we discover what is already on His heart.

The promises God makes about prayer are often misunderstood and taken out of context. For example, we are told, *Whatever you ask in My name, that will I do, so that the Father may be glorified in the Son* (John 14:13). To ask in Jesus' name is not a mechanical formula tacked on to the end of our prayers. Rather, it is asking as He would ask on the basis of His character and finished work on our behalf. The context of our asking is seen in John 15:7, *If you abide in Me and My words abide in you, you will ask what you desire and it shall be done for you.* If we are in that abiding relationship that bears fruit in Christ and His word is abiding in us, we will not be asking for things outside of His will. Our asking will not be self-centered but Christ-centered. As James says, we will not be asking to *spend it on your own pleasures* (James 4:3). This is confirmed again by John, *Now this is the confidence that we have in Him, that if we ask anything according to His will, He hears us. And if we know that He hears us, whatever we ask, we know that we have the petitions that we have asked of Him* (1 John 5:14).

Jesus shows us the relationship between God's burden and prayer when He taught in the model prayer, *Your kingdom come, your will be done, on Earth as it is in heaven.* Our praying should be to discover the will of God on earth from the God who rules in heaven and initiates His will from heaven to our hearts on earth.

A good example of God's burden in heaven and prayer on earth is seen in the praying of Elijah. *Elijah was a man with a nature like ours, and he prayed earnestly that it would not rain; and it did not rain on the land for three years and six months* (James 5:17). Elijah did not just come up with a great idea one day to pray that God would shut up heaven that it might not rain. Before Elijah prayed with a burdened heart, God had already revealed His will to Elijah. The Law of Moses said that if Israel broke God's covenant, God would shut up heaven and that it would not rain. Elijah just prayed back to God what God said He would do if they broke His covenant with them (Deuteronomy 11:16-17).

- Many pray simply for what they want.
- Many pray to change God's mind.
- Many pray in hope until hope turns to faith.
- Many pray based upon the general promises of God.
- Sometimes we pray, surrendering to God that which we ask for.

CHALLENGE

- God has a burden for your family, for your church, for your city, for your country, for specific nations and peoples. Whenever God has a burden in heaven, he looks for an individual on earth through whom He can accomplish great things: *For the eyes of the LORD run to and fro throughout the whole earth, to show Himself strong on behalf of those whose heart is loyal to Him* (2 Chronicles 16:9).

- Would you be one of those with whom God shares His burden? Will you respond with a loyal heart to Him?

- Have you ever had what you might describe as God's burden come upon you for a person's salvation?

- Have you ever felt that you began to know the heart of God for your specific purpose and calling in life?

What is God's burden like?

- It is bigger than you. The only explanation for it can be that God is at work.
- God will always get the glory and praise. He does not share that with man.
- God and not man always initiate God's burden.
- God's burden is always specific and is related to God's greater purpose in Christ.
- God's burden is always in accord with God's holiness.
- God's burden is not always measured in great numbers or events. God does not measure by "bigger and better," but only by that which He wills.
- God's burden is always founded on Scripture.
- God's burden is always confirmed by the working of the Holy Spirit.

4.   WHAT IS THE RELATIONSHIP BETWEEN GOD'S BURDEN AND OUR PATIENCE?

Hannah was a follower of those who *through faith and patience inherited the promises* (Hebrews 6:12). But that didn't mean it was easy. Remember what happened? *And her rival also provoked her severely, to make her miserable, because the LORD had closed her womb. So it was, year by year, when she went up to the house of the LORD, that she provoked her; therefore she wept and did not eat* (1 Samuel 1:6-7).

Mother's Day at our church was the worst Sunday of the year for my wife. Connie had a great burden for children, but the hope that she would hold a child of her own in her arms grew dimmer each year. But every year the burden in her heart got heavier. Mother's Day was the saddest day of the year for Connie. As the mothers in our church were honored with a flower, she was reminded of the cruel reality of her inability to have children.

I did not understand the strong instinct that God put in her life to have children. I was content and could accept not having children, but Connie could not. I talked with her, prayed with her, and like Elkanah, tried to comfort her —but still her burden was persistent and would not go away. Even after the doctor told her she would never be able to conceive, the burden for children persisted and only grew stronger.

One day after eight years of marriage, Connie prayed with tears that seemed much like Hannah's prayer of surrender, *"God, if You do not want me to have children, then You have to take this burden from me. The burden is too heavy for me to carry."* But the burden did not go away and, for the first time in our barren state, we prayed about adopting children. As soon as we felt that it was God's burden for us to adopt, God opened the very difficult doors of adoption. In a little over four months we had a call that our son had just been born and we were to pick him in less than a week. We named our first adopted son Matthew that means *"gift of God."* After all those years of a persistent burden, God had given us the gift of a beautiful baby boy. Then two years later, another son was born and we adopted Jeremy, and then another two years later we adopted Hope to complete our family. God had seen the faith and patience of Connie and had given her the children she had longed for all her life.

If God has impressed your heart with His burden, then you will need both faith and patience till it becomes a reality. If the desire is self-motivated, God will not answer. You may find yourself like Sarah, substituting a man-made solution instead of receiving God's promise. You may be like Peninnah and be able to produce fruit through the flesh through your natural talent and the motivation of religious works. But it will not be God's promised provision.

If your burden is from God, you must allow God's timing and God's way to be accomplished in you. You may not yet be broken and fully surrendered to the great work that God wants to do through His spiritually barren children.

Hannah needed patience to wait on God. Hannah was not only barren and battered, but she was bruised in the same place over and over again without relief. She had to first battle anger at Peninnah. We are told that her adversary *provoked her severely.* The word for *provoked* can also be translated *anger.* Hannah got mad! This word first appears in Deuteronomy 4:25, where Israel's sin provoked God to anger. *"A review of the uses of this verb shows that around 80 percent of them involve Yahweh's "being provoked to anger" by Israel's sin, especially its worship of other gods."* [23] Too often, we think that anger is always wrong. But God's anger was certainly not sinful. When God is provoked to anger, it is always in righteousness. Our anger can turn into hate and bitterness – but God's anger is always consistent with His holy character.

It would be natural for Hannah to become angry at Peninnah's taunting and mocking. Relentlessly, Peninnah would kick her while she was down. But Hannah seemed to give her provoking to God and did not grow bitter. She patiently endured, trusting God because of His promises to her. Her focus had to remain on the Lord or she would miss the grace available to those who humble themselves before God. God triumphed and Hannah praised Him by saying, *Talk no more so very proudly; let no arrogance come from your mouth, for the LORD is the God of knowledge; and by Him actions are weighed* (1Sam. 2:3).

---

23 Vine, W. E. ; Unger, Merrill F. ; White, William: *Vine's Complete Expository Dictionary of Old and New Testament Words.* Nashville : T. Nelson, 1996, S. 1:191

At first Hannah may have been tempted to be angry with Peninnah. But as the years went on and God did not intervene to give relief, perhaps Satan tempted her to be angry with God. Have you ever been tempted to be angry with God? Remember Job. He patiently trusted God – and eventually God restored Job's fortunes and increased all that he had twofold. [24] God ultimately blessed Hannah with her firstborn, Samuel, and then fulfilled His promise by giving her even more children. [25]

APPLYING PATIENCE TO YOUR LIFE

Do you have a burden that will not go away? Have you been patient with God? Love is patient. We manifest our love for God by patiently waiting and trusting Him.

Has God not taken the burden away from you? Is your heart right before Him? Are you free of your personal bias as to what you want? You may be experiencing God giving you His burden for your life. You must wait for God's perfect timing. Follow those who through faith and patience received what God had promised.

There are a few rare believers who only desire what God desires and often they know God's will by their sanctified desires. I certainly do not walk with God on that level of sensitivity and surrender on a daily basis. However, this is how I want to walk with God.

What are the possibilities regarding your deep desire or burden before God? There are several possibilities:

- Self and not the Holy Spirit may motivate your desire.
- You were the one who initiated your desire, and now you are expecting God to bless it.
- God gave your desire to you and it will not go away until God answers your prayers.
- You have prayed for an answer, but God has said no. You are to endure, living with it much like Paul did. The good news is that God said to Paul, *My grace is sufficient for you* (2 Corinthians 12:9). And His grace will be sufficient for you as well.
- You die daily to self. The desires that come to your heart are normally God's desires.

QUESTIONS

- Have you loved God by being patient with Him as He works in your life?

- Have the attacks of the enemy turned you to God? Or have they made you angry to the point where you have lost focus and are now becoming bitter?

24 Job 42:10-17
25 1 Samuel 2:5

- Has time made you forget your burden? Or does it remain persistent in your life?

- Have your learned to discern the difference between selfish desires and the desires that God places on your heart?

In the next chapter, we will look at three more questions to understand the burdens that God places on our hearts.

CHAPTER 9

Burdened — Part 2

So it was, year by year, when she went up to the house of the LORD, that she provoked her; therefore she wept and did not eat (1 Samuel 1:7).

THE FOURTH TEST OF FAITH

When God chooses to work His will on earth, He shares the burden of His heart from heaven to a receptive heart on earth. Hannah was given God's burden because He had chosen to bless her and through her, to raise up Samuel as God's prophet.

> *The test of faith was not to let discouragement or her own private burden distract from the burden of God.*

When it is the Lord who has shut the womb then it is only God who can open the womb. When it is God who has closed some door in your life, it is only God who can open the door of fruitfulness through you. Do not allow discouragement to lead you to despair. Let your burden lead you to greater faith in God.

In the previous chapter, we looked at four questions to understand the burdens that God places on our hearts. Let's continue with question number five.

5. WHY ARE THOSE WHO SHARE GOD'S BURDEN FROM HEAVEN PERSECUTED ON EARTH?

Hannah was hurt over and over without relief. Can you tell the difference between your own discouragement and a burden from God and between your suffering and the sufferings of Christ in you? (Phil. 3:10) Do you react to the persecutor or respond to God who allows persecution to mature us? *And her rival also provoked her severely,* **to make her miserable,** *because the LORD had closed her womb* (1 Samuel 1:6; emphasis mine).

WHAT – OR WHO – IS BEHIND PERSECUTION?

The Bible describes Satan as *our* a*dversary,* who seeks to *devour us* (1 Peter 5:8). He is the *accuser of the brethren* (Revelation 12:10), and desires to *sift us* (Luke 22:31) and *destroy us* (1 Corinthians 10:10).

Do you want a Bible promise you can count on every day? Here's one from the lips of Jesus: *If they persecuted Me, they will persecute you also* (John 15:20). If we accept the burden of God and want the blessing of God, then we will be persecuted. That persecution can come from Satan and his demonic forces, from people of the world, and even at times from the people of God. To have God love and choose you to bear fruit is to have Satan to mark you and abuse you. The servant is not above His master. If they persecuted the Lord Jesus, they will also persecute those that love Him and do his will.

Just as Job did not understand that the direct cause of his problems was Satan, Hannah may not have understood that Peninnah was an arrow in Satan's quiver. Believers are not immune to his strategies:

- Peter opened his mouth and out came Satan's thoughts in Peter's voice. Jesus' direct rebuke was simple: *Get behind Me, Satan! You are an offense to Me* (Matthew 16:23).
- David sinned when he took a census of the children of Israel. But behind his actions we read, *And Satan stood up against Israel, and moved David to number Israel* (1 Chronicles 21:1).
- Saul thought he was serving God when he persecuted the church and participated in the stoning of Stephen. After his conversion, Saul, now the Apostle Paul would remind us that *we do not fight against flesh and blood, but against principalities and powers, against the rulers of the darkness of this age, against spiritual hosts of wickedness in the heavenly places* (Ephesians 6:12).

If we fail to see that our battle is a spiritual one, then we fall into Satan's trap and miss the grace and faith needed to endure the fiery trial that we may face on our way to supernatural fruitfulness.

WHY DOES GOD ALLOW PERSECUTION?

Persecution is not to make us fret but to make us fruitful. Hannah's prayer of praise testified that while the adversary provoked and persecuted her, God sustained her. She testified, *He will guard the feet of His saints* (1 Samuel 2:9).

God had His unseen purpose by directly and actively shutting up the womb of Hannah. He does not owe us an explanation of His purposes. He simply asks us to trust His heart. We can become so angry at our problems and enemies that we thwart God's purposes and miss God's best for us in the future. When we react horizontally – to man or the circumstances in our lives – we miss the grace that God has reserved for us. If, however, we respond vertically and see God as the One sovereignly over all things, we find that our circumstances are simply like a raging river designed to carry our boat at a faster pace to God's preordained harbor of rest and fruitfulness.

Peninnah's provoking made Hannah miserable. The King James Version says that it made her *fret*. The word carries the connotations of irritation, anger, to make to roar, thunder trouble.[26] The New King James version reads, *And her rival also provoked her severely, to make her miserable.... * The NRSV reads, *Her rival used to provoke her severely, to irritate her, because the Lord had closed her womb.* The enemy was looking to irritate Hannah so much that she would get a violent reaction and sin.

Hannah was tempted to turn inward and grow discouraged and bitter. We play into the enemies' strategy if we become so violently agitated or irritated with anger that we do not continue to cry out to God. We lose our focus and become consumed with our situation rather than with His sufficiency.

Notice Satan's strategy: the "goal" was to make her fret, worry and irritated. The "means" to that end was to provoke her day after day. Notice the phrase, *to make her fret* precedes the phrase *because the Lord had closed her womb.* For the believer who understands God's character and ways, when the cause of our closed door is God, we should rejoice. Satan's strategy was to keep Hannah from the grace to endure the trials of faith by causing her to sin. Hannah's prayer of praise shows us something of how she dealt with the situation until God had put down her rival. *And Hannah prayed, and said, My heart rejoices in the LORD, my horn is exalted in the LORD. I smile at my enemies, because I rejoice in your salvation* (1 Samuel 2:1). She *smiled* at her enemies because she was full of God's grace to believe Him and trust Him. Therefore, by faith she rejoiced in God's salvation even before God opened her barren womb. It is this rejoicing by faith and not by emotional feelings that brings God glory and brings us God's blessings.

---

26   Strong, James: *The New Strong's Dictionary of Hebrew and Greek Words.* Nashville : Thomas Nelson, 1997, c1996, S. H7481

HOW DO YOU RESPOND?

- When others provoke you do you ever consider that there is a spiritual warfare going on? Do you see Satan at work – or do you simply fight against flesh and blood?

- What is your natural tendency when you are provoked over and over? Do you become angry? Discouraged? Or are you driven to a deeper dependence upon God?

- Do you feel that you react against people or respond to God in those situations?

- Are you aware that Satan can use people to discourage you, cripple your faith, and make you lose focus?

DO NOT TAKE PERSECUTIONS PERSONALLY

It is natural for us to want everyone to like us. However, if we get serious about following Jesus, we will soon learn that Jesus is the *"Great Divide."* When I began to tell others about Jesus, I soon discovered that many felt uncomfortable with me and some began to dislike me. Why is that? Consider the words of Jesus:

If the world hates you, you know that it hated Me before it hated you. ¹⁹ If you were of the world, the world would love its own. Yet because you are not of the world, but I chose you out of the world, therefore the world hates you (John 15:19).

I have given them Your word; and the world has hated them (John 17:14).

The world cannot hate you; but it hates Me because I testify of it that its works are evil (John 7:7).

And you will be hated by all for My name's sake (Luke 21:17).

If we are to walk with Jesus we must be prepared to identify with His persecution and sufferings as well. Remember His promise: *all who desire to live godly in Christ Jesus will suffer persecution* (2 Tim. 3:12).

PERSECUTION IS THE RESULT OF THE CONFLICT OF TWO NATURES

Hannah's conversation with the prophet Eli is very interesting. He misinterpreted her grief, thinking she was a drunken, evil woman. However, she was simply pouring out her soul before the LORD. She answers him and says, *I am a woman of sorrowful spirit. I have drunk neither wine nor intoxicating drink, but have poured out my soul before the LORD. Do not consider your maidservant a wicked woman, for out of the abundance of my complaint and grief I have spoken until now* (1 Samuel 1:15-16).

Hannah probably knew well the history of conflict between Sarah and Hagar (Genesis 16). It was Sarah's lack of faith to wait for God to open her barren womb that led to her sin and put in motion the self-initiated plan of the flesh. From this fleshly act of Abraham and Sarah, God illustrated the conflict and persecution that would come to believers through false professors of faith. *But as he who was born according to the flesh then persecuted him who was born according to the Spirit, even so it is now* (Gal. 4:29) Paul called the event with Ishmael and Isaac an allegory of two covenants: one of the Law and one the New Covenant in Christ's finished work of redemption. When Ishmael mocked Isaac, it was more than one man's persecution of another (Genesis 21:9). It revealed that all of those born in the flesh would persecute those born again of the Spirit.

Religious people attempt to control things. When they discover they cannot control the work of God in your life, they will get angry and take action. Many nominal Christians do not face much persecution because they are not a threat to Satan's kingdom and they are not manifesting the life of Jesus in the world. Silent Christians do not stand on the front lines of God's army.

Do not be discouraged when religious people in the church persecute you. There are always tares among the wheat and the tares will persecute the wheat of God. There are many Ishmael's who were like the seed on stony ground that only appear to believe but will persecute the true believers.

David had a heart after God. He faced Goliath with faith, not fear, and God gave him a great victory over the giant. Saul's son, Jonathan, also had a great faith in God and God gave him a great victory over the Philistines. Is it any wonder that these two warriors for God became great friends? When Jonathan saw the faith in David's life, his heart was drawn to him and he became an encourager and friend to God's anointed. This attraction was because they both had a heart after God. In contrast, Saul became an enemy of David because he did not have faith in God and sought to build his own kingdom. He even had conflict with his own son, Jonathan.

When we meet a believer who is fully committed to God, our hearts are drawn together in a special relationship. However, when we encounter those who are walking according to the flesh, there is a natural conflict.

So we have good news and bad news. The good news is that if we forsake all to follow Christ, God will always draw to us close friendships among other like-minded believers. The bad news is if we forsake all to follow Jesus, we will always have those who oppose us. We are promised a combination of blessings and conflicts. This is exactly what Jesus taught:

Assuredly, I say to you, there is no one who has left house or brothers or sisters or father or mother or wife or children or lands, for My sake and the gospel's, who shall not receive a hundredfold now in this time—houses and brothers and sisters and mothers and children and lands, with persecutions—and in the age to come, eternal life (Mark 10:29-30).

As a boy, I loved to play with a set of magnets. Magnets have two poles – positive and negative. Unlike poles attract and like poles repel. I could position two magnets in such a way that they would be drawn together. But if I made a change in only one and turned it around, the other would repel it. Sometimes I tried to work against the nature of the magnets and tape them together artificially against their nature. But as soon as I removed the tape they repelled. If I just followed the nature of the magnets, they did not need my help to hold them together. An unseen force held them together. That unseen force that holds true believers together is Christ. When we are born of the Spirit, God has turned us from the old nature of Adam's children and made new in Christ. As a result, we have a supernatural attraction to others who are also part of His family.

When the Holy Spirit is at work in two believers they will be attracted to one another. That is the good news. The opposite is also true: the world will love its own. Do not expect them to continue to vote you the most popular in the class.

In the church we have many artificial relationships where people are taped together by church activities, programs, ministries, and social activities. Yet when the Spirit of God moves, some believers are attracted to a deeper fellowship in Christ. It is the love for the Lord and His Word and ministry in Jesus' name that attracts and holds without the artificial tape of religion. Other church members have the artificial tape come off and they become uncomfortable around those that are the most excited about Jesus. It has been the history of the church that when revival comes to a church the tape comes off and many church members splinter into two groups based on their ultimate attraction to the Lord Jesus. I will take ten deep friendships in Christ to one hundred artificial friendships.

TAKE A LOOK AT YOUR RELATIONSHIPS

- Do you have deep, kindred-spirit friendships with other believers who are walking with Christ? Who are your best friends? How can you deepen those relationships?

- What kind of person is attracted to you? What kind of people are you attracted to?

- Have you seen some relationships that have deteriorated because of your commitment to Jesus Christ? In what ways have those friendships suffered?

THE SUNDAY SCHOOL TEACHER LEARNS A LESSON

One Sunday a teacher came into my office and slammed her Sunday School book down on my desk and said, *"I quit!"* Her class shared the same space with the church day care center. The day care worker of that particular class was also a church member, and knew that they were supposed to respect the Sunday School space. They had discussed sharing the space several times before, but problems and misunderstandings continued. The teacher felt she was being taken advantage of and could not handle it anymore.

I had recently read 1 Peter 2:20 where Christians were to endure patiently and suffer well when wrong was done to them. I asked if what her sister did was wrong. She readily agreed it was wrong. I asked her if she had ever been arrested for teaching the children about Jesus, or had ever lost her job because she taught children in Sunday School. I then had her read 1 Peter 2:20. She began to weep as she saw the pettiness of having a table or chairs out of place. She recognized that what she was experiencing was nothing in comparison to the persecution Satan threw at the early church to get them to stop ministering in Jesus' name.

I asked her what lesson she taught her children by her outburst that morning. I prayed with her and then she picked up her Sunday School book and said she had to go and apologize to the children and teach her Bible lesson. She learned a great lesson that day. She got her focus off the minor irritations she was experiencing and back on the children she was teaching.

Can you imagine God listening to that Sunday School teacher feeling persecuted because a piece of the children's puzzle of Daniel in the Lion's Den was missing? The teacher was missing a greater piece of the puzzle by not realizing that God wanted *her* to learn from Daniel's faith.

It's easy to react wrongly and get angry when our rights have been violated. That's where we need the power of the Spirit of God to control our thoughts, emotions and responses. Learn to keep the main thing the main thing – and to not sweat the rest of the details!

6. WHAT BLESSINGS ARE PROMISED TO THE BURDENED AND PERSECUTED?

THE BLESSING OF JOY

Did you ever notice that it was the religious professions who gave Jesus the most trouble? They were constantly criticizing Him, attacking Him, and even attributing His miraculous powers to the devil. Jesus was no stranger to persecution. And so He had credibility when He told His followers,

> *Blessed are those who are persecuted for righteousness' sake, for theirs is the kingdom of heaven. Blessed are you when they revile and persecute you, and say all kinds of evil against you falsely for My sake. Rejoice and be exceedingly glad, for great is your reward in heaven, for so they persecuted the prophets who were before you…. I say to you, love your enemies, bless those who curse you, do good to those who hate you, and pray for those who spitefully use you and persecute you* (Matthew 5:10-12. 44).

Before we say that no one could face persecution and rejoice, we must remind ourselves of the apostles who were beaten because they preached Christ. They went away rejoicing that they had suffered shame for the sake of Jesus' name (Acts 5:40-42). Paul and Silas were beaten and put in stocks in prison, yet they sang praises to Jesus at midnight (Acts 16:16-43).

Paul found His source of joy in God. He writes, *I have learned in whatever state I am, to be content: I know how to be abased, and I know how to abound. Everywhere and in all things I have learned both to be full and to be hungry, both to abound and to suffer need. I can do all things through Christ who strengthens me* (Philippians 4:11-13). How did Paul learn to be content even through suffering?

Notice all that Paul endured:

> *Are they ministers of Christ? —I speak as a fool—I am more: in labors more abundant, in stripes above measure, in prisons more frequently, in deaths often. From the Jews five times I received forty stripes minus one. Three times I was beaten with rods; once I was stoned; three times I was shipwrecked; a night and a day I have been in the deep; in journeys often, in perils of waters, in perils of robbers, in perils of my own countrymen, in perils of the Gentiles, in perils in the city, in perils in the wilderness, in perils in the sea, in perils among false brethren; in weariness and toil, in sleeplessness often, in hunger and thirst, in fasting often, in cold and nakedness—besides the other things, what comes upon me daily: my deep concern for all the churches. Who is weak, and I am not weak? Who is made to stumble, and I do not burn with indignation?* (2 Corinthians 11:23-29).

EVALUATE YOUR RESPONSE OF JOY

* Have you ever rejoiced when persecuted?

* Have you prayed for those who provoke you?

* Have you experienced the Holy Spirit giving you His joy, His peace, and His love for the persecutor?

THE BLESSING OF COMFORT FROM GOD

Throughout the Bible, God promises comfort to His children. *This is my comfort in my affliction, for Your word has given me life* (Psalm 119:50). *For I will turn their mourning to joy, will comfort them, and make them rejoice rather than sorrow* (Jeremiah 31:13).

God is described as *the God of all comfort* (2 Corinthians 1:3). The Holy Spirit is described as a *comforter* or *helper* in John 14:16.

Are you able to distinguish between your own discouragement and a burden from God, and between your suffering and the sufferings of Christ in you? There is a difference. Paul said that he knew *the fellowship of His sufferings* (Phil. 3:10). It is in that experience that we understand the comfort of God.

I would guess that most of what we call a burden comes from our own desires and wants. We want to be blessed without having to go through the process of sanctification. We want to be fruitful without abiding in the vine and going through the process of cleansing and pruning (John 15). We want the glory without the cross. We want life without death to self. We want a message without studying the Word. We want a ministry without trials. We want strength without weakness. We want exaltation without humbling. We want to be full without ever hungering for God. We want to sit with princes without identifying with the beggars in the garbage heap. We want supernatural fruit without barrenness.

But the way of God is clear. Strength, fruitfulness and fulfillment do not come to us naturally. They are produced supernaturally as God works sovereignly in our lives through the circumstances we endure.

Hannah learned this lesson. God closed her womb but continued to reinforce in her heart His burden for children. She knew the difference between her natural desire for a child and God's burden that could not be ignored. She never got sidetracked from the call of God. She was brought low to be brought up again by the power of God. God was her rock and she would depend completely on Him. It was in that state of dependency where God became her comfort and sufficiency.

The Apostle Paul experienced a similar process. He was given a thorn in the flesh, which he also described as *a messenger of Satan*. This was sent to him by God to keep him humble. We are never told what that thorn was — and it doesn't matter. Each of us has our own thorns that we know about all too well. The issue isn't the identification of the thorn. The issue is dependency on the Savior. Notice the maturity in Paul's life as he writes about the lesson he learned:

> *Concerning this thing I pleaded with the Lord three times that it might depart from me. And He said to me, "My grace is sufficient for you, for My strength is made perfect in weakness." Therefore most gladly I will rather boast in my infirmities, that the power of Christ may rest upon me. Therefore I take pleasure in infirmities, in reproaches, in needs, in persecutions, in distresses, for Christ's sake. For when I am weak, then I am strong* (2 Corinthians 12:8-10).

Did you see the lesson? *When I am weak, then I am strong.* It's a paradox: we release our weakness and give it to God. In exchange, He infuses our lives with His power and strength. That's where divine comfort comes into our lives.

I certainly am not at the point in my life where I have learned to rejoice and boast in my weaknesses. It's a process … and I'm still growing. But I have learned that when we kick against the goads and resist the path where God is leading us, we hurt ourselves and miss His strength, comfort and grace.

I like the way of grace better than the way of the law and flesh. The comfort of the Holy Spirit, the insight into the Word of God, and the fellowship of His sufferings are for those who identify with Christ in their trials of faith.

HAVE YOU EXPERIENCED GOD'S COMFORT?

- Have you sought comfort in God's Word and found strength and peace?

- Have you experienced the fellowship of His sufferings as the Holy Spirit gave you comfort?

- Have you experienced His strength in your weakness?

THE BLESSING OF THE FELLOWSHIP OF CHRIST'S SUFFERING

I was just called to a new church. The Pastor Search Committee and the Finance Committee had presented a salary package that was lower than what they wanted to give our family, but they promised to make the proper adjustments in a few months. When it came time for the budget to be approved those two committees kept their word and had included the increase in the new budget. In the process of approving the budget, one elderly lady became an adversary to me. She protested loudly that *she* was not getting a raise. She argued that the church had just called me and I should not be given a raise so soon. She pointed out that there were many retirees in the church who were not getting raises. The committee tried to explain their reasons to her, but she would have none of it. I kept silent and did not comment at all. After a divisive debate, the church yielded to the majority and gave me the increase in my salary package. It still was not enough to live on without my wife also working.

This was an older church and set in its ways and this woman stirred up some gossip. On Wednesday night as the church was assembled for a prayer meeting, she went to the homes of church members, leaving a letter comparing her income to mine and protesting the approved increase. I returned home to find my special autographed copy at my door. The chairman of the deacons, the finance chairman, and other key leaders of the church received copies as well and immediately called to encourage me. When I read the letter, I was filled with amazing joy. You could have sent me a birthday card with a gift in it and this would have been better. Why? This woman was not my issue. Even the Great Adversary behind her was not my issue. I knew I was sent there by God and did not allow this to upset me. This was His burden and it was light. I began to experience *the fellowship of His sufferings.*

At that point, God impressed me with what to do. At the end of the worship the following Sunday, I thanked the church for the salary package increase, but said that we would not accept it. We wanted our salary to remain as it was initially. Where did that response come from? I had preached about *The Blessing of Barrenness* from the life of Hannah weeks earlier at the church – and now I had the opportunity to demonstrate a godly response in a hard situation. Instead of responding in anger and lashing back at my attacker, I chose to rejoice in God and trust our future to Him.

The next week we received several anonymous letters from what I assumed were members of the congregation, each with cash in it. By the end of that week, we had received more money than the raise I had refused. God proved Himself faithful – and we rejoiced in His provision.

It burdens my heart as a pastor that most Christians never discover this great truth. They have refused to share in the sufferings of Christ that He has for them. The secret of fruitfulness comes through suffering. Let us learn from Hannah's example. The broken heart precedes the blessing of fruitfulness.

7. ARE YOU PREPARED TO REMAIN FAITHFUL TO GOD AND FOLLOW HIS BURDEN EVEN IF IT BRINGS PERSECUTION?

PERSECUTION IS COMMON

After I experienced personal revival in my life, I was hungry to grow in Christ. My pastor gave me a reading list of Christian books. Among the many great books I read, two books on persecution prepared me for ministry in an unusual way. One was *Fox's Book of Martyrs,* the history of the persecuted church. The other was *Tortured for Christ* by Richard Wurmbrand. It was difficult to compare my level of Christianity with Christians who have really suffered for Christ.

As a result of their stories, I was better prepared for the rejection and ridicule I would at times face in the ministry. I was even able to rejoice, because I knew God was in control. I began to sense a pattern in door-to-door evangelism: when someone cursed me at one house, it usually meant Satan was trying to scare me away from the great fruit that awaited me a few doors down the street. When I began to serve in the church and faced criticism, gossip, lies and false accusations, I was better prepared for it. Compared to what the persecuted church has and is experiencing in other nations, my troubles were petty.

American Christians have great religious freedom. We do not know the kind of persecution that the church has known throughout its history. Our Christian forefathers came to America to escape religious oppression and persecution in Europe. But today in many nations, Christians are still persecuted for their faith. Thousands of Christians around the world die for their love of Jesus. In some Muslim nations, it is against their law for a Muslim to convert to Christianity. There are some nations that carry the death penalty to those who convert to Christianity.

I have called all my persecutions little in comparison to Scripture and persecuted Christians in some other nations.

 ## LUNCH WITH A CHAMPION OF THE FAITH

One day David Nelms and I were discussing the possibility of our church sponsoring several TTI church-planting schools in Nagaland, India. He arranged for me to have lunch with Greg Kappas and one of TTI leaders from India. I listened to John's testimony [27] and was amazed at the grace that God gave him as he faced persecution. John came to Christ out of Hinduism and began preaching Christ in his village. He was beaten and told not to preach Christianity anymore. When he recovered from his beating, he again preached Christ and this time he was beaten to the point of death. Had his wife not rescued him and taken him to a hospital, he would have died a martyr's death. As John was sharing his story, I felt a little ashamed of fretting over my big problems that seemed to become so small and petty compared to what other believers face in some parts of the world. I wondered if I would continue to preach Christ at the risk of losing my life. John continued his story, that after months of recovery, he again went and preached Christ. This time the persecutors came and burned his house down. Since then, God has greatly blessed this simple servant of His. This champion in the faith is responsible for several hundred new church plants in India. I asked him if he would be willing to go to Nagaland and organize church planting schools that we would sponsor through TTI and he agreed. Within a few months, 120 pastors had enrolled and agreed to start 120 new churches.

God wants all of us to remain faithful and not be sidetracked by the provocations of our enemies or the persecutions of Satan. Supernatural fruitfulness awaits those who fully surrender to God and believe Him for great things.

RESPONDING TO PERSECUTION

- Think back to a time when another Christian easily offended you. How would you feel if you were sitting at lunch with John, listening to his story of persecution and faith?

- Has someone ever responded harshly to you because you tried to tell them about Jesus? How did you feel? Did you shrink back and become silent? Or were you emboldened to proclaim the Gospel even more?

---

27   His name has been changed for security reasons.

CHAPTER 10

Brokenness – Part 1

… then I will give him to the LORD all the days of his life … (1 Samuel 1:11)

 ## THE FIFTH TEST OF FAITH

The fifth test of faith tells us:

> *God will break us in order to mold us; His ultimate goal*
> *is to shape us to conform us to the image of Christ.*
> *Will we trust Him and learn the lessons He has for us?*

God brought Hannah to the exact point He wanted her to be. She was faced with the question, *Who does my womb, and the fruit of my womb, belong to: to God or to me?*

1. THE PURPOSE OF BROKENNESS

God desires to break us – not to hurt us, but to heal us. For, you see, we have a problem. Even as adopted children of God, we still have a fleshly, sinful nature that wars within us (see Paul's record of his experience in Romans 7). Our heavenly Father, who loves us and does all things well, desires us to live fully submitted to the Lordship of Jesus Christ. Getting us there requires a process … and part of that process is breaking us.

Simply put, God's purpose of breaking us is to bring our will into submission to His, bringing us to the point where we willingly submit to Him as slaves of Jesus Christ.

It is important to note that being broken by God is not anything like being broken by the world.

- God breaks us to humble us. The world breaks us to destroy and defeat us.
- When God breaks us, it is by design and with a good purpose. When the world breaks us, it is simply the result of living in a fallen, sinful world.
- When God breaks us, we surrender control. When the world breaks us, we rely on our self-sufficiency; often maintain control, insisting on our own way.
- When God breaks us, we are broken in the right place and in the right way. It is for our good and His glory. When the world breaks us, we are damaged, hurt and fractured.

Hannah found herself in bondage to her circumstances and to herself. Real liberty did not come to her soul by seeking independence from Peninnah, Elkanah, God's burden, or her own problems. Real liberty came when she gave up her independence to a new, loving Master, the Lord of hosts. In complete and sweet surrender to the Lord, Hannah found that brokenness led her to real liberty.

Notice Hannah's attitude of submission and obedience as she describes herself as *God's maidservant:*

> Then she made a vow and said, "O LORD of hosts, if You will indeed look on the affliction of **Your maidservant** and remember me, and not forget **Your maidservant**, but will give **Your maidservant** a male child, then I will give him to the LORD all the days of his life, and no razor shall come upon his head."

In the process of her grief and struggles, Hannah learned an important lesson: *God was God and she was not!* Three times in that one verse, she described herself as *God's maidservant.* Her life was not her own. She had been bought with a price and belonged to Him.

 ## THE BROKEN HORSE

A wild horse is of little value to its owner. It strength and speed can even be a danger, when not brought under control. Psalm 147:10 says, *He (God) does not delight in the strength of the horse; He takes no pleasure in the legs of a man.* Strength in battle belonged to the horsemen, and the strongest muscles in the body were in the legs of men. But God says He is impressed with neither. He does not delight in our self-confidence in our strength and independence. He is pleased only when we live by faith, in surrender and trust.

The solution to the independent nature of the wild horse is to break it. But a good cowboy knows he is not hurting the horse – he is simply breaking its spirit so that it can be brought under control. If the wild horse is broken and learns that its greatest security and care comes from its service and friendship to its master, then the horse can be of great value.

The process of breaking the will of the wild horse is often painful. The movie "The Horse Whisperer," showed a scene in which one of the front legs of a horse was tied to the saddle horn to prevent the horse from bucking. It was made to hobble around the training ring in exhaustion until it submitted to the trainer. Once it submitted, the young rider and her horse became like one.

What others may not have understood was that was God was hobbling Hannah, breaking her for God's glory, her good, and our instruction. 1 Samuel 1 used words like *severely provoked, miserable, grief, affliction, weeping and sorrow.* The process was painful to endure … but once Hannah had learned the lessons God had for her, she was His vessel, crafted and designed by Him for His honor.

I was at a church-wide retreat where one of the recreation electives was horseback riding. In my morning quiet time that day I had read in Psalm 32:8-9, *I will instruct you and teach you in the way you should go; I will guide you with My eye. Do not be like the horse or like the mule, which have no understanding, which must be harnessed with bit and bridle, else they will not come near you.*

This verse came alive to me later that day when I had the opportunity to ride a horse. The owner gave very clear instructions about his horse: *"He is well trained and well disciplined. In his mouth is a bit connected to the bridle, but don't pull on it because it causes pain in his mouth. You do not have to hurt him or cause pain to get him to respond to you."* He said, *"This horse is trained and very sensitive to the rider. If you want to go left, all you have to do is shift your weight in the saddle and apply some weight to your left foot in the left stirrup and the horse will go left. If you want to go right, shift your weight to the right, apply weight in the right stirrup with your right foot and the horse will go to the right. If you want to stop, just lay the reins gently across its neck. It will feel the weight of the reins. It is sensitive to the reins, and it will stop. If you want to go, just lift the reins from its neck and say, go."*

This horse did not need a rough kick to get going. I simply had to lift the reins and gently say, *"Go!"* I was amazed. I leaned to the left, the horse went left; I leaned to the right, the horse went right; I laid the reins across its neck, it stopped. I thought, *"This is a smart horse!"* He made it easy – and it was a joy to ride that horse.

While riding, the verse that I had read in my quiet time came alive to me and God taught me a great lesson. God wanted me to be submissive and sensitive to the point that He could guide me with His eye – not through the pain of the bit and bridle (Psalms 32:8, 9). God wanted me to hand over the reins of my life and trust Him with it.

When we see Hannah in 1 Samuel 1 and 2, she has been broken and become sensitive to God's leading in her life. Notice again the three times she refers to herself as *God's maidservant* (1 Samuel 1:11). In like manner, Abigail bowed before David and four times call herself *God's maidservant* as she was used of God by her submission to stop David and his armed soldiers from destroying her house and servants. David himself would also use this word in reference to his own surrender to God as *the son of Your maidservant* (Psalms 86:16). Each of them found liberty in submitting to God.

None of us can in a natural sense find liberty in slavery. The key is the object of our submission. Who is our Master? To most, their master is sin and self, leading not to freedom but to bondage (Romans 6). To some their master is Satan and he enslaves to destroy (John 10:10). However, those who have given over the reins of their lives to Christ as their Master have found the only true liberty on planet earth.

The Law of Moses had a most unusual and touching ritual regarding a Hebrew who on the seventh year of his bondage to a Hebrew master could go free if he chose to. However, there were some who chose to bind themselves to their master for life because they found their master to be gracious. Here is how Moses recorded the ceremony:

> *If you buy a Hebrew servant, he shall serve six years; and in the seventh he shall go out free and pay nothing. If he comes in by himself, he shall go out by himself; if he comes in married, then his wife shall go out with him. If his master has given him a wife, and she has borne him sons or daughters, the wife and her children shall be her master's, and he shall go out by himself. But if the servant plainly says, 'I love my master, my wife, and my children; I will not go out free, then his master shall bring him to the judges. He shall also bring him to the door, or to the doorpost, and his master shall pierce his ear with an awl; and he shall serve him forever* (Exodus 21:2-6).

The writers the New Testament picked up on this theme. As they wrote, they identified themselves as *bondservants of the Lord Jesus Christ.* Consider the following:

- *Paul, a bondservant of God and an apostle of Jesus Christ* (Titus 1:1).
- *Simon Peter, a bondservant and apostle of Jesus Christ* (2 Peter 1:1).
- *Jude, a bondservant of Jesus Christ* (Jude 1).
- *James, a bondservant of God and of the Lord Jesus Christ* (James 1:1).

For centuries, followers of Jesus have understood all that Jesus has done for them. Because of His sacrifice and great love for them, they willingly sacrificed their freedom and said, *"I love my Master and will be His slave for my entire life."*

Hannah reached the point in brokenness that she said, *"I do not want to be my own. Lord, here is my ear, mark me and Lord here are my desires for children. I recognize that my life is not my own. I belong to you. Do as you please. I am your maidservant."*

In submission, Hannah found a loving and trustful Lord of hosts. Peninnah was only a rod in the hand of Satan to provoke her as part of the process of brokenness. But unknown to Satan or Peninnah was the Master Chessman who was moving them like little pawns with the greater purpose that through brokenness would come great blessings to Hannah.

God's purpose of brokenness in our lives is to bring us to the true liberty of the Holy Spirit that God's great assignments may be accomplished through a submissive love-relationship with the Lord.

I wish I could tell you that through my own brokenness I have always given the Lord the reins of my life daily. After trusting the Lord one day, I have often taken the reins back another day and grieved the Holy Spirit. When I have failed to be sensitive to His whisper of love, He has, as a gracious Father, picked up the reins and through the bit and bridle turned me back to Him.

APPLYING THE PRINCIPLE OF BEING A BONDSERVANT

- How much has Jesus Christ done for you? What would be your eternal destiny if Jesus had not died for you?

- In light of His great sacrifice, what is the logical response? Have you ever come to the point in your life where you have said you would willingly give up your freedom to follow Jesus as a bondservant for the rest of your life? (Romans 12:1-2).

- If you knew that your master was kind, gracious and did all things well, would you freely submit to the uncomfortable times and trials of faith knowing that God was working His purpose in your life? (James 1:2-5).

- Sometimes only a wounding can take us where God wants us to go. Can you point to a time when God wounded you to do in your life what He wanted to do?

- Can you call yourself a bondservant of Jesus Christ?

2.   THE PROOF OF BROKENNESS

Then I will give him to the Lord is a key phrase in understanding the point that God has now brought Hannah. Before this time, she may have been content to dedicate a portion of her life to the Lord. Then she may have been willing to give her womb unto the Lord, if she believed that it would be fruitful. Would she be willing to give God her womb, if she thought that He would then shut it up and make her barren? In the process of brokenness comes a surrender of the ownership of our lives. The proof that brokenness has brought Hannah to absolute surrender is her willingness to give Samuel the Lord.

Hannah remembered and drew strength from the long test of faith of her father Abraham. His first test of faith was to trust God and follow Him wherever He led. He was asked to leave his family and go to a strange land that God promised to give to him and his descendants. He was told that he would be blessed in the Promised Land, but then encountered a famine. Instead of trusting God by faith, Abraham relied on that which he could see and left the Land of Promise to find relief in Egypt. In His grace, God continued to work in Abraham's life, sending him back into the Land of Promise to wait for the promised son through barren Sarah. The trial was long and in an attempt to fulfill the promise through natural means, Abraham and Sarah had Ishmael, the son of the flesh through Hagar. God told them this was not to be the son of the promise, and had them wait on God for the impossible. At age 99, Abraham received a reconfirmation of the promise from God, and Isaac was born a year later. However, a greater test of faith awaited Abraham a few years later.

Abraham loved Isaac deeply. He was the son he had waited for all of his life. At the appropriate time, God asked for Isaac back. However this was more than a command to *"dedicate Him to Me."* Abraham was asked to *sacrifice him* to God. *"Then He said, "Take now your son, your only son Isaac, whom you love, and go to the land of Moriah, and offer him there as a burnt offering on one of the mountains of which I shall tell you."* God was asking the impossible: that Abraham kill the son he had waited for all of his life. The phrase *your son, your only son Isaac, whom you love,* evidenced the magnitude of this command. At this point, Isaac was over 20 years old, and with his death, the Abrahamic Covenant would be ended.

Abraham had given God everything and now God asked for that which would break his heart. It would be with a broken heart and trust in God that Abraham would lay his Isaac down on God's altar of absolute surrender. Yet, Abraham trusted that God would have to raise Isaac up from the dead to fulfill God's promise to him. Abraham walked with Isaac up Mount Moriah with a broken heart, but he came down the Mount with joy having received back from God the son that he surrendered to God.

Brokenness is a process. It often involves the death of a dream. But it is rooted in the power of the Gospel, where Jesus died the death of deaths for us, paying for our sins, and triumphing over death by His resurrection. As a result, Christians know they have been *bought with a price and that we are not our own* (1 Corinthians 6:19-20). God did not free us from bondage to sin and Satan to simply send us on our merry way, claiming our lives as our own. The lifestyle of the unbroken is filled with the language of *"my"* and *"mine"* instead of the sweet surrender of *"Yours."* It is my money, my time, my pleasure, my dreams, my plans, my things, my talent to those who have not come to the place where their lives are completely His.

"My" and *"mine"* is the language of the prideful and selfish. Jesus Christ, the Creator of the whole Universe comes to each of us and asks for our lives. We respond by putting limits on our sacrifice, by lowering the bar of our devotion. Until we can give back to God that which He gave to us, we cannot be entrusted with God's true riches. God does not entrust His blessings to those who hold on tightly to their possessions.

God will not share His glory with another. His great assignments are not given to us until we are broken and willing to sacrifice all. Otherwise, without brokenness, the thing we desire to possess would possess us.

Without brokenness, Leah named her first three sons all in relationship to her rivalry to her sister Rachael. She envied Rachael's beauty and the love that Jacob had for Rachael to the point that the names Reuben, Simeon, and Levi were related to her focus on *"my need."* She was obsessed with her sister, and it was not until Leah's fourth son, through whom the Messiah would come, that her focus shifted away from her needs, her problems, and her sister. Worshipping the Lord, she called him Judah, saying, *Now will I praise the LORD"* (Genesis 29:31-35).

Remember this key principle: it is so much better not to interpret our lives through our problems but through our praise for the Lord.

You must learn from the process of brokenness to come to the point of absolute surrender in your Christian walk. Take your hands off of your life and do not focus on your problems. Begin to focus on the Lord, rejoicing in His salvation. *No one is holy like the LORD, for there is none besides You, nor is there any rock like our God* (1 Samuel 2:1, 2).

Why must God bring us to humility and brokenness to bear much fruit?

- Without brokenness, God's glory is marred.
- Without brokenness, man is praised.
- Without brokenness, God's gifts are abused.
- Without brokenness, we rely on our abilities and strengths and miss the mighty power of the Holy Spirit working through us.
- Without brokenness, we produce the works of the law and not the fruits of the Spirit.
- Without brokenness, our ministry is built around us instead of Jesus.
- Without brokenness, we divide the body of Christ through petty rivalries, envy, and exaltation of self.
- Without brokenness, we become proud, bitter, and discouraged when we encounter problems.
- Without brokenness, we are blinded to our spiritual pride and zeal.

In seminary, I signed up for a prison ministry that required getting up early on Sunday and going the city jail to teach a Bible study for jail inmates. The Chaplin who had been in charge of the ministry for years gave each of the team members the book from which we were to teach a certain section of the jail. By the second week I had decided that "I felt led of the Lord" to preach rather than teach the assigned Sunday school lesson. Some of the inmates informed the Chaplin and he reminded us to teach the lesson as agreed upon. I then began to plead my case of "feeling led" of the Holy Spirit to fulfill my ministry of preaching. God had called me to preach. I explained that I would be more effective preaching than teaching a lesson. Since the Chaplin could not understand what I felt was a better plan for my ministry, I returned his Sunday school quarterly and took my Bible and went home. At the time I really thought I was right and that the Chaplin just did not understand the leadership of the Holy Spirit. My spiritual pride and lack of brokenness had left me with blind spots of pride that I did not see. But others did.

In God's continual process of using trials of faith, problems, and the Word of God, I looked back on that experience to recognize spiritual immaturity and pride on my part. Now that I have been in leadership positions like that Chaplin, I have seen myself in the mirror of many team members who had their own agenda as well. The thing about blind spots of spiritual pride is that others who have been there before recognize them while you do not. Thus without brokenness, the self-will of the "Big My" can be in our preaching, teaching, singing, serving, and in every relationship. The sad thing is that we may not even recognize it while others see it clearly.

Most of us have had similar experiences where we seek to serve the Lord but manifest too much of our self-life. It appears in every ministry of our churches. Some young Christians in their zeal have a great new idea that they feel that the Lord has given them. Many of these ideas come from our flesh, from natural talent and zeal. Others are truly motivated by God. The proof of humility and brokenness is seen in two areas:

- How we respond to our leaders, when they ask us to do something different from our personal dreams and desires.
- How we respond to those who are not excited about following us in our self-generated plans.

This selfish motivation appears in older believers as well, when things do not go as planned or when there is a lack of support for ministries and ideas that they introduced. It appears in mature believers as well who yesterday were walking with God but today take their focus off Him and respond out of the flesh.

Jesus reminded the disciples that they were not to be like the Gentiles who seek greatness by seeking to be served. Jesus taught them to serve others and take the focus off themselves. *Now there was also a dispute among (the disciples), as to which of them should be considered the greatest. And He said to them, "The kings of the Gentiles exercise lordship over them, and those who exercise authority over them are called 'benefactors.' But not so among you; on the contrary, he who is greatest among you, let him be as the younger, and he who governs as he who serves. For who is greater, he who sits at the table, or he who serves? Is it not he who sits at the table? Yet I am among you as the One who serves* (Luke 22:24-27). Isn't that amazing? The one person in the entire universe who deserves all praise, glory, honor and service came as a servant. He said in Mark 10:45, *For even the Son of Man did not come to be served, but to serve, and to give His life a ransom for many."*

One of the proofs of brokenness is a servant's heart in ministry. Those who seek to be served, or to be recognized, or to have the limelight, have not been broken in humility. When you are broken, you do not care who gets the credit. You do not have a personal agenda. You only care about Jesus receiving the praise and glory.

 ## BECOMING A SERVANT

- Do you feel that you have the grace to give back to God that which He gives to you? Have you ever come to the point where you lay your gifts, abilities, dreams, concerns and passions on God's altar and give them to Him?
- The lifestyle of the unbroken is filled the language of *"my"* instead of the sweet surrender of *"Yours."* How much of your prayer life sounds like *"Give me what I want"* as opposed to *"Not my will, but Yours be done"*? Until we can give back to God that which He gave to us, then we cannot be entrusted with God's true riches.

- When we come out of a time of brokenness, we do so having learned valuable life-lessons that God imparts. Can you identify with the following statements:
  ○ The great assignments of God are not given to us until we are broken, lest we take glory from God.
  ○ The thing we desire to possess will possess us without brokenness.
  ○ It is so much better not to interpret our life through our problems but through our praise for the Lord.

3. THE PROCESS OF BROKENNESS

Just as God led Israel through a series of trials of faith to prove them, humble them, make them to know their heart, and to finally do them good in the end, Hannah was led through a similar process to glorify God and build her faith (Deut. 8: 2-3,16).

Peninnah or Satan did not break Hannah God broke her. Others may bruise us and batter us, but they cannot break us in our spirit. Only God can bring us to brokenness before Him.

Brokenness is the deep work of God's Spirit in our lives. There is a great difference between the godly sorrow that comes from experiencing His discipline and the type of sorrow that comes because of pain, loss, and persecution. Paul contrasted these two types of sorrows when he wrote, *For godly sorrow produces repentance leading to salvation, not to be regretted; but the sorrow of the world produces death* (2 Corinthians 7:10). God can use a broken heart over a broken relationship or loss, but it cannot be sorrow that turns inward and does not lead to repentance. Many are sorry for the consequences of their sins, but do not have a godly sorrow that leads to repentance and change by God's Spirit. Sorrow without brokenness can lead to depression, grief, or bitterness. But when we turn completely to God in our brokenness, it can lead to a supernatural opening of our lives to a new dimension of living.

Brokenness brings with it *indignation* against our sin, and not so much the sins of others against us. It creates within us a *vehement desire* for a closer relationship with God and our focus is not on those that offend us. The *revenge* spoken of here is not against others but is against our own sin as we are *ready to punish all disobedience when your obedience is fulfilled* (2 Corinthians 10:6).

Brokenness is a result of humility of spirit before God's holiness. It is surrendering willingly to His Lordship and sovereignty over our lives. It is the grace to abandon all faith in ourselves. Brokenness is the clay becoming pliable in the potter's hands. It hears the words of Jesus *"Blessed are the poor in spirit"* (Matthew 4:3).

BROKENNESS IN THE PSALMS

The book of Psalms, Israel's songbook of worship, contains many references to being broken before God.

*Make me hear joy and gladness, that the bones You have **broken** may rejoice…. The sacrifices of God are a **broken** spirit, a **broken** and a contrite heart— these, O God, You will not despise* (Psalm 51:8, 17; emphasis mine).

The background of Psalm 51 is most significant. David had sinned against God by committing adultery with Bathsheba, and murdering Uriah. For one year, he wasted away in grief, guilt and conviction. When God sent the prophet Nathan to rebuke him and say *You are the man*, David was brought face to face with his sin – and ultimately repented and came back to God. In verse eight, *the breaking of his bones* was a figure of speech, indicating that David's entire being had been brought low by guilt.

Phillip Keller tells that a shepherd sometimes broke the front leg of a straying sheep and then bound up the broken leg. He then carried him until the leg healed. Once healed the straying sheep would always walk next to the shepherd. [28] David was made to realize that God indeed accepts the one who comes before Him with a broken and contrite spirit.

*The LORD is near to those who have a **broken heart**, and saves such as have a contrite spirit. Many are the afflictions of the righteous, but the LORD delivers him out of them all* (Psalm 34:18-19; emphasis mine).

*O LORD, do not rebuke me in Your wrath, Nor chasten me in Your hot displeasure!... I am feeble and severely **broken**; I groan because of the turmoil of my heart. But my enemies are vigorous, and they are strong; and those who hate me wrongfully have multiplied* (Psalm 38:1, 8, 19; emphasis mine).

*Save me, O God! For the waters have come up to my neck. I sink in deep mire, where there is no standing; I have come into deep waters, where the floods overflow me. I am weary with my crying; my throat is dry; my eyes fail while I wait for my God.... Reproach has **broken my heart**, and I am full of heaviness; I looked for someone to take pity, but there was none; and for comforters, but I found none. They also gave me gall for my food, and for my thirst they gave me vinegar to drink* (Psalm 69:1-4, 20-21; emphasis mine)

*Praise the LORD! For it is good to sing praises to our God; For it is pleasant, and praise is beautiful. The LORD builds up Jerusalem; He gathers together the outcasts of Israel. He heals the **brokenhearted** and binds up their wounds* (Psalm 147:1-3).

This theme continues throughout the lives of the prophets. Here is Jeremiah's record:

*My heart within me is **broken** because of the prophets; all my bones shake. I am like a drunken man, and like a man whom wine has overcome, because of the LORD, and because of His holy words. For the land is full of adulterers; for because of a curse the land mourns. The pleasant places of the wilderness are dried up. Their course of life is evil, and their might is not right. "For both prophet and priest are profane; Yes, in My house I have found their wickedness," says the LORD* (Jeremiah 23:9-11; emphasis mine).

You must remember that brokenness is a work of God's Spirit. It is not emotional sorrow over the loss of a car, a ring, a friendship, or anything else. It is not centered in self-praise and the embarrassment that comes from the lack of man's approval. It is not centered in self-pity over the "woe is me" syndrome that comes when things do not go our way. If the trouble that we are experiencing is not centered on the Word of God, then it is not brokenness. If our sorrow is

---

28   Phillip Keller, *A Shepherd Looks at Psalm 23*. Grand Rapids, Zondervan Publishing Company, 1996.

worry and self-pity by telling people how bad things are going for us or how someone has hurt us, then it is centered in our emotions and flesh. Brokenness drives us to God and His Word. One who is broken by God will be in God's Word, praying without ceasing, and loving people like never before.

When God breaks us, it is often in one or more of the following areas:

- We are to be broken over our sins.
- We are to be broken over the things that break God's heart.
- We are to be broken over the lost.
- We are to be broken over our stinking flesh.
- We are to be broken in the presence of God's holiness.
- We are to be broken over the sins of our nation.

It is true that when we have sorrow, grief, sadness, and hurts, God does care. And we should comfort those who are emotionally down. However, brokenness goes further than the simple encouragement we may receive during such times. We are broken to change us and prepare us for God to work through us.

In Luke 7:36-50, there is woman who comes and breaks an alabaster box of perfume at Jesus' presence, weeping and washing His feet with her tears. She was broken over the love of Christ for her and for the awfulness of her sins. The perfume filled the room and Jesus was pleased with what He saw in her broken heart. However, one of the Pharisees named Simon expressed his great displeasure, judging Jesus for allowing a sinful woman to touch Him. Simon reasoned that if Jesus knew what sort of woman she was, he would have never allowed it. But Jesus, knowing all things, received her act of worship and love. He blessed her and said, *Your faith has saved you; go in peace.* When we are broken of our pride and self-sufficiency, we are free to worship Jesus in complete abandonment. "Religious people" will never understand us. But take heart: they never understood Jesus either!

Finally, without a broken heart, we do not have a ministry to hurting and broken people. God uses us to comfort and encourage others to trust Him through the breaking process.

LET'S REVIEW

- Others may bruise us and batter us, but they cannot break us in our spirit. Peninnah or Satan did not break Hannah. She was broken by God, and entrusted her soul to Him.

- Brokenness is the deep work of God's Spirit.

- Brokenness is a result of humility of spirit before God's holiness. It is surrendering willingly to His Lordship and sovereignty over our lives.

- Brokenness is not emotional sorrow over the loss of possessions or relationships.
  Brokenness is not centered in self, but in Christ.

 ## PROUD, UNBROKEN PEOPLE VERSUS BROKEN PEOPLE

The following lists [29] contrast two types of people: the proud and unbroken, and the broken and humble. Read through these lists carefully, asking the Spirit of God to shine His light of truth into your life. Follow His promptings to repent and trust God to break you and mold you into the person He desires you to be.

PROUD, UNBROKEN PEOPLE

- Focus on the failures of others
- Are self-righteous, have a critical, fault-finding spirit, look at their own life/faults with a telescope but others with a microscope
- Look down on others
- Are independent, have a self-sufficient spirit
- Maintain control; must have their way
- Have to prove that they are right
- Claim rights
- Have a demanding spirit
- Are self-protective of time, rights, reputation
- Desire to be served
- Desire to be a success
- Desire for self-advancement
- Are driven to be recognized and appreciated
- Are wounded when others are promoted and they are overlooked
- Think "the ministry is privileged to have me!"
- Think of what they can do for God
- Feel confident in how much they know
- Are self-conscious
- Keep people at arm's length
- Are quick to blame others
- Are unapproachable
- Are defensive when criticized
- Are concerned about what others think
- Work to maintain image and protect reputation
- Find it difficult to share their spiritual needs with others
- Want to be sure no one finds out about their sin
- Have a hard time saying, "I was wrong. Would you forgive me?"
- Deal in generalities when confessing sin
- Are concerned about the consequences of their sin
- Are remorseful for being caught

---

29   Originally developed by Nancy Leigh DeMoss for a presentation to the staff of Campus Crusade for Christ in Ft. Collins, Colorado.

- Wait for the other party to come and ask for forgiveness in a conflict
- Compare themselves with others and feel deserving of honor
- Are blind to their true heart condition
- Don't think they have anything of which to repent
- Don't think they need revival (think everybody else does)

BROKEN PEOPLE

- Are overwhelmed with their own spiritual need
- Are compassionate toward all people, have a forgiving spirit, look for the best in others
- Esteem all others better than self
- Have dependent spirit; recognize others' needs
- Surrender control
- Are willing to yield the right to be right
- Yield rights
- Have a giving spirit
- Are self-denying
- Are motivated to serve others
- Desire to be faithful to make others a success
- Desire to promote others
- Have a sense of unworthiness; are thrilled to be used at all; are eager for others to get the credit
- Rejoice when others are lifted up
- Think, "I don't deserve to serve in this ministry!"
- Know that they have nothing to offer God
- Are humbled by how much they have to learn
- Have no concern with self at all
- Risk getting close to others; are willing to take the risks of loving intimately
- Accept personal responsibility, can see where they were wrong
- Are easy to be entreated
- Receive criticism with a humble, open heart
- Are concerned with being real
- Know all that matters is what God knows
- Die to their own reputation
- Are willing to be transparent with others
- Are willing to be exposed; know that once broken, there's nothing to lose
- Are quick to admit fault and to seek forgiveness
- Deal in specifics when confessing sin
- Are grieved over the root of their sin
- Are repentant over sin and forsake it
- Take the initiative to be reconciled; gets there first
- Compare themselves with the holiness of God and feel desperate for mercy
- Walk in the light
- Have a continual heart attitude toward repentance
- Continually sense their need for a fresh encounter with the living God

CHAPTER 11

Brokenness – Part 2

… then I will give him to the LORD all the days of his life … (1 Samuel 1:11)

THE FIFTH TEST OF FAITH

Again the fifth test of faith tells us:

> *God will break us in order to mold us; His ultimate goal*
> *is to shape us to conform us to the image of Christ.*
> *Will we trust Him and learn the lessons He has for us?*

God brought Hannah to the exact point He wanted her to be. She was faced with the question, *Who does my womb, and the fruit of my womb, belong to: to God or to me?*

In the previous chapter, we covered The Purpose of Brokenness, The Proof of Brokenness, and The Process of Brokenness. Now we move on to point four, The Pattern of Brokenness.

4. THE PATTERN OF BROKENNESS

Hannah's prayer to God came after years of affliction. Each year she would come to the House of the Lord and each year she would return empty handed. She was provoked by Peninnah, by Satan, and by her own losing battle with her flesh and discouragement. The process of God's trial of faith was long – but it was with purpose.

A Song We Can All Sing

What Hannah did not yet understand was heaven's viewpoint of her brokenness. She did not understand how her life was linked to all the other women of God who struggled with infertility. Like Sarah, Leah, Rachael, Rebecca, and other women of faith, Hannah did not fully understand what God was doing through her trials. That's why some things are best understood after the fact. [30] She did not yet understand that God had chosen her for a demonstration of His supernatural power, to give hope to all who long for supernatural fruitfulness.

Trusting God, while silently suffering, is one of God loudest forms of praise. Through Hannah's suffering came a song that reflected the depth of intimacy with God that had been developed over the years of suffering. Hannah's praise song reflects some of the greatest principles of grace and the way of God in all of Scripture. She begins her song with a greater understanding of God: *No one is holy like the LORD, for there is none besides You, nor is there any rock like our God* (1 Samuel 2:2). It was through the process of faithfully enduring the trials of faith that Hannah understood God better. She saw Him as holy … unlike any other … like a rock that she could depend on every day of her life. The middle part of her song declares God's victory over the wicked. It also tells one of the greatest lessons Hannah learned: *for by strength no man shall prevail* (1 Samuel 2:9). She learned that God's way of victory was through total dependence upon Him, and not our own strength. She ends her praise song with a prophecy of the coming King who is Christ the Lord Jesus Himself; *He will give strength to His king, and exalt the horn of His anointed* (1 Samuel 2:10).

Hannah was not the only one in Scripture who learned dependence on God through the things they suffered.

- Abraham and Sarah had been given a clear promise that God would raise up the chosen seed through Sarah's barren womb. Abraham and Sarah's main test was that of patience.
- The wife of Manoah was given a clear promise and specific instructions regarding Samson who was to be born from her barren womb. [31] God did not delay in opening her barren womb.
- Jacob did not know that when he cried, *All these things are against me,* that from heaven's viewpoint God was working all things for Jacob's good in his apparent loss of Joseph. [32]
- Job suffered in silence, not knowing the discussions God was having with Satan regarding his servant Job. Job did not know that God was writing a book about Job to one day bless millions of His children. [33]
- David's great songs of trust in the LORD did not come in the easy days. They came when he was running for his life from Saul, when his friends had misunderstood him,

---

30   It was John Flavel who said, *Some providences of God, like Hebrew letters, are best understood backwards.*

31   Judges 13

32   Genesis 43-44; cf. Genesis 50:20

33   Job 1

and when he despaired of life itself. Through his sufferings, he was drawn closer to the heart of God. In a similar way, Hannah was drawn into deeper fellowship with God through her sufferings.

- In fact, Jesus Himself, though the Son of God and sinless in character, *learned obedience from the things which He suffered.* [34] There are some lessons that can only be learned in the crucible of suffering.

The way God dealt with Hannah gives us new lessons of faith. God would not give her an explanation of His purpose, but did give her His burden for a son. In brokenness with no strength left in her, Hannah surrendered her future to the unknown purpose of God. She trusted God with the unseen, unheard, and unknown, knowing only that God is God and that she was His child.

 ## HANNAH'S PRAYER AND HER TRIAL OF FAITH

Hannah had no strength left to hold onto. Her dream of a child reached a point of brokenness where she was willing to surrender her dream for a child to God. She was willing to entrust Her future to God for His purposes. Out of weakness, she would be made strong:

- She surrendered her stumbling weakness for the power of God (v. 4).
- She opened her hungry mouth and let God feed her (v. 5).
- She surrendered her desire for children and saw God bring a full and complete set of children into her life (v. 5)
- She was brought down to be raised up by God (v. 6).
- In poverty, she would only be content when God made her rich (v. 7).
- She sat with the poor and the beggars on the garbage heap bearing the shame of her barrenness before she was exalted by God to sit with princes (v. 8).

She was barren, battered, burdened, and now broken – but she was also at the dawn of God's supernatural blessings. In brokenness she received from Eli's lips a promise from God that would forever change her life: *Go in peace, and the God of Israel grant your petition which you have asked of Him* (1 Samuel 1: 17). With that word she moved from her broken condition and believed. At that moment she trusted in that word as a personal promise from God and ceased from her own works to enter into God's rest. [35]

 ## UNDERSTANDING THE CONTRAST BETWEEN PENINNAH AND HANNAH

Now let us look again at Hannah's prayer from a different perspective. God allowed Peninnah to be a catalyst to Hannah's brokenness and full surrender to God.

- While Peninnah provoked, Hannah fretted.
- While Peninnah was fruitful, Hannah was barren.

---

34   Hebrews 5:8

35   Hebrews 4:9-10

- While Peninnah boasted over and over of her fruitfulness, Hannah wept.
- While Peninnah had a mighty bow for battle, Hannah was made to stumble.
- While Peninnah was full from feasting at the House of the Lord, Hannah fasted.
- While Peninnah womb was alive, Hannah's was dead.
- While Peninnah was exalted, Hannah was brought low.
- While Peninnah was rich, Hannah was made poor.
- While Peninnah seemed to receive children without crying out to God, Hannah is reduced to holding out her hand all the day to God as a beggar.
- While Peninnah boasted in the light, Hannah sat silently in the darkness before God.

 ## Our Faith-Walk with God

We fail to make a good application of the comparison and contrast between Peninnah and Hannah if we don't realize that it will apply to our walk with God as well. Like Hannah, we are spiritually barren, and cannot bring forth spiritual fruit.

There was a time when the Apostle Paul was caught up into heaven and showed things that no human had ever before seen. But notice what happened to him after that vision:

> *And lest I should be exalted above measure by the abundance of the revelations, a thorn in the flesh was given to me, a messenger of Satan to buffet me, lest I be exalted above measure. Concerning this thing I pleaded with the Lord three times that it might depart from me. And He said to me, "My grace is sufficient for you, for **My strength is made perfect in weakness.**" Therefore most gladly I will rather boast in my infirmities, **that the power of Christ may rest upon me.** Therefore I take pleasure in infirmities, in reproaches, in needs, in persecutions, in distresses, for Christ's sake. **For when I am weak, then I am strong** (2 Corinthians 12:7-10; emphasis mine).*

Hannah sang, *For by strength no man shall prevail.* Paul understood the same principle when he said, *when I am weak, then I am strong.* I call this paradox the "Secret to Fruitfulness," not because it is a secret, but because it is the direct opposite of how we serve God in religion. It is a hard lesson to learn. The Christian life does not consist of the great things we do for God, but what God does through us by the Holy Spirit. Paul appeals to us to follow his walk with God as a pattern.

If Paul were to visit many of our modern churches, he would be grieved at so many Christians who boast of how fruitful they are, when it is more the fruits of religion than the fruits of the Spirit. Remember the words of Jesus to the Laodicea church,

> *I know your works, that you are neither cold nor hot. I could wish you were cold or hot. So then, because you are lukewarm, and neither cold nor hot, I will vomit you out of My mouth. Because you say, 'I am rich, have become wealthy, and have need of nothing'—and do not know that you are wretched, miserable, poor, blind, and naked— I counsel you to buy from Me gold refined in the fire, that you may be rich; and white garments, that you may be clothed, that the shame of your nakedness may not be revealed; and anoint your eyes with eye salve,*

that you may see. As many as I love, I rebuke and chasten. Therefore be zealous and repent (Revelation 3:15-19).

A FEW SIMPLE QUESTIONS

- Have you struggled to understand God's purposes in your trials?

- When you don't know the purpose of a long trial, it is easy to begin to question God. Have you ever done that?

- Will you trust Him in the midst of the trial – and continue to learn the lessons He has for you?

5.   THE PRINCIPLE OF BROKENNESS

Have you ever said, *"I don't deserve this"*? Maybe it was getting fired from a job, losing out on a promotion, being the victim of theft, or any number of other trials. We say, *"I want JUSTICE!"* But do you really?

The LAST thing we want is justice. If God were to give us what we truly deserve, He would send us to hell ... immediately. That's what we *deserve*. No, we don't want justice. We need *grace*.

We know the principle that *no good thing dwells in me.* [36] We are totally incapable of pleasing God in our flesh. That is why we must be filled with the Spirit and walk in His power moment by moment. [37] But coming to that point of conviction is not easy. That is why God must break us ... to teach us to be fully dependent on Him.

DAVID'S BATTLE WITH HIS FLESH

David, the man after God's own heart, had his periods of walking with God and showing mercy and grace. He constantly battled with Saul. When Saul sought to kill him, David turned his face to God and saw the smile of God's pleasure on his life. He refocused on God and His grace, and therefore was able to smile himself. But through those trials, God used Saul in David's life to prepare him for his ministry as the Shepherd over Israel.

---

36   Romans 7:18

37   Ephesians 5:18; Galatians 5:16-25

However, after Saul was dead, David would soon discover that his greater problem was not Saul but his own flesh. Without Saul hunting David every day, he was not as alert to his greater enemy of his own flesh. He let his spiritual guard down. Being at ease in Zion, he soon became more like Saul.

David's flesh was not one bit different from Saul's flesh. He took multiple wives against God's command. In pride and self-reliance, he yielded to Satan's temptation to number Israel to know the potential strength of his army rather than rely on God. He committed adultery with Bathsheba and stole another man's wife. Looking into the mirror of his soul, his flesh looked just like Saul's. He murdered Uriah to hide his sin. In the Psalms, he asks God to judge Saul for trying to take his life. Now he must ask God for mercy as he took the life of Uriah. *Have mercy upon me, O God, according to Your lovingkindness; according unto the multitude of Your tender mercies, blot out my transgressions.* (Psalms 51:1). David needed grace.

If God is to use us in ministry, we must learn this truth as well. We should look at people and say, *"If God saved me, then He can save them as well."* One of the hardest lessons for Christians to learn is that our flesh after salvation is just as rotten as it was before salvation. God gave us a new heart, but He did not change our flesh. This is why we must die to self every day. It may be shocking for you to realize this important truth: you are every bit as capable of sinning as greatly as the worst of sinners. Do you think that King David ever thought he would become a murderer like Saul? But he did!

I studied and preached from the life of David for nearly a year. While preparing to teach one section, I understood more deeply the attitude of brokenness in the life of the believer. The context was after David experienced true repentance and brokenness over his sin with Bathsheba and Uriah as expressed in Psalms 51. God's loving chastening humbled David and brought him to the point where God wanted him to be. Part of God's chastening included his son Absalom driving David from the throne of Israel. As David and his loyal men were leaving Jerusalem, a descendant of Saul by the name of Shimei took advantage of the moment and cursed David.

Now when King David came to Bahurim, there was a man from the family of the house of Saul, whose name was Shimei the son of Gera, coming from there. He came out, cursing continuously as he came. And he threw stones at David and at all the servants of King David. And all the people and all the mighty men were on his right hand and on his left. Also Shimei said thus when he cursed: **"Come out! Come out! You bloodthirsty man, you rogue! The LORD has brought upon you all the blood of the house of Saul,** *in whose place you have reigned; and the LORD has delivered the kingdom into the hand of Absalom your son. So now you are caught in your own evil, because you are a bloodthirsty man!"*

Then Abishai the son of Zeruiah said to the king, "Why should this dead dog curse my lord the king? Please, let me go over and take off his head!"

But the king said, "What have I to do with you, you sons of Zeruiah? So let him curse, because the LORD has said to him, 'Curse David.' Who then shall say, 'Why have you done so?'"

And David said to Abishai and all his servants, "See how my son who came from my own body seeks my life. How much more now may this Benjamite? Let him alone, and let him curse;

for so the LORD has ordered him. It may be that the LORD will look on my affliction, and that the LORD will repay me with good for his cursing this day." And as David and his men went along the road, Shimei went along the hillside opposite him and cursed as he went, threw stones at him and kicked up dust. Now the king and all the people who were with him became weary; so they refreshed themselves there (2 Samuel 16:5-14; emphasis mine).

Notice David's attitude and spirit of brokenness:

- David restrained his soldier from killing Shimei.
- David did not try to debate or defend himself against Shimei's lies.
- David looked behind the cursing and expected a blessing from God.
- David saw Shimei as part of God's process of chastening and restoring him.
- David humbly endured the cursing, the stones, the dirt, and the humiliation before his men.

What really spoke to me was David's humility in the face of Shimei's accusation. *Come out! Come out! You bloodthirsty man, you rogue! The LORD has brought upon you all the blood of the house of Saul.* There were many things Shimei could have accused David of that would have been true – but he chose the area of David's life where he was the most sensitive to God. David had been faithful to leave Saul in God's hands. Saul had hurt David in a hundred different ways, yet David did not sin against Saul. Even when David could have justified killing Saul to save his own life, he did not touch Saul but left him in God's hands and timing. David was accused of that which he was innocent of. Despite the trial, David faithfully waited for God to exalt him to the throne that Saul occupied.

Shimei accused David falsely. But David knew that he was secretly guilty of a greater sin. He was indeed a bloody man. It was not the blood of Saul that he shed but the blood of Uriah, who David killed to hide his adultery. David knew it and God knew it. David was guilty of far greater sins than Shimei ever knew.

When Nathan confronted David about his sin in 2 Samuel 12, he told the story of a rich man who had taken one lamb from a poor man. David immediately became angry at this injustice ... until Nathan pointed out, *You are the man.*[38] Without brokenness, we judge the sins of others. Nathan was speaking of us: *we are the man.* When we read Scripture, we must see ourselves in the stories we read. You must see yourself in Adam and in Christ, noting the contrast of the old nature of sin and the new nature we have in Christ.

MY CHALLENGE OF FAITH

Over thirty years ago I was going through a deep trial of faith and the chastening of the Lord. I felt I was innocent, yet wronged. It was this passage in 2 Samuel 16 that God used to give me greater understanding of how He wanted me to respond. Though it took all my strength, I did not fight back or defend myself. Like Peter commanded, *Therefore let those who suffer according to God's will entrust their souls to a faithful Creator while doing good* (1 Peter 4:19).

---

38 2 Samuel 12:5-7

In that moment God let me see my accuser differently. I learned that no matter what I am accused of, I am a greater sinner and guilty of more than I have ever been accused of. I must learn to remind myself that, though the facts I am accused of may not be true, I am still guilty. I should say to myself, *"He sure has got his facts wrong and I am not guilty of this. But he does not know the tenth of my failures and sins!"*

For example, suppose I am accused of lying about a certain matter. The accuser's facts may be completely wrong, and I can be sure that I have not lied. But one thing is sure: God and I know that I have lied in the past. My first response should be to thank God for His forgiveness and mercy. I need to remember that if I think I stand today, then tomorrow I may fall.

Each of us has the capability of sinning greatly. Have you not lied in the past? Have you not had impure thoughts? Have you been critical of someone in the past? Me too. And we must come to God in complete dependence on Him. Apart from Him, we are powerless to respond correctly. Godly responses need God's power.

I have since learned to take the accusations of the enemy to God. *"Lord, You know that I am not guilty of this gossip, but today I humble myself before you and admit that in the past I have been guilty of many things much worst. I know that in my flesh dwells no good thing. There are many secrets sins that You have forgiven and covered that no one knows about. Today I am looking to You to keep me from stumbling and falling into that of which I am accused. I could easily sin in the manner that I have been accused. I know that I am in my flesh capable of sinning as I am falsely accused. I know that in my flesh dwells no good thing and I could fall tomorrow if not for your daily grace. Lord take this cursing and turn it into a blessing. I also pray for my accuser that you will have mercy upon them because you died for them. If you saved me, one of the chief of sinners, then You can save them."*

 ## KNOW WHO YOUR ENEMY IS

Most believers do not yet understand that when they look at their enemy, God is giving them a disgusting look at themselves. Every demonstration of sin in the lives of Bible characters is evidence of what we are potentially capable of doing. We must come to the place where we are more disgusted with our flesh than any of our accusers. If not, we will always see ourselves as victims rather than victors. It is only through the illuminating work of the Spirit of God that we can come to the point of brokenness.

Open your Bible and sit once again at the Cross and remember His sufferings for you. It was at the cross that we are reminded, *For He (God the Father) made Him (God the Son) who knew no sin to be sin for us, that we might become the righteousness of God in Him* (2 Corinthians 5:21; explanations mine). When you hear Christ's own words regarding you, you will be brought to brokenness.

What can someone do to you that you have not done a hundred fold more to Christ? Understanding the sin and shame that Jesus carried for you on the cross is key to brokenness. I have often reminded myself of my great sin as I saw myself in the faces of those who crucified Christ. I must see myself in the faces of all sinners that day and feel the rage, not against sinners, but against myself until in brokenness, I can only feel the compassion of Christ for those who crucified Him.

Until Christ's words *"Father forgive them,"* echo through my heart to all sinners, then I have not fully understood both my position in Adam, having no righteousness, and my new position in Christ, having the very righteousness of God imputed to me through faith in Christ.

I have looked into the eyes of Peter and seen that I, too, could have denied my Lord. I have warmed myself by the fire on that cold night and said, *"I do not know the man."* I have plotted with the Pharisees to put Christ to death. I have seen myself in the faces of those that covered His face. I have slugged Him with my fist and said, *"Prophesy who hit You."* I have seen myself pressing the crown of thorns upon His head and then beating Him with the reed, and mocking, *"Hail King of the Jews."* I have seen myself in Pilate, choosing political correctness over righteous justice and sentencing Jesus to be crucified. I have washed my bloody hands of my part in the death of Christ just like Pilate and my words, *"I am innocent of this man's blood,"* were the darkest of lies. I did not just cry, *"Crucify Him, crucify Him"* before Pilate. I held the whip in my hand and stripped His flesh from His back.

At the cross, I became the chief offender, the vilest of sinners, and the worst of the mockers of Christ. I took the hammer and nails and pierced His hands and feet. I spat upon Him and cursed and mocked Him. I did not just watch him die; I help crucify him and have found myself guilty of crucifying the innocent.

We need to see more than the sins we have committed. We must see the sin nature that is within our flesh. When Christ saved me, I was not just a little innocent third grade boy for whom He died. I have now seen myself in the faces of those who crucified the Lord and it has given me a different perspective on what others do or say about me. I was one of those vicious dogs that surrounded Jesus at the cross. [39]

Until you despise your own flesh more than you despise your enemies, you have not allowed God to break you. Look at your adversary with pride and without brokenness, and you will eventually become like the one you focus on. Only when we die to our flesh will the life of Christ be manifest through us.

No Good Thing

Look at your adversary with humility and you will cry out to God for help.

> *"Lord I know in my flesh dwells no good thing. Everything that I despise in my enemy is potentially in my wicked flesh. Lord, you said that the one who thinks he stands should take heed that he does not fall. You have allowed me to see in my enemy what I can become tomorrow unless I abide in You daily. Lord, I do not want to be known as one who is bitter, but one who is better because I have been through Your refining fire.*

"There go I but for the grace of God" should be our response to the life of every Bible character that God has recorded for us.

---

39   Psalm 22:16

As you read through the Bible, you must look beyond the immediate context to find God's universal principles that apply to all of us. Discovering those life-principles will provide even more understanding and application. One of those filters that I like to use is the two positions that every believer passes through: *"Once in Adam, but now in Christ."* Several years ago, I wrote a poem contrasting my former position in Adam and my present position in Jesus Christ. Entitled *Seeing the First and Last Adam*, it is included as Appendix 1 because of its length. However, it would be very beneficial for you to turn there and read it now. Remember that every sin and flaw revealed in the people of Scripture is potentially in us as well. When we judge the sin of another remember that we can commit the same sin tomorrow.

As a young Christian, I would hear some church members express shock when others committed certain sins. And I wondered how a church member could fall into such a sin. I felt that there were some sins that I would never succumb to. Later in my walk with God, I discovered that the closer I got to Jesus, the greater sinner I had become in my own eyes. It wasn't that I actually committed more sins. Rather, I became sensitive to the depth of the depravity that had always been in my flesh. My failed struggle to defeat minor battles with the flesh proved to me that I could not defeat my flesh through will power or religious resolve. It was after being defeated over and over by my flesh that I saw the Scriptural truth that we cannot defeat the flesh. We must die daily to our self-life. Through all this, I came to identify with Paul's cry: *O wretched man that I am! Who will deliver me from this body of death?* (Romans 7:24).

The answer is, of course, not me! As Paul goes on to say in that chapter, *I thank God – through Jesus Christ our Lord!* (Romans 7:25). It is only by the power of the Gospel and the work of the Savior through the enablement of the Holy Spirit that we can see the victory.

When Paul said that he was *"the chief of sinners,"* he came face to face with the absolute depravity of the flesh. When he wrote that *none are righteous, no not one,* he understood the undeniable holiness of God.

Do you see those two truths: *the absolute depravity of the flesh* and *the undeniable holiness of* God? Seeing this twofold truth brings humility and brokenness to our lives. Generally those who have seen God's holiness are the first to despise their own flesh and sin while having mercy and compassion on others' sins. Without brokenness, we become more judgmental of some, condoning some sinful behavior while condemning other sinful behavior.

James and John, two of the disciples closest to Jesus, asked permission to call fire down from heaven and consume certain people because they did not receive the message of Jesus. Jesus rebuked them saying, *You do not know what spirit you are of.* [40] It is possible to experience Jesus' grace and salvation and even walk with Him daily, and tomorrow wake up with judgmental thoughts that come from the flesh.

Without brokenness, we preach at people from an elevated pulpit rather than sitting with them and sharing as one beggar to another who has found *"the Bread of Life."* Without brokenness, we become Pharisaical in relationship to the Law – keeping it outwardly without ever dealing with our inner sinfulness.

---

40   Luke 9:51-56

A HYMN THAT COMMUNICATES TRUTH

Growing up in London, Robert Robinson (1735–1790) [41] lived a rebellious life, involved with the 18th century version of gangs. At the age of 17, he heard evangelist George Whitefield preach. Robinson had gone to the meeting with the purpose of "scoffing at those poor, deluded Methodists" and ended up professing faith in Christ as his Savior.

Soon after his conversion, God called him to preach the Gospel. He became the pastor of a large Baptist church in Cambridge, England. Robinson became known as a faithful pastor and scholar. But he was most famous for several of the hymns he wrote, including these words written when he was just 23 years of age:

Come, Thou Fount of ev'ry blessing, tune my heart to sing Thy grace; streams of mercy, never ceasing, call for songs of loudest praise. Teach me some melodious sonnet sung by flaming tongues above; praise the mount—I'm fixed upon it—mount of Thy redeeming love.

Here I raise mine Ebenezer—hither by Thy help I'm come; and I hope by Thy good pleasure safely to arrive at home. Jesus sought me when a stranger wand'ring from the fold of God; He to rescue me from danger interposed His precious blood.

O to grace how great a debtor daily I'm constrained to be! Let Thy goodness like a fetter bind my wand'ring heart to Thee: Prone to wander—Lord, I feel it—prone to leave the God I love; here's my heart—O take and seal it; Seal it for Thy courts above.

That last verse is the one I'd like to have you notice for just a moment. Can you feel the emotional struggle that Robinson had? Each of us faces the same thing. Sometimes we are *Prone to worship—Lord, I feel it—prone to serve the God I love.* Other times, we are *Prone to wander—Lord, I feel it—prone to leave the God I love.*

There is a daily battle that we face: walking by the flesh … or walking by the Spirit. Where are you today?

QUESTIONS TO CONSIDER

- In what ways have you battled with your flesh?

- How does God produce victory in your life? (See Romans 8:37; 1 Corinthians 15:18).

---

41   Osbeck, K. W. (1990). *Amazing Grace : 366 Inspiring Hymn Stories for Daily Devotions* (343). Grand Rapids, Mich.: Kregel Publications.

- Take the words of the hymn *Come Thou Fount of Every Blessing,* and turn them into a prayer to God, asking Him for the spiritual strength to walk by the Spirit every day.

- Have you ever seen that, "In your flesh dwells no good thing"?

CHAPTER 12

Brokenness – Part 3

… then I will give him to the LORD all the days of his life … (1 Samuel 1:11)

THE FIFTH TEST OF FAITH

As we again look at the fifth test of faith, we are reminded:

> *God will break us in order to mold us; His ultimate goal*
> *is to shape us to conform us to the image of Christ.*
> *Will we trust Him and learn the lessons He has for us?*

God brought Hannah to the exact point He wanted her to be. She was faced with the question, *Who does my womb, and the fruit of my womb, belong to: to God or to me?*

In this third and final chapter on brokenness, we will consider two important truths.

6. THE PAIN OF BROKENNESS

*And she was in **bitterness of soul**, and prayed to the LORD and **wept in anguish**. When she made a vow and said, "O LORD of hosts, if You will indeed look on the affliction of Your maidservant and remember me, and not forget Your maidservant, but will give Your maidservant a male child, then I will give him to the LORD all the days of his life, and no razor shall come upon his head" (1 Samuel 1:10-11).*

Hannah's pain emanated from deep within her soul. She could not let go of the burden to have a son. Her pain and tears were real.

 ## OUR STORY

All three of our children were adopted at birth. Connie did not have to go through the nine months of pregnancy, morning sickness, weight gain, and finally the labor pains that precede birth. Connie had the mother's heart long before she became a mother by adoption. Her pain and tears were also real.

In our situation God graciously opened the door for an adoption agency to interview and accept us as prospective adoptive parents. But it wasn't easy. Initially all of the adoption agencies we called in Portland said they were not accepting any new applications. However, at one agency, the lady who normally answered the phone was out of the office when we called. She had previously told us that they were not accepting any new applications for adoption. In God's providence, there was a different woman who answered the phone that day. She, too, told us that they were not taking any new applications. But then she asked my wife where I worked. When she found out that I was a Baptist pastor, she showed us favor because she was the daughter of a Baptist pastor and we were accepted for an interview. We prayed fervently, faithfully and consistently until the day that we received the phone call to come and pick up our son.

We named our first son Matthew. His name means *"gift of God."* Our second son we named, Jeremy after the prophet Jeremiah which means *"Jehovah has appointed."* Our third child was a little girl who we named Hope, which means *"expectation of good from God."*

God was so good to answer our prayers. As we bonded with our new son, we began to pray for the young teenaged girl that had made the right choice not to abort her child but to give him up for adoption. According to the strict adoption guidelines of our state, we could never know who the birth mother was, only that she was a young teenage girl. Also, Oregon had a law that there was a waiting period in which the birth mother could ask for her child back. We could not imagine how we could handle losing the son that we had prayed for years for God to give us. Finally the deadline passed and we went before the Judge, who sealed the records and made it official that we were the legal parents to our adoptive son. He gave us our son's adoption certificate listing us as the parents. We celebrated on the way home from the Portland courthouse by stopping by a local restaurant. There God would give us assurance that not only would our son be fine, but so would the birth mother.

The young woman behind the counter took our order and noticed our young baby boy. I left our booth for a moment and when I returned, before we had even eaten our meal, Connie said, *"We must leave now."* I asked why and she said she would tell me in the car.

While I was away from the table, the young woman who had taken our order left her position behind the counter to come and look at our beautiful baby boy. She said to Connie, *"I hope I am not disturbing you, but I have such a soft spot in my heart for babies now because I just gave my son up for adoption."* Connie's curiosity turned to nervousness as all of my wife's questions made it clear that this was no chance meeting. *"When was your son born? What hospital was he born in? Who was your adoption agency?"* Not only did every question match Matthew, but also our son looked just like this young girl.

As we sat in our car, we asked ourselves what had just happened. We were convinced that the young lady was Matthew's birth mother. What were we supposed to do? The adoption agency had stressed the privacy issues that neither the mother nor we were to know each other. We prayed again for the young birth mother of our son. *"Lord, why did you arrange this encounter today?"* The answer came from the young lady herself. Connie had first asked her why she chose adoption. Her answer reassured us, *"Because I had to do what was best for my baby and I was sure that adoption was best for my son. I was sure that he would be given to loving parents."* God was good, not only to give our son to us, but also to give us the assurance that the birth mother would be okay.

God led Hannah to give her son wholly to the LORD. Her son would be adopted by God Himself and live in the House of the Lord, not in Hannah's house. The choice Hannah made followed God's plan exactly, though this would obviously result in the pain of separation for Hannah. This was the third painful experience related to Samuel:

- First, she waited for years to get pregnant.
- Second, she experienced the physical labor pains with his delivery.
- Third, she bonded with the son she loved and then had the pain of separation as she gave him up to be adopted by God.

Connie and I experienced labor by proxy as our daughter gave birth to her first son, Trace. We watched and waited for hours as the labor pains intensified and grew more frequent. I held Hope's hand and when the pain came, she squeezed my hand with such intensity that I knew that her pain was great. It was hard for me to watch the pain process, and I often left the room for short walks down the hallway. Finally the doctors decided that the labor was too long and the stress on the mother and baby was too great for a natural birth. They took her back to surgery for a C-section. I thought to myself that if we had lived in Bible times, a difficult labor like this might have killed both the mother and child. My daughter could have died in labor.

Because of her sin, God told Eve that birth would come through pain. *To the woman He said, I will greatly multiply your sorrow (pain) and your conception; in pain you shall bring forth children …* (Genesis 3:16; comment mine). The word sorrow here commonly refers to physical pain.

Hannah not only knew the physical pain of childbirth, but she also knew a greater pain – the pain of brokenness before God. The pain that Hannah went through to reach brokenness and to pour out her soul to the Lord was much like Abraham's pain as he gave Isaac to God. The labor pains of birth could not be compared to the years of sorrow and pain that Hannah experienced before she received God's promise of a son.

Looking at the six Hebrew words used to describe Hannah's burden, we gain deeper insight into the pain of brokenness that she was experiencing. Those words are:

- Bitterness of soul
- Affliction

- A sorrowful spirit
- Pour out her soul
- My complaint
- Grief

Let's take a closer look at each of these six aspects.

 ## BITTERNESS OF SOUL

*And she was in **bitterness of soul**, and prayed to the L*ORD *and wept in anguish* (1 Samuel 1:10; emphasis mine).

This word is first used to describe the bitter cry of Esau when he learned that Isaac had given his blessing to the deceitful Jacob. *When Esau heard the words of his father, he cried with **an exceedingly great and bitter cry**, and said to his father, Bless me—me also, O my father!* (Genesis 37:34; emphasis mine). Notice the double reference to *me* in that verse. Esau was lamenting his loss. He was bitter and sought revenge against his brother for stealing his birthright. There is a bitterness that does not make us better because it does not include godly sorrow that leads to repentance.

The same word was used when God turned Job's bitter cry into a blessing of praise. *Why is light given to him who is in misery, and life to **the bitter of soul**, who long for death, but it does not come, and search for it more than hidden treasures* (Job 3:20-21; emphasis mine).

Hannah's pain was similar to the bitter cry of Mordecai. He wept before God when he learned of the decree to destroy all the Jews. *When Mordecai learned all that had happened, he tore his clothes and put on sackcloth and ashes, and went out into the midst of the city. He **cried out with a loud and bitter cry*** (Esther 4:1; emphasis mine).

Hezekiah experienced a similar pain when Isaiah was sent by God to announce his death. He cried out to God with tears and was immediately answered by God.

> *Remember now, O L*ORD*, I pray, how I have walked before You in truth and with a loyal heart, and have done what is good in Your sight." And Hezekiah wept bitterly. And the word of the L*ORD *came to Isaiah, saying, "Go and tell Hezekiah, 'Thus says the L*ORD*, the God of David your father: "I have heard your prayer, I have seen your tears; surely I will add to your days fifteen years…' What shall I say? He has both spoken to me, and He Himself has done it. I shall walk carefully all my years **in the bitterness of my soul**. O Lord, by these things men live; and in all these things is the life of my spirit; so You will restore me and make me live. Indeed it was for my own peace that I had **great bitterness**; but You have lovingly delivered my soul from the pit of corruption, for You have cast all my sins behind Your back* (Isaiah 38:3-5, 15-17; emphasis mine).

Finally, this same word is used in a most unusual passage in the law regarding jealousy. If a husband suspected his wife of adultery but had no proof, then he could bring his wife before the priest who would have her drink bitter water. If she was guilty of adultery, then a curse would come to pass and her belly would swell and her thighs would rot. However, if she was innocent, then the priest's words would bring a blessing and she would conceive and have a child. [42]

As we have seen, men and women down through the centuries have experienced this bitterness of soul. For those of us who are in Christ and trust the sovereign hand of a loving Father, the curse is made a blessing and the trials of faith are designed to refine us. We cry out to God in the process and pain of brokenness and God blesses us with great fruitfulness. To others who do not trust God, the problems of life make them bitter and they cry with grief.

 ## AFFLICTION

*When she made a vow and said, "O LORD of hosts, if You will indeed look on the **affliction** of Your maidservant and remember me, and not forget Your maidservant …* (1 Samuel 1:11, emphasis mine).

This word *affliction* was used repeatedly by Job to describe his suffering. It was used by David in 2 Samuel 16:12 when Shimei cursed him, saying, *It may be that the LORD will look on my **affliction**, and that the LORD will repay me with good for his cursing this day* (emphasis mine).

Affliction was often the word of choice by David in the Psalms. Consider how David used it when he said,

> *Turn Yourself to me, and have mercy on me, for I am desolate and afflicted. The troubles of my heart have enlarged; bring me out of my distresses! Look on my **affliction** and my pain, and forgive all my sins* (Psalm 25:17; emphasis mine).

Though this word speaks of the deep sorrow of the soul, it was also a word that gave hope. *Affliction* was used in Exodus 4:17 where God looked upon the affliction of His people in slavery to Pharaoh. Hannah picked up this same word to describe the pain she was experiencing, remembering that her forefathers had also been in great affliction in their bondage to Pharaoh and their cry came to the heart of God.

 ## SORROWFUL SPIRIT

*But Hannah answered and said, "No, my lord, I am a woman of **sorrowful spirit**"* (1 Samuel 1:15; emphasis mine).

Hannah knew the pain of a sorrowful spirit as she described herself to Eli, who thought that she was drunk.

This Hebrew word is translated *"hard"* in describing the cruel bondage of Pharaoh's slavery of the Hebrews. *And they made their lives bitter with **hard** bondage— in mortar, in brick, and in all manner of service in the field. All their service in which they made them serve was with rigor* (Exodus 1:14; emphasis mine).

---

42   Numbers 5:27

The word is translated *"heavy"* to describe the burden that Solomon put upon Israel when his own heart was hardened against Israel because of his idolatry. [43] *Your father made our yoke **heavy**; now therefore, lighten the burdensome service of your father and his heavy yoke which he put on us, and we will serve you* (2 Chronicles 10:4; emphasis mine).

Perhaps Hannah could have had more faith and not become a slave to her sorrow. But we must understand that her sorrow was painful, deep, and a heavy burden, like the burden of a slave. However, she came to the Lord and poured out her soul to God. He turned her sorrow into joy. I think of the words of Jesus to His disciples:

> *Most assuredly, I say to you that you will weep and lament, but the world will rejoice; and you will be sorrowful, but your sorrow will be turned into joy. A woman, when she is in labor, has sorrow because her hour has come; but as soon as she has given birth to the child, she no longer remembers the anguish, for joy that a human being has been born into the world. Therefore you now have sorrow; but I will see you again and your heart will rejoice, and your joy no one will take from you* (John 16:20-22).

The disciples were weeping one day – but through the victory of the cross, God turned their sorrow into joy at the realization of the Resurrection. That same type of joy ought to characterize our lives because we know the One who was dead and who is now alive forevermore. [44] He takes our hard, heavy burdens that cause a sorrowful spirit and turns them into joy.

POURED OUT MY SOUL

*No, my lord, I am a woman of sorrowful spirit … I have **poured out my soul** before the LORD* (1 Samuel 1:15; emphasis mine).

This phrase, *poured out,* was used when the priest took the sacrifices to the Lord and poured out the blood at the altar. Five times in Leviticus 4 we read that the priest was to pour out the blood of the sacrifice around the altar. How fitting is this word to describe Hannah's predicament. She was at the place in the House of the Lord where the priest would pour out the blood on the altar.

We find a great contrast in that the bloody hands of Eli's sons, Hophni and Phinehas, who also poured out the blood – but God rejected them because of their immorality. In contrast, Hannah poured out her soul with a broken heart and God accepted her sacrifice. Surely the words of David apply, *The sacrifices of God are a broken spirit: a broken and a contrite heart, O God, You will not despise* (Psalm 51:17).

Have you ever poured out your soul in brokenness to the Lord? Be assured of this: as surely as God answered Hannah, He will answer you.

COMPLAINT

*Do not consider your maidservant a wicked woman, for out of the abundance of my **complaint** and grief I have spoken until now* (1 Samuel 1:16; emphasis mine).

43   In the KJV translation, the word is *grievous.*

44   Revelation 1:17-18

The pain of brokenness can also be seen with this Hebrew word that is translated *"complaint."* Hannah was the first person to use this particular word in Scripture. This *complaint* is different from the complaining Israel did in the wilderness. They complained against Moses, and their unbelief angered God. The complaint that Hannah registered was more like Job's complaint when he was seeking God.

Job used this word five times as he sought to understand how God was working in his life. One example is in Job 10.

> *My soul loathes my life; I will give free course to my* **complaint**, *I will speak in the bitterness of my soul. I will say to God, 'Do not condemn me; show me why You contend with me* (Job 10:1-2; emphasis mine).

David also used this word as he sought God in his many trials and troubles. *I pour out my* **complaint** *before Him; I declare before Him my trouble* (Psalm 142:2; emphasis mine).

Many of the psalms begin with a superscription or title. Psalm 102 begins with these words, *A prayer of one afflicted, when he is faint and pours out his* **complaint** *before the LORD* (emphasis mine). God is instructing us here that it is proper to *complain* before Him when we cry to Him out of brokenness, asking Him to miraculously deliver us. Hannah was not a bitter complainer, moping around in her misery, complaining to people and to God. Hers was a complaint and burden for God to show mercy and grace. She did the right thing with her complaint – she brought it to God.

What do you do with your complaints? Do you take them to God?

GRIEF

Do not consider your maidservant a wicked woman, for out of the abundance of my complaint and **grief** *I have spoken until now* (1 Samuel 1:16; emphasis mine).

Notice how both Job and David brought their grief to God. God answered both of them in His time and His way.

> *Then Job answered and said: Oh, that my* **grief** *were fully weighed, and my calamity laid with it on the scales!* (Job 6:1-2; emphasis mine).

> *I am weary with my groaning; all night I make my bed swim; I drench my couch with my tears. My eye wastes away because of* **grief**; *it grows old because of all my enemies* (Psalms 6:6-7; emphasis mine).

I've often wondered: *what if every mother refused to give birth because of the anticipated pain she would experience?* The human race would have been extinct thousands of years ago! I have known many women in our church who compare the labor pains to the joy of their newborn. Their pain was forgotten and quickly replaced by the joy of their newborn child. Why would a woman have six children if the pain were so great? Jesus said the pain is forgotten because of the joy of the child. [45]

Let's make the analogy to being spiritually fruitful. Will you refuse more fruit because you do not want the vinedresser to cut away some needless leaves in your life? God prunes every branch in the vine of Christ. [46] Just as the Creator has chosen physical birth through pain, even so God has chosen that we identify with the sufferings of Christ if we are to bring forth much fruit. [47] If the church refuses the pain of brokenness, we will not know the great harvest of souls that awaits us.

Choosing the Bus Kids

As a young pastor I attended a conference where I heard Jack Hyles speak. At that time he was the pastor of the largest church in America. He told a story that made me realize that sometimes in ministry the pain of brokenness precedes great fruitfulness. His church had begun to grow with hundreds of people being saved. Many of these were the results of a fast-growing bus ministry that the church had begun. Some leaders in the church, many of whom were part of the financial base of the church, became upset with the bus ministry and gave Jack an ultimatum, *"Make a choice between us or the bus kids."* Jack said he walked the streets of Chicago for hours and found himself in an alley where he agonized throughout the night. When God finally spoke to him he rose to his feet, relieved of the burden and had peace from God about the situation. He cried out saying, *"I'll take the bus kids."*

As he told this story, he described how many pastors and missionaries across America and the world came from his church. From where did God raise them up? Not from the wealthy members who sought only their own personal interests. They came from the scores of bus kids who God saved from all over the city. Those bus kids who became pastors and missionaries were the fruitful result of agonizing prayer.

Hannah went through the "pain of brokenness," to bring Samuel into this world. There are many Christians who are afraid to go through the labor pains of God to bring forth the greater fruitfulness that God desires for us. As a young man, I was afraid that if I turned my life over to God's complete control He might send me to Africa as a missionary. But we must remember that He loves us and has the best plan for our lives – no matter where that may take us.

Have you ever feared God's will? Remember those who have gone through great trials of faith. God's blessing of fruitfulness awaits you.

7.   The Product of Brokenness

We have spent a lot of time in these three chapters talking about brokenness. Let's finish with one question: What does brokenness produce?

---

45   John 16:21-22

46   John 15:2

47   Philippians 3:10

THE TRIALS OF JOB

After enduring countless trials, Job testified, *But He knows the way I take; when He has tested me, I shall come forth as gold* (Job 23:10).

- The first phrase in that verse, *But He knows the way I take,* not only speaks of God being aware of Job's situation; it also describes the fact that God *led* Job through those paths. His trials were God-initiated, God-designed, and God-directed. Nothing could affect Job's life that was not filtered through the will and plan of his heavenly Father.

- The second phrase, *when He has tested me,* tells us there are both a purpose and an end to those tests. Job knew that God had a design for what he was going through. He also knew there was a God-ordained conclusion to the trials, and that they would be over once their purpose was accomplished.

- The final phrase, *I shall come forth as gold,* tells us the product of God's tests. They were to refine Job, to purify him, to make him, in the words of the New Testament, more conformed to the image of Jesus Christ.

That is the product of brokenness. God breaks us, not to hurt us or to harm us, but to conform us, to change us, and to mature us. God develops us over a lifetime. That development is where God uses a combination of events and people to impress lessons upon us that we need to learn.

Eugene Peterson, the author of *The Message* translation of the Bible, has written,

> *It's odd that a religion that carries the cross as its central symbol should require a crash course in suffering. But it does. Oh how it does. We have somehow ended up with a country full of Christians who consider suffering, whether it comes from a broken body or a broken heart, a violation of their spiritual rights. When things go badly in body or job or family, they whine and complain endlessly. Sometimes they protest vehemently. In between complaints and protests, they seek out the company of those who anesthetize them with soothing words and soft music. They have no difficulty finding such aestheticians — pain killing spiritualities are a glut on the market. The only cross they seem to have any acquaintance with is a piece of cheap jewelry.... Brokenness does not diminish a life of faith but deepens it.... Suffering is not evidence of God's absence, but of God's presence and that it is in our experience of being broken that God does His surest and most characteristic salvation work.*[48]

FRUITFULNESS PROMISED

The Apostle Peter was writing to a group of first-century believers who were undergoing incredible trials. One of his purposes was to give them hope and perspective that God was in control.

Grace and peace be multiplied to you in the knowledge of God and of Jesus our Lord, as His divine power has given to us all things that pertain to life and godliness, through the knowledge

---

48   Eugene Peterson, writing in the Preface of *Broken in the Right Place,* by Alan E. Nelson.

of Him who called us by glory and virtue, by which have been given to us exceedingly great and precious promises, that through these you may be partakers of the divine nature, having escaped the corruption that is in the world through lust (2 Peter 1:2-4).

Notice *He has given to us all things that pertain to life and godliness.* God does not keep His children spiritual paupers. He blesses us exceedingly. [49] We have *everything* we need to live the victorious Christian life. Peter goes on to say,

> *But also for this very reason, giving all diligence, add to your faith virtue, to virtue knowledge, to knowledge self-control, to self-control perseverance, to perseverance godliness, to godliness brotherly kindness, and to brotherly kindness love* (2 Peter 1:5-7).

Here Peter reminds us that we must grow. And he lists the character qualities that are essential to enable us to grow into Christ likeness: *diligence, faith, virtue, knowledge, self-control, perseverance, godliness, brotherly kindness,* and *love.* There is a progression from one quality to another. That progression is spelled G-R-O-W-T-H.

Then he makes an incredible promise:

> *For if these things are yours and abound, you will be neither barren nor unfruitful in the knowledge of our Lord Jesus Christ* (2 Peter 1:8).

Isn't that incredible? Peter says that if we cooperate with God and allow Him to grow us, change us and mature us through the trials we experience, WE WILL BE FRUITFUL! Actually, Peter writes it in the negative, *You will be neither barren nor unfruitful.* I often wondered why he wrote it negatively rather than stating it positively. Peter is emphasizing that the true nature of the believer is *never* to be barren or unfruitful. God purposes us to be fruit-bearers. But there are times where we seem to be barren and unfruitful – those are the times we are going through His process of brokenness. But we don't stay there. Peter says that if we are living by faith and trusting God, *we will not (remain) barren nor unfruitful.*

Finally Peter addresses those who aren't bearing fruit:

> *For he who lacks these things is shortsighted, even to blindness, and has forgotten that he was cleansed from his old sins* (2 Peter 1:9).

Are these people Christians? Yes, of course. Have they lost their salvation? No, that is not possible. Then what is the reason for their unfruitfulness? Peter says it's because they are *shortsighted ... blind ... and have forgotten.*

What is it that they have forgotten? They have forgotten what Jesus did for them on the cross, that He died and paid for *all* of their sins. When you know that you are fully forgiven, you will respond to God in loving trust. And if you do that, you will grow (v. 5-7) and become fruitful (v. 8).

Alan Nelson writes,

---

49   See also Ephesians 1:3; 3:20-21.

I am sure that He (God) sees things somewhat differently than we do, probably most of the time…. I find myself staring at the mirror too often, wondering how others view me…. Brokenness is about death; the cessation of the unbridled spirit. Anyone who is in a time of brokenness, or who vividly remembers the pain and disillusionment of the process, knows it as a time of solemnity…. I pray that God will use these thoughts and words to expand your capacity for Him, to make sense of the seemingly paradoxical events which transpire in times of breaking, and most of all, that you understand the processes through which He seeks to tame your soul…. Because the former pain has a beautiful result, the emergence of new life. [50]

So What?

- Do you really grasp all that Jesus has done for you on the cross? Do you live moment-by-moment with an awareness of His marvelous grace and blessing toward you?

- If you've forgotten or grown numb to the Gospel, repent. Return to a steadfast understanding that you have become a new creation in Christ, [51] that you are blessed with every spiritual blessing in Christ, [52] and that you are forgiven, [53] redeemed [54] and forever secure in Him. [55]

- Look up the Bible references located in the footnotes at the bottom of this page. After reading and meditating on them, take time to thank God for His indescribable gift of salvation in Jesus Christ.

A Note to Pastors about Brokenness

There is a special type of brokenness that God has designed for pastors and teachers of His Word. That brokenness is found in the paradox of human responsibility and divine enablement. Though it is true that we must *study to show ourselves approved before God* [56] (we put in the effort), we must also die to ourselves and trust Him completely (we know that it is ultimately God's Spirit who must speak to the hearts of men and women). We must be broken of self-reliance on our giftedness, personality and experience.

---

50   Alan E. Nelson, *Broken in the Right Place*, p. 4-5.

51   2 Corinthians 5:17

52   Ephesians 1:3

53   Colossians 2:13; Ephesians 1:7

54   Romans 3:24-31

55   Romans 8:35-39

56   2 Timothy 2:15

In his outstanding book, *The Supremacy of God in Preaching*, John Piper describes his approach to preparing a message for his congregation. He follows this during the week, and also reviews this during the last two minutes before he stands up to preach. He calls it his "APTAT" approach:

- Admit – my utter helplessness not only for the task at hand, but even to breathe without Him.
- Pray – for help. Beg for insight, power, humility, love, and memory. (Piper suggests rising 3.5 hours before worship, and spending two hours in prayer over your text.)
- Trust God – to empower for His glory based upon specific promises in His Word.
- Act – in confidence that God will be with you to fulfill His word for His glory.
- Thank God – for the privilege of preaching His word. [57]

Piper writes, *"Gladness and gravity should be woven together in the life and preaching of a pastor in such a way as to sober the careless soul and sweeten the burdens of the saints."* [58]

I call on my fellow pastors and teachers to come each week, broken before God, crying out for His touch, relying on His Spirit, and looking forward to the fruit that only He can provide.

---

57   John Piper, *The Supremacy of God in Preaching*, revised edition, pp. 48-49.

58   Ibid., p. 52.

CHAPTER 13

Blessed – Part 1

Then Eli answered and said, "Go in peace, and the God of Israel grant your petition which you have asked of Him" (1 Samuel 1:17).

THE SIXTH TEST OF FAITH

The sixth test of faith is to find God's will and receive the promise.

As we begin this chapter, notice Hannah's actions and faith:

- Hannah sought God in prayer continuously year by year with patience and endurance.
- She poured out her soul to God.
- She reached a point of brokenness and absolute surrender of her desire for children.
- Three times she called herself the *maidservant* of the Lord as she bowed to God as His servant.
- Her attitude was not her own. Her life – and her legacy – belonged to God.

She now had both a sensitive heart and ears to hear God speak to her. Her heart was open to the slightest whisper of God. She was in the right place at the right time with the right heart to hear a word from God that she could claim by faith.

Hannah's heart was so sensitive to God that she looked beyond the unfaithful priest Eli, to a faithful God who spoke to her through Eli's anointed office as High Priest. When he told her to *go in peace*, that *God (will) grant your petition*, she knew she had heard from God. Eli's words may have simply been a comforting salutation that he gave to many who came to worship the Lord. However, Hannah heard God clearly.

Finding God's specific will was a long process for Hannah. But the process of discovering God's will transformed Hannah. Samuel needed a mother who was focused on God and His will, not her personal desires. He needed a mother who would pray for him as he served in the House of God. He needed a godly role model, so that he could courageously walk with God and lead the nation back to Him.

THE QUESTION PASTORS ARE MOST FREQUENTLY ASKED

If you ask pastors around the country, *"What is the most frequent question people ask you?"* you are likely to hear: *"How do I know God's will?"* Followers of Jesus in America – and around the world – are consumed with knowing God's will. Unfortunately, not too many of them are equally committed to *doing* His will once they find out what it is. That's why Jesus said, *If anyone wills to do His will, he shall know concerning the doctrine, whether it is from God or whether I speak on My own authority* (John 7:17). We want Jesus to operate under the *"I'll-show-you-and-then-you-can-decide-whether-or-not-to-do-it"* plan. But He doesn't! He says, *"Are you willing to do My will? If so, I'll show you. But only if you are ready to obey."*

How do we hear from God a specific answer to our prayers? In this chapter we will answer that question by looking with wisdom at specific questions about discerning God's will:

- How do we move from general hope in God to faith in a specific promise from God?
- How do we find the will of God for our lives?
- How does doing the general will of God for all believers relate to finding the specific will of God for my life personally?
- How do we get to the place in our own hearts that we can hear and discern the specific will of God for our lives without personal bias or preference?
- Is it possible to find and do God's will one day and then another day be deceived and miss God's will?

1. HOW DO WE MOVE FROM GENERAL HOPE IN GOD TO FAITH IN A SPECIFIC PROMISE FROM GOD?

DEFINING TERMS

Let's first define what we mean by the term *general hope*. God continually invites us to believe Him and trust Him. The believer who has general hope is demonstrating an attitude of faith in the character of God and is continually responding to the Gospel. Note: many Christians assume that the Gospel is only for *non-believers*, calling them to come to repent of their sins and come to faith in Christ as Savior and Lord. That is certainly true ... but the Gospel is also for *Christians,* as God continually calls us to repent from the sins we commit as believers and to continue to trust Christ as Savior and Lord. That is *general hope.*

Hope and faith are inseparable. Hope in God is the inspiration and motivation to find a specific promise to exercise faith in. *Now faith is the substance of things hoped for, the evidence of things not seen* (Hebrews 11:1). The New American Standard Bible reads, *Now faith is the realization of things hoped for and evidence of things not seen.* [59] The Message translation renders this verse; *The fundamental fact of existence is that this trust in God, this faith, is the firm foundation under everything that makes life worth living. It's our handle on what we can't see.* [60]

The second term to define is when we move from hope in God to *faith in a specific promise from God.* There are over 7,000 promises in the Bible. Many of them were made to specific individuals at specific times in specific situations. For example, if I tell my children I will pay for their dinner at a restaurant, that it a specific promise. I'm not volunteering to pay for *every child* to eat dinner. Just mine. Some promises are specific.

However, there are many promises in the Bible that are for *everyone.* For example, Isaiah 26:3 states, *You will keep him in perfect peace, whose mind is stayed on You, because he trusts in You.* That is a promise that believers can claim for themselves.

Beyond that, the Spirit of God can take the Word of God as He chooses, and impress it upon our hearts and minds. People ask today, *"Does God still speak?"* The answer to that question is both simple and complex. Yes, God still speaks. He has not become mute. I believe that God still guides His people. He still works *personally* in their lives. His spirit is resident in each believer … how could that Spirit who resides in our lives 24/7/365 *not* speak to us and guide us? Certainly He does!

However, I believe there are times when believers claim that God has spoken to them when He has not. I've seen times when the message they claim to have received from God directly contradicts the clear teaching of Scripture and the unchanging character of God. I can say with complete confidence that God has *not* spoken to them. He does not contradict Himself.

Hannah was given both the grace and patience to move from general hope in God to faith in a specific promise from God. Hannah heard one word from God, *"Go in peace and the God of Israel grant thee the petition that thou has asked of him,"* and moved from hope in the general character of God to a specific promise from God.

FROM HOPE TO FAITH

Romans 8:24 teaches that *hope that is seen is not hope.* In other words, if you can physically see something, you don't have to believe God for it. If I am in need of $300 to pay bills, and you give me $300, I don't have to *hope that God will send me $300.* I've already received it. Hannah moved from hope to faith. Faith was now the realization of her burden and the answer to her prayer. Faith had her *see the unseeable.* Faith had made the future the present and her dead womb

---

59   *New American Standard Bible,* copyright © 1995 by The Lockman Foundation.

60   *NIV / The Message Parallel Bible,* copyright © 2004 by The Zondervan Corporation.

alive. Hannah left God's house with evidence that she would have the answer to her prayer. That evidence was not hope but faith in the specific promise of God to her. That word was to Hannah God's birth certificate even before Samuel was conceived in her womb.

It was God who put the burden of heaven in Hannah's heart for a son. Her prayers were lifted to heaven by that God-given burden. However, heaven seemed to be silent. Hannah continued to pray persistently with a burdened heart until, in one moment, the burden was lifted from her heart and God exchanged it with peace and assurance. She was commanded to *go in peace, and the God of Israel grant your petition which you have asked of Him* (1 Samuel 1:17).

In one moment Hannah had crossed the long bridge of "*hope in God for a child*" to "*faith in God for the son of promise.*" From that moment on, she would believe that God had answered her prayer. She would stand on the promise of God as her assurance that she was a mother before she had conceived Samuel. She had moved from *"I hope so"* to *"I know so."* She would call things that were not as though they were (Romans 4:17).

How do you reach a point where you can believe with such deep faith? How do you know that God has answered your prayers and that you are not just presuming or hoping that He has?

KNOWING, NOT HOPING

I believe that Hannah had faith in God's character and therefore she continued to seek Him. She had the general promises of God to give her hope. Hope in God and His promises are a foundation for faith. (Hebrews 11:1) Hannah first had hope that God would open her barren womb before God gave her a promise that He would. It was this hope that kept her coming back to God again and again.

Hannah did not have the clear promise of a son like Abraham and Sarah had. Abraham's test of faith was not to waver in his faith, even though he would wait twenty-five years until the age of one hundred before Isaac was born. Think about that … here's what Abraham and Sarah were up against:

- He was 99. She was 89. And they still weren't pregnant.
- They had been trying for years and years. And let's face it, people that old just don't get pregnant!
- God had promised an heir earlier, but He hadn't come through. They were probably tempted to believe that their earlier faith had simply been wishful thinking.
- Since Abraham had left Ur of the Chaldeans, it had been almost 25 years. He had been 75 at that time. [61] Now He was 99 … and no baby.
- There had only been a few times [62] that God had even showed up to speak to Abraham and reinforce the promises He had made. The last time (Genesis 18), Sarah laughed.

---

61   Genesis 12:4

62   Genesis 15; 17; 18

Here's what they did have going for them: *God.* That's it. But Abraham believed God. That's faith.

In the case of Manoah's wife, the angel gave her specific instructions that her son would be a Nazirite from the womb. *And the Angel of the LORD appeared to the woman and said to her, "Indeed now, you are barren and have borne no children, but you shall conceive and bear a son. Now therefore, please be careful not to drink wine or similar drink, and not to eat anything unclean. For behold, you shall conceive and bear a son. And no razor shall come upon his head, for the child shall be a Nazarite to God from the womb; and he shall begin to deliver Israel out of the hand of the Philistines"* (Judges 13:3-5). Mrs. Manoah did not have to wait long to receive the specific answer. But she did have a clear, specific, and unmistakable promise given her by God.

WHAT HANNAH DIDN'T HAVE

Think about the difference between Hannah and these other women:

- Hannah did not have the clear promise of a son like Abraham and Sarah had.
- Unlike Mrs. Manoah, Hannah did not have the clear appearance of an angel to announce the conception of her promised son.
- Unlike Sarah and Mrs. Manoah, Hannah did not have a specific promise that God would open her barren womb and give her a son.

Sarah had faith in God but she also had a specific promise from God that from her barren womb would come the "Promised Seed." Mrs. Manoah had a specific promise that from her barren womb would come a deliverer for Israel from the Philistines. Hannah had faith in God and in His Character and God's general promises, but she did not have a specific word from God regarding a promised son. It was her faith in God and her specific hope for a son from the barren womb that led to her receiving a specific word from God.

It is more likely that, in our prayers, we will experience what Hannah did ... she sought God but did not receive a clear promise. But she still believed. And so must we.

APPLICATION

- What are you hoping for? Does your hope come from God as His burden or was it generated by your own desires?

- Are you obeying the revealed will of God for all believers?

- Do you have a specific promise from God about your prayers?

- Have you ever like Hannah made faith in the Word of God your evidence of God's answer before you received the answer?

2.   HOW DO WE FIND THE WILL OF GOD FOR OUR LIVES?

Many books have been written to help believers discern the will of God for their lives. Thousands of sermons have been preached to both warn and exhort believers in their search for the specific will of God. [63]

As a young Christian I heard a preacher speak on knowing the will of God. He described a dangerous channel where ships had been shipped wrecked by the hidden rocks as they attempted to enter the port. In order to provide a way for ships to safely navigate that channel, three lighthouses were built in a straight line with the channel and at a distance from one another. As long as the ship's captain lined all three lighthouses up in a straight line, he could be confident that he would arrive safely at his port. He then talked about three "lights" of knowing God's will: *The Word, The Witness,* and *The Way.* His application point was that when we line up these three lighthouses of God's will, we, also, have the assurance that we are in the will of God.

THE FIVE WS

I have amplified and added to that simple outline of finding the will of God. The more of these elements we line up, the clearer the will of God will become for us.

- **The Word of God**

  The will of God is revealed through the Word of God. God will never lead you to do that which is in conflict with the clear teachings of Scripture. However, we can in our personal bias take Scripture out of context or even twist Scripture to fit our own desires. In 2 Peter 3:16, Peter described those in the first century who would distort the clear Scriptures to their own destruction.

  What are some examples?

  ◦ Husbands are told to *love your wives, just as Christ also loved the church.* A man doesn't need God to "speak to him" about how to treat his wife. God has already told him to love her sacrificially, forgive her freely, faithfully meet her needs, and to patiently care for her.
  ◦ Wives have been commanded to *be submissive to your own husbands so that even if any of them are disobedient to the word, they may be won without a word by the behavior of their wives* (1 Peter 3:1). Wives, you do not have to preach a sermon to your husband. God calls you to be a living sermon. The greatest sermon your husband will hear will be as you live out the character of God in front of him.
  ◦ Throughout the Epistles, there are dozens of *one another's: love one another, bear one another's burdens, encourage one another, forgive one another,* etc. I believe if

---

63   For a more detailed discussion of how to find and do the will of God see the author's book, *God's Greater Purpose in Christ.*

church members were to be obedient to the clear, revealed will of God in the *one another's,* 100% of the problems in the church would disappear and the world would sit up and take notice of *how they love one another.*

- ○ Every believer is called to be a witness of the Gospel and the grace of God in their lives. You are not expected to be able to answer every question; you are not called to "convert people." That's God's responsibility. But you are called to open your mouth and give testimony to what God has done for you and to tell others how they can be saved. Do you know ANY church in America where 100% of their members are fulfilling that command? Personally, I don't know of any where 25% of the members are fulfilling that command. No wonder the church of God in America is impotent. We are living in clear disobedience to the revealed will of God!

According to Jesus' words in John 7:17 that we looked at earlier in this chapter, if we are not willing to do His will that we know about, God is not obligated to give us any future light. We've already proven to be disobedient to the light we have. That's why our obedience is so important.

- **The Witness of God**

The Holy Spirit who indwells every believer will lead and bear witness to His will. If we have confessed our sins and our hearts are right with God, we should have the deep peace of God regarding His will.

However, if we are not doing the will of God, we are grieving the Holy Spirit. We will not have the spiritual sensitivity to follow His leadership (see Galatians 5:16; Ephesians 4:30).

How does the Holy Spirit bear witness in our lives? Look for a moment at Romans 8.

- ○ *The Spirit Himself bears witness with our spirit that we are children of God* (Romans 8:17). His Spirit speaks to our human spirit.
- ○ *Likewise the Spirit also helps in our weaknesses. For we do not know what we should pray for as we ought, but the Spirit Himself makes intercession for us with groanings which cannot be uttered. Now He who searches the hearts knows what the mind of the Spirit is, because He makes intercession for the saints according to the will of God* (Romans 8:26-27). He *helps us ... He prays for us ... He searches our hearts ...* and He does all of this *according to the will of God.*

- **The Way of God**

God's hand of providence is involved in the will of God. God is the one who will open the doors that He sends us through and closes the doors that we should not walk through. Look for people, places, resources, and events to confirm the will of God. However, we can in our own strength misinterpret persistent perseverance for presumption and force doors open that God did not open. It is a mistake to walk as we please and expect God's providence to close the wrong doors we choose.

- **The Wisdom of God**

  It is also important that we seek godly counsel to help confirm the will of God. Wise men and women expose our misunderstanding of the will of God. There are many godly believers who can help us with a biblical and unbiased advice. However, we in our personal bias can always find some that agree with our own will. We are not to put faith in man, but we are to listen for God's confirmation among the mature believers in the church and family.

  ○ We are to seek wise counselors.

    The way of a fool is right in his own eyes, but he who heeds counsel is wise (Proverbs 12:15).
    Without counsel, plans go awry, but in the multitude of counselors they are established (Proverbs 15:22).

  ○ We are to develop wisdom ourselves.

    *Oh, how I love Your law! It is my meditation all the day. You, through Your commandments, make me **wiser** than my enemies; for they are ever with me. I have more **understanding** than all my teachers, for Your testimonies are my meditation. I have more **insight** than the ancients, because I keep Your precepts* (Psalm 119:97-100; emphasis mine).

    Do you notice the three words I highlighted, *wisdom*, *insight*, and *understanding?*

    Wisdom is the ability to look at life and its difficulties through God's point of view.
    Insight is the ability to see through the surface level to the real problems of life.
    Understanding is the ability to respond correctly with the right attitudes. [64]

    We need each of these elements to clearly discern God's will for our lives. How are these elements developed? We develop them by spending time with God – and by spending time in His Word. Stop watching so much TV. Get off the internet for a while. Stop playing video games and start investing your life in things that matter for eternity!

- **Our Walk with God**

  If we are to know the specific will of God for our lives, we need to be walking daily with Jesus in obedience to the Word of God.

---

64 These three definitions come from Charles R. Swindoll, *Growing Strong in the Seasons of Life.*

- It is normally while doing the revealed will of God that we discover more of the will of God.
- It is while we are applying the truths of Scripture that more of the Scripture is open unto us.
- As we are faithful in a little, God will make us faithful with much.
- If we are not walking in obedience to God, then we will have a difficult time finding God's specific will.
- Do not expect for God to be specific with you if you are not walking in agreement with His will. *Can two walk together, except they be agreed?* (Amos 3:3). It is while we are bearing fruit that we are pruned to bear more fruit and much fruit.

Oh Wait ... There's More!

There are many other factors in finding the will of God that are also important. Though a complete discussion is beyond the scope of this book, I will highlight seven additional principles.

- **Learning from Examples**

  Look at the examples of mature believers that God has blessed with the character of Christ and fruitfulness. I have often asked myself, *"Is this a pattern of other servants of Christ?"* As a pastor, I look at the lives of great men of God like Billy Graham, Jerry Vines, and John McArthur. If what I am choosing to call the will of God leaves me out in left field while the great examples of the faith are in right field, then I am probably in the wrong field!

- **Walking in Submission**

  In doing the will of God we will be submissive to God. In the application of that submission, we will have a servant's heart in all of our relationship to others. Consider the authorities that God has placed all of us under:

  - Children are to submit to parents. I have had zealous teenagers tell me that God wanted them to go on a mission trip with the church and I had to remind them that in their submission role to the Lord, they would have to submit to their parent's decision (see Ephesians 6:1-4).
  - After God instructs husband and wives to be filled with the Spirit, He tells them both to submit to one another under the Lordship of Christ. Then the wife is told to submit to her husband (Ephesians 5:18-33). One wife told me that it was God's will that she tithe her husband's paycheck. When I asked if her husband was giving his willing approval, she said he was not. This was not a case of *"obeying God rather than man,"* but rather an issue of obeying God by mutual submission to and with her husband.

- o Employees are to submit to a degree to their employer. One of the big issues on finding the will of God to join our team on a mission trip to India, Brazil, or Columbia is not only God providing the resources but the time off from work. Our mission team prays that if it is God's will for a believer to be part of our mission team that God would give him favor with his employer and he would be given the vacation time to go. If an employer says that you are needed at your job, then we encourage the employee to consider that God has used the role of submission to help give direction about the specific will of God for the mission trip (Eph. 6:5-8).
- o Citizens are to submit to the government authorities that God has placed over us (Romans 13:1-7). In general, we are to be law-abiding citizens. We should think twice before we say it is the will of God that we do a certain thing if it means that we will secretly violate your conscience and the law.
- o There is a submissive role within the church to leadership. The church has delegated authority from its head, Jesus Christ. The pastors and elders find their delegated authority in overseeing the church only as they submit and align with the teaching of Scripture. They are not to find their authority as lords over the flock of God, but as submissive examples to the church (1 Peter 5:1-4). God confirms their role of *"ruling over, leading, going before,"* in Hebrews 13:7, 17, and 24. It is a wise believer that reexamines his assurance of what he calls the will of God if his pastor or elders have warned him that he may be missing the will of God.

The church also often delegates ministry heads and committees to do the will of God in decency and order. Often individual believers will claim that it is God's will that they serve in a certain leadership or ministry role but those in leadership do not recognize it. Unless there is submission, then there is a wedge of division in the church.

From the experience of being a pastor for 41 years and speaking with hundreds of pastors, I can say that most of the churches problems come from independent believers who, rather than submitting to the Lord and the church leadership, have their own private agenda in the church. Sadly they are blind to the power of personal bias to influence what they determine is the will of God for their lives.

- • **The Chastening of God**

Chastening is one of the most important and often overlooked factors in finding the will of God. Even if we are not actively pursuing the will of God for our lives, God is pro-active in our chastening. What I mean by that is God is actively leading into His will those that want to do His will, and God is actively correcting those who are missing God's will. As our Father, God chastens, corrects, trains, disciplines, reproves, and spanks all of his children (Hebrews 12:1- 17).

God chastens in love, in wisdom, and by degrees. Chastening is a mark of our salvation and if we are without God's chastening, then we have deceived ourselves and are not truly saved. If we are not pursuing the will of God, then God will pursue us until we do. If we are walking outside of the will of God, He rebukes us and even disciplines his children. It is important that we remember that God is sovereign and what we call accidents, mishaps, unrelated events and circumstances, may well be the correcting hand of God to redirect us into the will of God.

- **The Glory of God**

If it is God's will for our life, then it will meet the glory-of-God test. That test answers the question, *"Will this bring glory to God or simply satisfy my desires, ego, pride, or even lusts?"* Immature believers seek their own glory and honor. Mature followers of Christ seek His glory above all else.

- **The Unity Principle**

Unity of God's people is critical. God devotes an entire chapter of the Bible, Psalm 133, to describe the importance of unity. Verse one says, *Behold, how good and how pleasant it is for brethren to dwell together in unity!* To that, I would simply add that it is good and pleasant for the "sistern" to dwell in unity also! If something is the will of God, it will unite the body of Christ and not divide it. And that unity will become a witness to the world of the Gospel of Jesus.

- **Pattern and Purpose**

God's will never deviates from His pattern and purpose in Christ. When we discover God's pattern and purpose in Scripture, we never have to reinvent the wheel. God's will for our lives will always be after the pattern of Christ in evangelism, discipleship, service, giving, and prayer, etc.

- **The Principle of Joyful Surrender**

One of the keys in finding the will of God is to come the point of being neutral. Whatever God sets before us, we are willing to say, *"Not my will but Your will be done."* We do not reach this point without reaching the point of brokenness and full surrender.

APPLICATION QUESTIONS

- In seeking the will of God, have you ever lined up these three indicators: *The Word of God, The Witness of God,* and *The Way of God?*

- Are you currently walking with God in doing all that you know is the will of God before you ask God for specific direction?

- In what ways would you see yourself in submission to the Lord's delegated authorities in your life?

- Do you recognize God's chastening in your life as a means of directing your life into God's will?

- Would other church members say that your walk has been a source of unity and glory to God or would they honestly say it is self-promoting and divisive?

- What is one thing that you know is the will of God for all believers that you are not currently doing?

CHAPTER 14

Blessed – Part 2

Then Eli answered and said, "Go in peace, and the God of Israel grant your petition which you have asked of Him" (1 Samuel 1:17).

 ## THE SIXTH TEST OF FAITH

> *The sixth test of faith is to find God's will and receive the promise.*

In the last chapter, we discussed two factors in knowing and doing God's will:

- How do we move from *general hope* in God to *faith in a specific promise* from God?
- How do we find the will of God for our lives? We will discuss the 5 Ws: *The Word of God, The Witness of God,* and *The Way of God, The Wisdom of God,* and *Our Walk with God.*

Now let's move to a third factor in knowing God's will.

3. HOW DOES DOING THE GENERAL WILL OF GOD RELATE TO FINDING THE SPECIFIC WILL OF GOD?

The general will of God is that which applies to all believers regarding God's commands, promises, and principles, and examples of Scripture. In contrast, the specific will of God for an individual believer is a personal assignment from God and is always within the general will of God.

EXAMPLES

The general will of God for Joshua and Caleb and all the twelve spies was the same: to give a good report of faith. Only Joshua and Caleb gave that report of faith. In their faithfulness, God gave them both the same promise to possess the promise land. However, the specific assignment for Joshua and Caleb within the general will of God was different. God had specifically prepared and chosen Joshua to lead Israel in the conquest of the Promised Land. Caleb's was to claim his promised mountain and as an example of faith inspire his daughter and son-in-law for the next generation of leadership.

Another example of the general will of God for all believers is to be a witness of our salvation and to share the Gospel to the lost. Therefore, we should generally feel that every person we meet is one with whom we could share the Gospel. But God can also give us a specific burden, call, impression, to share the gospel with a specific person. For example, Philip shared Christ in Samaria as he fled from the persecution of Saul. In the midst of preaching Christ to an entire city, God would give him a specific call to go and share Christ to one Ethiopian in another region (Acts 8:29).

If we are to be in a position to receive the specific will of God as an assignment from God, then we need to be faithful in doing that which God has plainly commanded all believers to do. It is while we are faithfully doing the general will of God that we normally discover the specific will of God for our lives. As Paul was obediently doing missions, he received the specific call to take the Gospel into Macedonia (Acts 16:9).

One of the clearest pictures in all of Scripture regarding discovering the specific will of God for our lives as we daily do the will of God is seen with King Josiah. Consider that God had named Josiah and outlined part of His purpose for his life over 300 years before he was born.

Then he cried out against the altar by the word of the LORD, and said, "O altar, altar! Thus says the LORD: 'Behold, a child, Josiah by name, shall be born to the house of David; and on you he shall sacrifice the priests of the high places who burn incense on you, and men's bones shall be burned on you'" (1 Kings 13:2).

How did Josiah find himself at the altar of Bethel at the right time and place to do the specific will of God for his life? He was not given a command or special revelation to go to Bethel to fulfill this amazing prophecy regarding him. God had a specific purpose for Josiah that would not be a matter of him directing his own steps, but of discovering the will of God for his life as he allowed God to direct his steps in the Word of God and by a process of daily doing the will of God. *And he did what was right in the sight of the LORD, and walked in all the ways of his father David; he did not turn aside to the right hand or to the left* (2 Kings 22:2).

By the way, that's the same way we will find ourselves also at the right place at the right time with the right heart to do the specific will of God: by obeying God in the general things, He will lead us to His specific paths.

In reading the following passages we find a timeline of how Josiah found and did the specific will of God for his life. Please take the time to read through1 Kings 13:2; 2 Kings 21:19-24; 2 Kings 22-23; 2 Chron. 34-35; and notice the following about Josiah: [65]

- His father was evil and did not follow God as David did.
- He was born when his father was just 16.
- His father reigned as king of Judah for just two years and was murdered.
- He became king of Judah at the age of 8.
- He began to seek God actively at the age of 16 when God stirred his heart.
- At the age of 20, he brought about religious reform by beginning a campaign to destroy all idolatry in Judah and Israel.
- His zeal for God took his purging of idolatry beyond Judah and into the far reaches of Israel.
- For six years he faithfully destroyed all idolatry and burned the bones of the false priests on the false altars.
- At the age of 26, he had a deep desire to repair the Temple of Solomon.
- During the process of repairing the Temple he discovered a lost copy of the Word of God that Jehovah sustained. Notice that Josiah's name, which means *"Jehovah sustains"* reveals how God will always sustain His Word no matter how difficult the days in which we live.
- When he heard the Word of God read, he humbled his heart before God and tore his cloths as an outward sign of repentance.
- Upon hearing the Word of God, he recognized that the wrath of God was upon Judah because they had broken God's covenant and brought upon themselves the curses of the covenant.
- His sensitivity and obedience to the Word of God brought about a second wave of idol destruction.
- In the process of destroying idolatry, he came to Bethel and destroyed the altar of Jeroboam and dug up and burnt the bones of the false priests that offered sacrifices upon it during Jeroboam's day.
- From the age of 20 to 26, Josiah faithfully did what he knew was the will of God in destroying idolatry and repairing the Temple. In the process of walking with God, he discovered the unique and specific will of God for his life at the altar of Bethel.
- His commitment to walk with God led him to fulfill the greater purpose in Christ for his life. This was prophesied 300 years before he was born.
- He did not have to have a "burning bush" experience in order to be in the center of God's will. As he acted upon the light of the Word of God, he discovered the very thing that God had ordained that he do.

The principle we learn from Josiah's life is very simple: if we will faithfully do what we know to do from Scripture, we will discover God's greater purpose in Christ for our lives that He has ordained before we were born (Ephesians 2:10).

---

65   The following section regarding Josiah is taken from the author's book, *God's Greater Purpose in Christ*.

I can testify that many of the specific open doors for ministry came, not as I sat at home waiting, but as I was doing the will of God. When I followed the leading of God's Spirit to go on a mission trip to India in 2004, it put me in the right place at the right time to hear from God specifically and to have new doors of ministry opened in Brazil and Columbia.

The problem that most believers face is not how to discover the specific will of God, as much as it is just to be faithful and obedient to that which is God's clear will for all believers. We are all called to a private time with God in His Word. We are all called to love our families. We are all called to serve God in a local New Testament church. The Holy Spirit calls us all to give, witness, pray, and allow Christ to live His life through us. If we are not doing the will of God that is common to all believers, then we will miss the specific will of God and often be deceived about what God is calling us to do by our own selfish bias that is rooted in our flesh.

APPLICATION QUESTIONS

- In what ways are you currently following the general will of God for your life?

- How have you sensed God's Spirit directing you in His specific will for your life?

- Like Josiah, would you be willing to do the general will of God for over six years before finding part of the specific will of God for your life?

4. HOW DO WE GET TO THE PLACE WHERE WE HEAR AND DISCERN THE SPECIFIC WILL OF GOD FOR OUR LIVES WITHOUT PERSONAL BIAS OR SELFISH PREFERENCE?

Without brokenness and being poured out to God, we can, in our own zeal, presume on the specific will of God for our life. Without brokenness, our personal bias toward self-will often deceives us regarding the specific will of God.

In the section on brokenness, we saw the principle that our flesh is sinful, corrupt, and without any good thing. Not only does God reject the evil of our flesh, but he rejects what we might think are the good things that we see in ourselves (Romans 7:5-6, 17-25). The battle between the will of the flesh and the will of the Holy Spirit is real and constant:

> *I say then: Walk in the Spirit, and you shall not fulfill the lust of the flesh. For the flesh lusts against the Spirit, and the Spirit against the flesh; and these are contrary to one another, so that you do not do the things that you wish* (Galatians 5:16-17).

We must recognize that we are capable of presuming on the will of God. We can be deceived by the good intentions of our flesh, and the personal bias that we all have in the flesh toward ourselves. As a result, we can feel that we have received direction from God when we may have only rationalized and convinced ourselves.

Satan can deceive us all and the biased nature of our flesh in seeking the specific will of God about a particular matter. At times we presume upon God's will and seek to commit God to that which we have initiated.

When we come to a fork in the road, it's easy to choose the road that is the most comfortable and convince ourselves that we are on the right road walking with God. We have blind spots of pride that can cause us to assume we are in the will of God, yet not know that we have been subtly influenced by self-exaltation. We can have zeal without knowledge and boldly walk down a path that God did not send us. It is good to seek to do God's will, but the enemy has many side roads that we can take as a detour.

The amazing thing about God and His amazing grace is that …

> *He has not dealt with us according to our sins, nor punished us according to our iniquities. For as the heavens are high above the earth, so great is His mercy toward those who fear Him; as far as the east is from the west, so far has He removed our transgressions from us. As a father pities his children, so the LORD pities those who fear Him. For He knows our frame; He remembers that we are dust* (Psalm103: 10-14).

I have found that when I realized that I had been deceived and taken a deceptive detour off of the road of God's will, God in His great mercy allowed U-turns back into the center of His will. The key, of course, is in the character of God.

- Read through those verses from Psalm 103 once again. Circle every time David mentions something about God's character.

- What do you learn from that exercise?

🌿 How Do We Hear God?

- God speaks to us through the Scripture. This is the main way He speaks to us. 2 Timothy 3:16-17 states, *All Scripture is given by inspiration of God, and is profitable for doctrine, for reproof, for correction, for instruction in righteousness, that the man of God may be complete, thoroughly equipped for every good work.*

  If we read the Bible faithfully and systematically, we will be surprised how clear the will of God becomes to us. If we follow the general rules of interpreting the Bible (interpretation is known as the Biblical science of hermeneutics), we will discover the voice of God, not in our ear, but from the pages of Scripture.

- God speaks to us through pastors and teachers. Have you ever heard a sermon and felt that God was speaking directly to your heart? That's a common experience. God often speaks through gifted teachers to our hearts as they unfold the Word of God to us. 1 Thessalonians 2:13 says, *For this reason we also thank God without ceasing, because when you received the word of God which you heard from us, you welcomed it not as the word of men, but as it is in truth, the word of God, which also effectively works in you who believe.*

- God speaks to us through heart-impressions. He puts ideas in our minds and burdens in our spirits. Notice what Job tells us about how God speaks:

For God may speak in one way, or in another, yet man does not perceive it. In a dream, in a vision of the night, when deep sleep falls upon men, while slumbering on their beds, Then He opens the ears of men, and seals their instruction (Job 33:14-16).

We must be careful, however, in relying on inner impressions. There are two extremes to avoid: one is the error of the rationalist; the other is the error of the mystic:

- The rationalist denies that God ever speaks to us. He says God only speaks through the Bible and never personally leads an individual or gives them any impressions.

- The mystic thinks that every impression they get is from God.

Both extremes are wrong. God's impressions will always be in concert with and backed up by God's Word.

- God speaks to us through painful experiences. Proverbs 20:30 says, Blows *that hurt cleanse away evil, as do stripes the inner depths of the heart.* Sometimes it takes a painful experience to make us change our ways … and God can do that through the circumstances of pain. C. S. Lewis said, *"God whispers to us in our pleasures, He speaks in our conscience, but He shouts in our pain. It is His megaphone to rouse a deaf world."* [66]

WHY IS IT IMPORTANT TO HEAR GOD SPEAK?

- Hearing from God reminds me that I am a child of God. Jesus said, *My sheep hear My voice, and I know them, and they follow Me* (John 10:27). True followers of Jesus hear His voice. If you have never heard God speak to you (not audibly, but by the inner impressions we have been talking about), if you have never sensed Him speaking to you in your heart, you have every reason to doubt that you're a true believer and that

---

66   C. S. Lewis, *The Problem of Pain*, HarperCollins edition, 2001.

you are part of His family. But when I hear from God, I am reminded that I am His child.

Be careful here, because it takes time to learn to hear His voice. It takes time to tune our ears to the frequency of His Spirit. But know this: He is speaking. Are you listening?

- Hearing from God keeps me from making mistakes. Asaph wrote Psalm 73. [67] He tells us of his personal experience:

Truly God is good to Israel, to such as are pure in heart. But as for me, my feet had almost stumbled; my steps had nearly slipped. For I was envious of the boastful, when I saw the prosperity of the wicked.

If you listen, God will warn you in advance and you will avoid the traps, pitfalls and mistakes that Satan puts in our way.

- Hearing from God is the secret of a fruitful life. The more we depend on God's guidance, the more successful we will be. Jesus said, *If you abide in Me, and My words abide in you, you will ask what you desire and it shall be done for you. By this My Father is glorified, that you **bear much fruit**; so you will be My disciples* (John 15:7-8).

God desires us to be fruitful, to be prosperous, and to realize His purpose for your life. He made you to be fruitful.

APPLICATION QUESTIONS

- Have you recognized the personal bias toward your self-life that lives daily in your flesh?

- Do you remember a time that your zeal was so influenced by pride that you missed God's will?

- Do you need to make a U-turn now to get back into the will of God?

- Are you abiding in Christ? Are His words abiding in you? Are you experiencing the principle of *bearing much fruit?*

---

67   David wrote most of the psalms, but not this one. This was written by a Levite who led a temple choir (1 Chronicles 15:19; 25:1-2. He likely wrote Psalms 73-83 and also Psalm 50.

5. IS IT POSSIBLE TO DO GOD'S WILL ONE DAY AND THEN ANOTHER DAY BE DECEIVED AND MISS HIS WILL COMPLETELY?

King David certainly proved that you can one day seek God's will before making an important decision and the next day make a decision that takes you out of God's perfect will for your life (see 1 Samuel 27:1).

In the preface of this book, I told the story of sitting at a Shoney's restaurant in Laurel, Mississippi praying about my burden to pastor. I could identify with Hannah in that God had *"shut up the womb,"* but that day I applied the *"opening of the barren womb"* to my specific prayer and felt I had received a similar word from God: *Go in peace, and the God of Israel grant your petition which you have asked of Him.*

I was so sure that God had just given us a church that I immediately closed my Bible and went home and announced it to Connie. Within three hours I had received a phone call from the chairman of a pastors search committee and within three weeks we were preaching in our new church. All the elements of *The Word, The Witness* and *The Way* were present in this decision.

In this case the specific will of God was made plain to me. However, there would also be times when I would come to forks in the road and deceive myself, choosing the wrong road. I had gone through a similar process of seeking God's specific will and yet convinced myself that I was being led by the Lord when in hindsight, I now feel I missed God's best.

In the following two stories I want to contrast two tests of faith and seeking to discover the specific will of God about two decisions. In one instance, I was able to stand because I stood by faith on what I felt was God's promise to me. I remind you that only the Word of God is objective truth and stories are subjective and are interpreted through the bias of the individual. Yet, God uses our personal testimonies to encourage or warn other believers. We can learn principles from both the blessings and failures of members of the body of Christ and in doing so are challenged or warned to avoid similar detours in our common journey of faith.

STORY #1: STANDING ON PROMISES OF GOD

In 1970 my pastor ask me to pray about an opportunity of planting a new church some 2,600 miles away from our home in Baton Rouge, Louisiana. My home church purchased a round trip bus ticket for me to go up and meet with a Baptist church in Washington that was looking for a pastor to start a new church in a small neighboring farming community. I spent nearly seven days and seven nights on this journey to find the will of God. I read the Bible throughout most of those days and nights, asking God for clear direction. I witnessed to several people who sat next to me on the bus, and was able to hand out many Gospel tracts. From a physical perspective, it was a miserable trip. I sat on a bus seat for nearly a week. My rear end became numb. It was hard to sleep in a sitting position. I was often aroused at late night bus stops and had to wait in the bus station for the next connection. But finally I arrived at the church plant site.

I was brought to the vacated church building where we would hold services for the new church plant. I prayed with the sponsoring church pastor in that empty church building and then asked if I could have some time alone. There I pleaded with God to give me a clear promise to stand on if this was His will for my wife and I to move there and start this new church. I knelt at the first pew and prayed and read the Word. It was in the midst of this time of praying and reading the Bible that I opened to these words,

> *You therefore, my son, be strong in the grace that is in Christ Jesus. And the things that you have heard from me among many witnesses, commit these to faithful men who will be able to teach others also. You therefore must endure hardship as a good soldier of Jesus Christ. No one engaged in warfare entangles himself with the affairs of this life, that he may please him who enlisted him as a soldier* (2 Timothy 2:1-4).

I knew this was the plain teaching for every pastor to build his ministry upon, but God impressed me that it was also a specific application for me at this point. Based on this passage, I was convinced that it was the will of God for me to accept a call from the mother church to be their church planter.

It was the plain and general will of God for me to read my Bible daily and share Jesus with the people that God had brought into my path during that week long journey of faith. The general will of God is the same for all believers and is a matter of faith and obedience. However, I needed to know the specific will of God for me to be able to accept the call to be a mission pastor.

I had peace in my heart that God had called me to start the new church plant and made the week long bus trip back home to share with my wife who was willing to follow me as we left our hometown on our first mission assignment.

It was important to me to have a deep conviction that God had sent me and that I had correctly discerned God's specific will. Little did I realize how important it would be to have had 2 Timothy 2:1-4 as a strong foundation for the storm of testing I was about to face.

Connie and I moved to Washington, and I began to go door to door to invite the community to come to our new church start. I shared my testimony and the Gospel with whomever I could talk to. For our first service I was expecting several to join us, but no one came. It was just my sweet wife and me. She sat on the same pew on which I had prayed and discerned God's will some weeks before. Connie asked what we were going to do. I did not know any better than to say, *"We will have our first service with just the two of us."* I lead the singing from the Hymnal, we gave our tithe, and then I preached my first sermon as the mission pastor. We came back Sunday night to repeat the same scenario. I had even more incentive to visit the community and share Jesus. But still no one came to join our services. Week after week I visited in the community and then preached with just Connie and me.

The emotional toll on Connie was great. She could not hold back the tears. Instead of encouraging her, each of those eighteen services brought greater discouragement. Finally in one service when I was about to preach, Connie proposed a couple of inquiring observations: *"Perhaps we missed God's will and God did not send us here or there would have been people responding. You have a business degree from college. We could return home and you could get a good job. Perhaps God did not call you to preach."*

In looking back, this was one of the most critical moments in my ministry. Had I given in and given up at that moment, I may not have been in ministry today. But, like Hannah, I moved beyond hoping to faith and assurance regarding God's specific will. I remember many factors that confirmed God had called us there. One of those was the foundation of God's promise that I had applied from 2 Timothy 2:1-4.

I was able in that moment to reassure Connie that God had indeed called me to preach and that He had also called us to start our first mission there. I did not know the work that God was doing secretly or the life lesson that He was teaching for the future.

The next Sunday, several families that I had visited and witnessed to came to church. From that Sunday on, we increased week by week in numbers. One Sunday, soon after the trial of faith, Connie herself responded to the Gospel invitation and said to me, *"Truman, God has shown me that I am lost. Do not try to tell me that I am a Christian."* In that moment I knelt with my wife at the same pew where she had questioned me about God's call to the ministry and Connie received the Lord Jesus into her life. Connie was saved that Sunday and would be the first person I baptized in my ministry. I did not know that one of the reasons for the trial of faith was to bring my wife, who I thought was a true believer, to salvation. I am so thankful that God gave me a foundation of faith to stand on in the midst of the storm of testing. Kneeling at that same pew weeks before, I had taken 2 Timothy 2:1-4 and applied it to my prayer as one of the key pieces in determining the specific will of God regarding our first mission assignment. God had given me a deep peace on the land in the daylight as to the specific will of God for our first mission. That was the anchor that kept us from sinking in the night on the storm-tossed sea of testing.

6.   We Can Miss God's Will by Misinterpreting a Trial of Faith and Giving in to Personal Bias Because of Discouragement

Story #2: Misinterpreting God's Will

After our first trial of faith, we were seeing people saved and joining our church. While witnessing from door to door, I presented the Gospel to an older Catholic woman (I will call her Alice) who seemed to be under conviction of the Holy Spirit.

I phoned one of our senior ladies, whom I will call Sally. She often helped me with visitation follow-up. Sally had at one time been actively involved in a church but had stopped going to church for years over some problems in a previous church. I visited her in her home and she and her husband became involved in our new church plant. I called Sally and told her I felt that this Catholic lady was close to responding to Christ and asked if she would go by and share her testimony with Alice. After her visit, Sally called me back, praising God and telling me how Alice had prayed with her and how she led her to Christ. Sally then instructed me to go back and talk to Alice about baptism and church membership. I rejoiced with Sally and immediately visited Alice, whom I assumed had received Christ.

However, when I arrived and discussed Sally's good news, Alice told me a different story. She said that Sally was pushy and made her feel uncomfortable. She said that she was so persistent that she prayed the sinner's prayer with Sally just to get her out of her house.

I apologized for her bad experience and then had the opportunity to answer many of her questions. She came to an understanding of salvation by grace through faith in Christ's finished work in her behalf. Tears began to roll down her cheeks and I asked if she was ready to trust in Christ alone for her salvation. She prayed from her heart in her own words and immediately had the assurance of salvation.

When I called Sally, I did not tell her of Alice's bad experience with her. I told her that Alice shared with me that she had not received Christ. God then gave me the opportunity to go over the Gospel with her again and she came to understanding and had assurance of salvation and committed to be baptized and become a member of our church.

What happened next was shocking. I remember clearly her provoking words thundered in great anger: "How dare you convert my convert!" She then told me that I was too young to be a pastor. She then informed me that she was never coming back to church and said she was going to call all the other church members and tell them the same thing. She said she was also going to call the visitors list of those who had been visiting our church. I had never seen this side of Sally before. Up till that point, she had often bragged to others about my preaching and ministry. But now I was under a spiritual attack and was being provoked to worry, to be angry, and to quit.

That Sunday my heart broke as Sally's criticisms and gossip had been very successful. More than two thirds of the congregation chose not to come to church. I felt as though the wind had been knocked out of me. I began to make phone calls and many told me that Sally had called them and they did not want to get involved in church problems. I was being battered – and rather than allow the trial of faith to teach me, refine me, and prepare me for greater fruit, I aborted the work of God by running from my problem.

My first great day of discouragement in ministry was emotionally overwhelming. I knew that it would be wrong and sinful to quit and run from my call to the young mission. I was emotionally defeated and crushed. I did not want to pick up the pieces and build again. Have you ever noticed how subtle spiritual pride can be? I did not want to run from God like Jonah, so I had to convince myself that God had released me from the church. I did not want to feel like a failure, so I had to convince myself that the sheep would not follow the shepherd. I did not want to leave without a promise from God, so I manipulated Scripture to fit my preconceived desires. I can remember praying and randomly reading a passage in Daniel.

Daniel spoke of the three faithful Hebrews thrown into the fiery furnace and the Lord delivered them. Nothing was burned but the ropes, which bound them. Depending upon the state of my heart I could have made many applications from that passage to my life situation. I could have been encouraged to go through the fiery trial of faith and trust God to deliver me. However, I wanted to get out of the situation, so I tried to spiritualize the problem and claimed that God had burned the bands of this gossip and the church problem and I was free to leave.

Today I would have handled that day of discouragement differently but on that day there was no fight left in me to persevere.

God used this experience – and several others like it – to break me to better understand the deceitfulness of my flesh (self-life). It left me with a deep awareness that I can have my mind made up and then manipulate the will of God to endorse my desires in the name of my obedience to His will.

When I told my church that I was resigning and going to accept an invitation to start a church plant in a large city, many pleaded with me not to leave. One of those was Alice. But the roaring lion had roared and I ran from my burden and not to God. I had stood strong in the previous test of faith but failed when I let my fretting turn into discouragement.

Failure can be a great teacher

Failure is a great teacher when you see yourself in the faces and principles of Scripture. I now believe that I missed God's will. In the process of maturity, we must face many common tests of faith like those in Scripture. If we fail our test of faith, then God will strengthen us and arrange a new set of circumstances where we will face someone who will again challenge us. Every believer who seeks to bear fruit will face the persecutions of our great adversary Satan.

Israel failed in following God into the Promised Land. As a result of their unbelief, they wandered in the wilderness for forty years. By that point, Moses was dead, a new leader named Joshua had taken his place, and a new generation of Israelites was ready to follow him. God gave him this command:

> *After the death of Moses the servant of the LORD, it came to pass that the LORD spoke to Joshua the son of Nun, Moses' assistant, saying: Moses My servant is dead. Now therefore, arise, go over this Jordan, you and all this people, to the land which I am giving to them—the children of Israel. Every place that the sole of your foot will tread upon I have given you, as I said to Moses. From the wilderness and this Lebanon as far as the great river, the River Euphrates, all the land of the Hittites, and to the Great Sea toward the going down of the sun, shall be your territory. No man shall be able to stand before you all the days of your life; as I was with Moses, so I will be with you. I will not leave you nor forsake you. **Be strong and of good courage**, for to this people you shall divide as an inheritance the land which I swore to their fathers to give them. **Only be strong and very courageous**, that you may observe to do according to all the law which Moses My servant commanded you; do not turn from it to the right hand or to the left, that you may prosper wherever you go. This Book of the Law shall not depart from your mouth, but you shall meditate in it day and night, that you may observe to do according to all that is written in it. For then you will make your way prosperous, and then you will have good success. Have I not commanded you? **Be strong and of good courage**; do not be afraid, nor be dismayed, for the LORD your God is with you wherever you go* (Joshua 1:1-9; emphasis mine).

When God says something once, we should listen and obey, because it is His will. When He repeats it three times, like He did to Joshua, it must *really* be important. Joshua had to learn from Israel's failure … and to depend on the LORD to give him strength and victory.

We must faithfully endure until we hear God give us a promise to stand on. And it is on that promise that we must stand faithfully. Strength is built in times of failure.

APPLICATION QUESTIONS

- Have you ever misinterpreted the will of God because of personal bias?

- What have you learned from failure? How has failure been a good teacher to you?

- In what ways do you need to stand strong and be of good courage? What are you facing right now that challenges you to trust God more?

CHAPTER 15
Believing – Part 1

And she said, "Let your maidservant find favor in your sight. So the woman went her way and ate, and her face was no longer sad. Then they rose early in the morning and worshiped before the LORD, and returned" (1 Samuel 1:18-19).

THE SEVENTH TEST OF FAITH

The seventh test of faith asks,

> Can we rejoice and thank God before the promise is fulfilled,
> and can we walk by faith and not by our feelings?

As we begin this chapter, notice Hannah's actions and faith. This is the first time in the text that we find Hannah not carrying the heavy burden of her soul. Her burden was lifted. She had learned to say, in the words of Jesus that *His yoke is easy and His burden is light.* Hannah, whose name means grace, had found grace in the eyes of the Lord. Her long journey of faith has brought her to the point where she saw the unseen and rejoiced in the Lord. No longer burdened, she probably sang a song of praise to God. If she had been in our church today, she might have sung with real soul, *"God hath made me glad, Oh God hath made me glad!"*

Jesus taught that we should persevere in prayer. We should keep knocking, keep asking, and keep seeking. [68] Hannah did that. She kept knocking, kept asking, and kept seeking – and she finally received from God that for which she had been asking for so long. God favored her with faith. She believed His specific promise for her. And she received that which was promised.

68   Matthew 7:7-8

It is amazing what God does in the very nanosecond that we believe. The witness of the Holy Spirit can give us such a deep assurance of faith that we can know before we see. The seed of faith had been planted in Hannah's soul and she knew that she was pregnant before she was physically pregnant. Hannah's faith ruled over her emotions and she was filled with praise.

Hannah's experience can help us answer two important questions in our journey to strength, fruitfulness, and fulfillment:

- How do we learn to thank God by faith and rejoice in the promised blessing before we receive the blessing?
- How do we by faith learn not to allow our feelings to rob us of the joy of believing without seeing?

In this chapter we will consider the first question.

1. HOW DO WE LEARN TO THANK GOD BY FAITH AND REJOICE IN THE PROMISED BLESSING BEFORE WE RECEIVE THAT BLESSING?

Our heavenly Father has made incredible promises in His Word. Those promises are like solid rocks [69] upon which we can fully depend. Rather than depending on the quicksand of emotions and self-focused hope, Hannah built her house of faith on the solid rock of God's promise to her. When the winds, rains and storms beat, she stood strong. She did not waver. Her emotions did not revert back to sadness and self-pity. She rejoiced without wavering until she held Samuel in her arms.

If I had to apply a New Testament verse to Hannah's manner here it would be found in the words of Jesus, *Therefore I say to you, whatever things you ask when you pray, believe that you receive them, and you will have them* (Mark 11:24). Hannah asked and believed with rejoicing faith before she received her answer to prayer. This verse is a great promise and challenge for us as well. However, it must be kept in context of the whole of Jesus' teachings about faith and prayer.

FAITH AND PRAYER: THE FOUNDATION OF ASKING

- We ask out of an abiding relationship with Christ. *If you abide in Me, and My words abide in you, you will ask what you desire, and it shall be done for you* (John 15:7). If we remain in God's Word, we will not ask self-centered requests.
- We ask that the Father may be glorified in us bearing much fruit. *By this My Father is glorified, that you bear much fruit* (John 15:8).
- We ask according to the will of God. *Now this is the confidence that we have in Him, that if we ask anything according to His will, He hears us. And if we know that He hears us, whatever we ask, we know that we have the petitions that we have asked of Him* (1 John 5:14-15). When we are at the point where we want only God's will and glory, God's Spirit will take God's Word to reveal God's will to us.
- We ask prompted by the Holy Spirit. *Likewise the Spirit also helps in our weaknesses. **For we do not know what we should pray for as we ought**, but the Spirit Himself*

---
69   Matthew 7:24-27

makes intercession for us with groanings which cannot be uttered. Now He who searches the hearts knows what the mind of the Spirit is, because He makes intercession for the saints according to the will of God (Romans 8:26-27; emphasis mine). The most effective prayers are those that the Holy Spirit has burdened our heart to pray.

- We ask in Jesus' name, which encompasses asking within the framework of Jesus' character and work on the cross. *Whatever you ask the Father in My name He will give you* (John 16:23). Jesus, who had nowhere to lay His head, never asked for any self-indulgent luxuries. He was consumed with doing the will of His Father. In Jesus' name we have access and standing before the Father through His imputed righteousness and High Priestly intercessions for us (Hebrews 7:25).
- We ask in Jesus' name that the Father may be glorified in the Son in giving us what we ask for. *And whatever you ask in My name, that I will do, that the Father may be glorified in the Son* (John 14:13-14).
- We ask in Jesus' name that our joy may be full (John 16:24).
- We ask as we walk in fellowship with God with our sins confessed and our hearts clean or we cannot ask for the things God wills and desires (1 John 1:6-10; 2:1).
- We ask in faith without wavering (James 1:6).
- We do not ask for things to satisfy our own pleasures. *You ask and do not receive, because you ask amiss, that you may spend it on your pleasures* (James 4:3).
- We ask in the spirit of the model prayer that Jesus taught us (Matthew 6: 9-13). Therefore our prayers to God our Father include praise and worship, asking for things that advance the kingdom of God, asking for God's will to be done on earth, asking for our daily needs, asking for forgiveness as we forgive others, asking not to be lead into temptation and deliverance from evil.
- We ask knowing that our Father is good and will not give us a stone when we ask for bread but will answer us according to His goodness (Matthew 7:9-11).
- We ask with faithful perseverance and keep on asking with the assurance that God will surely answer (Matthew 7:7-8).
- We ask with the confidence that we do not have to change God's mind or will because He already knows what we have need of before we ask. Therefore we focus on serving and seeking first the advancement of God's kingdom knowing that as we do, *all these other things will be added to us* (Matthew 6:33).
- We ask and leave the results to God, knowing that God will do more than we ask. *Now to Him who is able to do exceedingly abundantly above all that we ask or think, according to the power that works in us* (Ephesians 3:20).

What True Faith Isn't

- Our faith is not faith in faith. It is not a blind leap into the dark.
- It is not self-initiated were we claim what we desire.
- It is not a mind game played by the mystic, where we ask for something we want and try to bring it into existence simply by wishful thinking.
- Rejoicing faith is not the wishful thinking of the "name it and then claim it" philosophy of receiving from God.

- It is not working up our emotions with a spiritual pep rally to get us to rejoice before we receive.

When we reach the point that we walk in fellowship with God with a clean heart and faith in the revealed will of God, whatever we ask will be that which God already desires that we ask and we can rejoice before we receive the blessing as though we had already received it.

Do We Limit God or Do We Experience His Unlimited Resources?

God was not limited by Hannah's barren womb. Hannah saw beyond her inability to conceive to a God who promised to provide. She saw God's clear promise to her – and she rejoiced.

Remember we are looking beyond the historical experience of Hannah to the eternal principles of faith that apply to us all. Here lies the key that unlocks the unlimited resources of God: how do we obtain from God by faith alone? If God's work on earth was limited to what we could do for Him, then we limit God. In the greater sense, God cannot be limited because He is the almighty God. However, God has chosen to work through man on the basis of faith. We are told that *without faith it is impossible to please God* (Hebrews 11:6). God had a greater purpose for Israel in the wilderness than they experienced because they limited God by their unbelief (see Psalm 78:41).

God wants to use us in this world. Our hearts should grieve with the possibility that we limit God by our sin of unbelief. However, if we can obtain from God by faith alone then we have entered the realm of Ephesians 3:20 where we can see God do *exceedingly abundantly above all that we ask or think, according to the power that works in us.* This is one of the greatest needs of the church today. How few of God's children have learned to draw upon the resources of God by faith alone. I am ashamed to say that my faith is little and I limit God. It makes me sick. I have a longing in my heart to know God like this. How about you?

The Story of George Muller

As a young Christian, I read several biographies of men of faith. I knew that this was a level of faith that few obtained. As I read of the faith of George Muller, I was convinced that all of God's children could obtain from God by faith alone. Here was a man whose prayer diary revealed that every prayer that he prayed for God's provision for his orphans and ministry was met. If you were to audit his prayer records, you would find that as he wrote one of heaven's checks on his prayer ledger, then – just on time – God would make a deposit on earth that answered his prayer. George Muller learned to obtain God's provision for God's work by faith alone. He never asked a man for a dime and never made known his needs, yet in his lifetime, he housed and provided completely for the care of over 10,000 orphans. [70]

---

70 Christian Biography Resources, J, Gilchrist Lawson.

Many have looked at George Muller's faith and thought that God would not do that for them. However, Muller was very clear that God wanted to demonstrate that any believer could obtain from God by faith alone.

> *This was his supreme passion: to display with open proofs that God could be trusted with the practical affairs of life. This was the higher aim of building the orphan houses and supporting them by asking God, not people, for money.*[71]

It was inspiring for me to learn that George Muller preached from 1825 to 1829 and felt that his preaching was without real fruitfulness. He was like most Christians, trying hard to serve God in their own strength and power. But he came to learn that it is not by human effort or good deeds that we receive from God – it is by faith alone. He discovered the great truths of grace and the enabling of the Holy Spirit, that without Him he could do nothing. It was this discovery of spiritual dependency that opened to Him the unlimited resources of God through faith and prayer.

George Muller inspired many by his life of simple faith. But he is not alone. There are many – including people today – who exhibit the same kind of faith. There is a lady in our church who has been totally dependent on God financially for the last three years. Her husband was deported and left her with no source of income. My faith has been challenged as I have seen God answer her prayers for provision so many times. Are you challenged to have greater faith by the faith of others? Or do you just grow numb, explaining that their lives of great faith are not relevant to you?

I think I am still in kindergarten regarding this unlimited potential of prayer. I have at times cashed a few of heaven's checks of promises. Not one has ever bounced. But I am grieved with myself when the need of our world is so great and I still have not learned to tap into the full resources of God that are available to us all. One of the purposes of this book is to challenge us to see that we limit what God wants to do in our world by our lack of faith. It is the Hannah's of God who have discovered the principle that God orchestrates the circumstances in our lives to bring us to the point of supernatural fruit. God wants to break us of our strength in self, to cause us to be totally dependent on Him, for *when we are weak, then we are strong* (2 Corinthians 12:10).

It took George Muller four years of fruitless ministry to discover the secret of fruitfulness. How long will we be satisfied with a little fruit when the world desperately needs Christians who have a manifestation of the life of Christ through them? In the next chapter we will learn that Hannah was bettered because of her barrenness because it brought her to a more fruitful walk with God. It is better for God to make us barren in order that we would become so desperate for God and true fruitfulness that we like Hannah will obtain by faith alone.

A few Sundays ago a sobering thought came to my mind: *"Do you want to be known as a great preacher or a great prayer warrior?"* I have heard great preachers and I do not put myself in that category. However, preaching is a passion that God has given me. I have heard many great preachers like Adrian Rodgers, W.A. Criswell, and Jerry Vines. Every time I heard these men

---

71   George Muller's Strategy for Showing God, Simplicity of Faith, Sacred Scripture, and Satisfaction in God, 2004 Bethlehem Conference for Pastors, © 2011 Desiring God.

speak, God used them to touch my heart and make application in my life. But who knows the names of great prayer warriors? God knows each of these great prayer warriors by name, but they are unknown by the common man. Not all of us can have gifts of great preaching, but we all can have a private place of prayer that can move mountains. It was the missionary William Cary who lived by the motto, *"Expect great things from God; attempt great things for God."* God has called each of us to live by that kind of faith to bring about His greater purpose in the world.

QUESTIONS TO PONDER

- What have you been asking God for? What kinds of spiritual checks have you been writing?

- Consider your own checkbook. If a stranger examined your checkbook, what kind of pattern of desires would he find? Is there any proof that your checkbook is advancing the kingdom of God?

- Is there any proof that what you ask in prayer is advancing the kingdom of God?

- Does God give you everything you ask for? What does that say about what we ask for?

- Do you have a testimony like Hannah where you can say that you believed and rejoiced before you received the actual answer to your prayers?

- Is there an area in your life where you feel that you have limited God?

- Do you believe that some believers like George Muller can have the kind of faith that receives from God consistently?

- Has God created a desire in your heart to see Ephesians 3:20 become a pattern for your walk with the Lord?

WRITING CHECKS ON GOD'S ACCOUNT

Months before God sent us to plant a church in Washington state, my pastor had been secretly praying about launching a campaign to pay off the church debt for its new building. He sought confirmation by asking God to send someone to him that felt burdened to give a special love offering above his or her tithe of $1,000 to the church. No one knew of this prayer but he and God, yet I received a burden to do that very thing. When I went to his office to tell him of my specific burden, he was filled with joy. He said he had thought one of the wealthy members might come to him – but not one of the poorest! That amount would be about a third of my income for 1970. I did not see how I could keep that promise without God doing something supernatural. When we arrived in Washington, our finances were even tighter, but we kept an accurate record of our giving above the tithe to keep our promise of $1,000. We had a year to fulfill our promise, and after several months, I looked at the reality of the situation and began to feel defeated. It was a sacrifice to give an extra $15 to $20 a month above our tithe. Without God doing something special, I could see no way of keeping my commitment to God.

I went to God in my discouragement and asked if I could be freed from my promise. I did not receive an immediate answer, and I could not get any peace in my heart. Over the next few weeks, I seemed to be hearing, *When you vow a vow to God, do not delay paying it, for he has no pleasure in fools. Pay what you vow. It is better that you should not vow than that you should vow and not pay* (Ecclesiastes 5:4-5).

Late one night, I complained to God about how I could not fulfill my promise. I had read Malachi many times before, but I was drawn to this passage:

> *Will man rob God? Yet you are robbing me. But you say, 'How have we robbed you?' In your tithes and* **contributions***. You are cursed with a curse, for you are robbing me, the whole nation of you. Bring the full tithe into the storehouse, that there may be food in my house. And thereby* **put me to the test***, says the* LORD *of hosts, if I will not* **open the windows of heaven** *for you and pour down for you a blessing until there is no more need* (Malachi 3:8-10; emphasis mine).

As I read those words, I was filled with the kind of faith that Hannah experienced with the word from Eli. It was as if I had been filled with faith and knew that God would certainly provide, as I trusted Him.

At that moment I got up and wrote a $100 check, and the next day went to the post office to mail it. Like Hannah, I was no longer sad but filled with such joy that I had become a cheerful giver (2 Corinthians 9:7). I could identify with Hannah rejoicing for the blessing before I received the blessing. When I arrived home from the post office, somehow I knew that God had something for us in the mailbox. We had not been receiving money in the mail, but that day there was a letter containing a check. Guess what the amount was – it was $100!

I was humbled by God's power. No one could convince me that God had not given the promise and faith to act upon His Word. I was convinced that this was not coincidence but the hand of God.

I immediately took that $100 and went back to the post office and sent it on its way to my home church. Three days later I received a second $100 check dated the same date that I wrote the second $100 check. It was plain to me God was teaching me something about faith. Over the next few weeks, each time we gave the $100 that God supernaturally provided, God would match it.

I decided to write a check for the odd amount of $133 and went to the post office. Somehow I knew that God had something waiting for us in our mailbox. As I open my home mailbox there were three letters each containing checks. The three checks totaled $135. With those three checks, I was able to go back to the post office and send my last check that completed the $1,000 promise. At that point the checks stopped coming in the mail. I had just become a channel through which God's blessings flowed. In that first year of ministry I was learning that God was my provider. The lessons learned were about building faith and dependence upon a Sovereign God who was able to control the sending and receiving of checks including the timing and amount to build my faith in the first year of ministry. I learned when God gives His burden and initiates anything, He will be faithful to respond to our faith and finish that which He began.

 ## FAITH LESSONS LEARNED

- We have seen how God gives His burden to one of His children.
- We have learned that the trial of faith is to refine us and wean us from our own desires so that what we ask from God is only what God already desires.
- We have learned that every believer is spiritually powerless and, without abiding in Christ, we can do nothing of eternal value.
- We have seen how hope precedes faith and is the motivation for us to seek God until we receive a specific promise from God.
- We have seen that we are to be followers of those who *through faith and patience inherited the promises* (Hebrews 6:12).
- We have emphasized that it is while we are in the path of obedience doing the general will of God for all believers that God normally comes to us with a specific burden to believe God for.
- We have learned that without brokenness we are self-seeking and that which we desire would mar the work that God desires to do.
- We have learned that through brokenness, we reach the point of absolute surrender. We have learned that the unlimited resources of God are not all ours until we can say we are not our own but have been bought with a price (1 Corinthians 6:19-20).

Now we learn that true faith rejoices today before tomorrow's blessings.

- True faith will believe before it sees (John 20:29).
- True faith will call that which is not as though it were (Romans 4:17).
- True faith will lift your burdens and cause you to enter into God's rest (Hebrews 4:9).
- True faith will change your behavior (James 2:14-26).
- True faith will make God and His Word the object of faith. We no longer depend on self, feelings, circumstances, or religion.

- True faith will hold the promises of God in its heart before they are received in your hands.

Let us look at some of those in Scripture whose faith resembles Hannah's faith.

🌿 The Centurion's Great Faith Contrasted with the Disciples' Little Faith

Jesus was supremely interested in developing the faith of the disciples. He rebuked them it because of their lack of faith. In Matthew 8:18-27, He directs them to get into a boat and go to the other side of the lake. As they traveled, a strong storm came up and almost sank the boat. Jesus was asleep through it all, and when the disciples woke him up, they were terrified and cried out, *Lord, save us! We are perishing!* Jesus' response was not to initially rebuke the winds and the sea, but to first rebuke the disciples: *Why are you fearful, O you of little faith?* (Matthew 8:25-26). He had placed them in a position to trust Him … and they failed the test.

Jesus had prepared the disciples for the storm the day before by illustrating the *great faith* of the centurion (Matthew 8:5-13; Luke 7:1-9). Why did Jesus say that the centurion had great faith? In reading Luke 7:1-9, we find he had some characteristics in his life that make faith flourish and grow.

- He had great humility: He said, *I am not worthy that you should enter under my roof* (7:6). Humility recognizes both who Jesus is – the King of Kings, and who we are – sinful, dependent, and unworthy. John the Baptist said that he was not worthy to even untie the Lord's shoelaces. Hannah had this same kind of humility. But hers came through a process of time and trials of faith. Hannah knew that God lifts up those that are brought low in humility. James echoes this when he writes; *God resists the proud but gives grace to the humble* (James 4:6). Pride and faith are like oil and water: they do not mix. If we are to have great faith, then we must have great humility.
- He had great love: He was a Roman soldier and yet he had love and compassion for his servant (7:2-3). It was rare for a Roman master to show mercy toward one of his servants. Great faith is void of selfishness. It produces a sacrificial love for others.
- He had a great understanding of the power and authority of Jesus. The centurion did not need a sign to believe. He did not even need to see the miracle in order to believe. He simply said, *Speak the Word and my servant will be healed* (7:7). Faith has its source and foundation in the Word of God. *Faith comes by hearing and hearing by the Word of God.* (Romans 10:13). The centurion believed without seeing or feeling. The moment Jesus spoke the Word he knew that his servant was healed.

We often use the difficult circumstances of life to justify our little faith when the Lord is expecting great faith from us. Most of us would see the disciple's actions, emotions, and words as understandable considering the life-threatening storm that they were in. We would say the disciples' fear was only natural. I would agree, but Jesus obviously had a higher expectation of them. *Why are you fearful, O you of little faith?* What did Jesus expect from His disciples? The same thing He expects of us – a supernatural response of faith in the midst of our storms.

- The great faith of the centurion was an object lesson for the disciples to prepare them for the storm that they were about to face. What are you learning today that will prepare you for tomorrow's storms?

- Are you more like the centurion with great faith or the disciples in their storm, filled with fear and little faith?

- Can you think of a time that you responded to a storm in your life as the disciples did with a natural response rather than great faith?

- Can you think of a time that you responded to a need in your life with great faith?

GIDEON'S LITTLE FAITH BECAME GREAT FAITH

Few of God's servants have great faith like the centurion. Most of us come to the point of great faith through a process. That process involves God patiently revealing more and more of Scripture to us – and it takes time for us to "get it." We're in good company here, as it took Gideon quite a bit of time to "get it" also.

Gideon was chosen by God to be one of Israel's judges and deliverers. Because of Israel's sin and idolatry, God had delivered them into the hands of the Midianites who oppressed them for seven years. In the midst of the oppression, God saw the heart of a man who longed for God to show Himself strong and deliver Israel from their oppressors. God came to Gideon and called him a *mighty man of valor* (Judges 6:12). God then called Gideon to be his servant to deliver Israel from the Midianites. *Go in this might of yours, and you shall save Israel from the hand of the Midianites. Have I not sent you?* (Judges 6:14). When Gideon questioned how God could use him in his weakness, God again confirmed that call to victory, *Surely I will be with you, and you shall defeat the Midianites as one man* (Judges 6:16).

Gideon's call was much clearer than that of the centurion; yet he still needed his faith to be strengthened. Gideon asked for a sign that the Lord was indeed calling him, and, as Gideon gave his offering to God, the Angel of the Lord touched the offering and fire came from the end of his staff and consumed the offering. Gideon had God clearly call him four times and still he was afraid and desired a sign from God. His first act of obedience was to destroy the altar of Baal in his father's house, but because of fear, he did it secretly at night.

When the Midianites came to war against Israel, Gideon again in weak and wavering faith questioned what God had already plainly told him four times: *If You will save Israel by my hand as You have said— look, I shall put a fleece of wool on the threshing floor; if there is dew on the fleece only, and it is dry on all the ground, then I shall know that You will save Israel by my hand,* **as You have said** (Judges 6:36-37; emphasis mine). Notice that the phrase *as you have said* makes it clear that Gideon was not like Hannah rejoicing in what God had already said was his guarantee of victory. God gave him a confirmation with this second sign and yet Gideon asked for a third sign to strengthen his faith. Again God granted the sign by having the dew have the opposite effect upon Gideon's fleece. Now God had clearly spoken to Gideon six times. Gideon did not need any more convincing about God's call and promise. Yet he still did not respond with great faith.

Gideon's little faith would be tested when only 32,000 of Israel responded to his call to war. Seeing the pride of man's heart, God instructed Gideon to give all who were fearful an opportunity to leave his army. God explained, *The people who are with you are too many for Me to give the Midianites into their hands, lest Israel claim glory for itself against Me, saying, 'My own hand has saved me'* (Judges 7:2).

Still God, who knows the hearts of all men, reduced Gideon's army to only 10,000. *But the LORD said to Gideon, "The people are still too many; bring them down to the water, and I will test them for you there* (Judges 7:4). At that point God spoke for the seventh time promising Gideon victory, *Then the LORD said to Gideon, "By the three hundred men who lapped I will save you, and deliver the Midianites into your hand"* (Judges 7:7). Certainly God's ways are higher than our ways, for who in his right mind would choose 300 soldiers over 32,000 to go to war. God was striping Gideon of any faith or confidence in his army or himself. Gideon was not among those that God rejected, for he still obeyed God's instructions, but he has not come to the point that he is rejoicing in faith before the victory.

The next scene in Gideon's preparation for victory shows how incredibly patient God is with us to nurture our little faith to the point that it is great faith. He tells Gideon for the eighth time that the victory is already won. Now God takes the initiative to strengthen Gideon's little faith to the point that he is saying what God says about the victory and is rejoicing in faith and counting the victory as past tense while he worships in the present tense. *It happened on the same night that the LORD said to him, Arise, go down against the camp,* **for I have delivered it into your hand.** *But if you are afraid to go down, go down to the camp with Purah your servant, and you shall hear what they say; and afterward your hands shall be strengthened to go down against the camp* (Judges 7:9-11; emphasis mine). Notice that God speaks as though the victory was assured and **calls the future tense as the past tense.**

God did the same thing with Abraham in Romans 4:17. He said, *I have made you a father of many nations…*and *calls those things which do not exist as though they did.* I like the way the King James Version describes God's actions here. It says that God *calleth those things which be not as though they were.* This is the kind of great faith that God wants to build in our lives. Hannah had it when she rejoiced in faith before she was pregnant with Samuel. The centurion had it when he simply believed the word of Jesus and counted his servant healed before he was healed. However, Gideon did not have that great faith at this point. But he will. Gideon demonstrated a bolder faith as he and his servant went into the camp of the thousands of Midianites by night. Upon hearing the dream and interpretation of two fearful soldiers of Midian, his faith was strengthened as he heard for a ninth time of victory assured. *Then his companion answered and said, "This is nothing else but the sword of Gideon the son of Joash, a man of Israel! Into his hand God has delivered Midian and the whole camp"* (Judges 7:14).

Now notice that the faith and confidence of Gideon has reached a new level, as he will call the future tense to be so sure that he calls it past tense, *And so it was, when Gideon heard the telling of the dream and its interpretation, that he **worshiped**. He returned to the camp of Israel, and said, "Arise, for the* LORD ***has delivered*** *the camp of Midian into your hand"* (Judges 7:15; emphasis mine). Gideon is now saying in faith before it came to pass what God had already said; ***The Lord has delivered*** (compare Judges 7:9 to 7:15).

God chose Gideon and called him a mighty man, yet it took a process of God building his little faith before he rejoiced in faith before the promise was fulfilled. I know we should believe God and simply take Him at His word. This is the kind of faith that God wants in our lives. However, if God sees a small amber that still burns in you, He will fan it into a great flame of fire and faith.

APPLICATION QUESTIONS

- Why do you think it took so many confirmations for Gideon to believe God's Word?

- Why do you think that God was so patient with Gideon?

- At what point do you think that Gideon had the kind of faith that rejoiced before the promised blessing like Hannah?

- I have heard many Christians say that they were putting out a fleece to find God's will like Gideon. How can that be dangerous for New Testament believers?

We do not need to ask God for a sign or a fleece to find God's will. Asking God for a sign can open one up to deception from the enemy. Jesus reproved those that came to Him asking for a sign. We also now have the complete revelation of Scripture that was already confirmed by signs and miracles. We do not ask for a sign to believe the Scripture. We have the indwelling Holy Spirit to direct us into God's will.

PETER: LITTLE FAITH TO GREAT FAITH BACK TO LITTLE FAITH

Jesus did not give up on his disciples with little faith in their first storm on the troubled sea. He continued to teach and mentor them, and then test them once again with yet another storm on the troubled sea. Even though the disciples still had a natural response and battled fear, Jesus again calmed them with the words, *Be of good cheer! It is I; do not be afraid* (Matthew 14:27). The words of Jesus immediately drove the fear from Peter's heart and replaced it with faith. Peter then asked Jesus for a word of faith to walk on water to Him. Jesus gave a single word, *"Come,"* and with that, Peter began walking on the water toward Jesus.

> *"Lord, if it is You, command me to come to You on the water." So He said, "Come." And when Peter had come down out of the boat,* **he walked on the water** *to go to Jesus. But* **when he saw** *that the wind was boisterous,* **he was afraid***; and beginning to sink he cried out, saying, "Lord, save me!" And immediately Jesus stretched out His hand and caught him, and said to him,* **"O you of little faith, why did you doubt***?" And when they got into the boat, the wind ceased* (Matthew 14:28-32; emphasis mine).

- Peter had seen the great faith of the centurion who was willing to simply believe the word of Jesus.
- Peter manifested fear and little faith in the first storm with Jesus, even though Jesus had promised they were to go to the other side of the lake. He did not say, *"Let us go to the middle of the lake and drown."*
- Peter again manifested fear in the second storm. This of course is the natural reaction of our hearts toward storms.
- Jesus walked on water to the disciples and calmed Peter's fears.
- Peter exercised great faith when he firmly stood on Jesus' command to come to Him. All that faith needs to support it is one word from God. Just as Hannah seized the word of Eli, *go in peace,* Peter seized the one word of Jesus, *come.*
- As he was walking on the water, Peter took his eyes off of Jesus and saw the waves. It was at that point he wavered in faith and fear returned and he began sinking. It is the natural state in our flesh to walk by sight and to be influenced by changing circumstances. Great faith will continue to stand firmly on God's promises and look to Jesus in spite of circumstances.
- When Jesus rescued Peter from sinking, He again issues a mild rebuke, *O you of little faith, why did you doubt?* (4:31).

Like Peter, we can exercise faith one day and waver the next. Because we are still battling the world, the flesh, and the devil, our faith can waver. Even if you have failed in the past to exercise great faith, do not lose heart. God is patient with His children. Notice the greater faith of Peter after he was filled with and empowered by the Holy Spirit on the Day of Pentecost. He boldly proclaimed the Gospel, even amidst much opposition. The same could be true of us if we die to self and yield ourselves to the control of the Holy Spirit.

 SARAH STRUGGLED THROUGH MANY YEARS TO COME TO A POINT OF GREAT FAITH:

Years after God gave a promise that He would provide the promised son through Abraham and Sarah, Sarah waivered in faith by offering Hagar as a surrogate wife to her husband. Abraham bought into this man-made solution, and Ishmael was born. However, God rejected Ishmael and this fleshly attempt to fulfill His promise through means of the flesh. At nearly ninety, even though God clearly said that Sarah would give birth to Isaac, she laughed in unbelief.

> *And He said, "I will certainly return to you according to the time of life, and behold, Sarah your wife shall have a son." (Sarah was listening in the tent door which was behind him.)* [11] *Now Abraham and Sarah were old, well advanced in age; and Sarah had passed the age of childbearing. Therefore Sarah laughed within herself, saying, "After I have grown old, shall I have pleasure, my lord being old also?" And the LORD said to Abraham, "Why did Sarah laugh, saying, 'Shall I surely bear a child, since I am old?' Is anything too hard for the LORD? At the appointed time I will return to you, according to the time of life, and Sarah shall have a son." But Sarah denied it, saying, "I did not laugh," for she was afraid. And He said, "No, but you did laugh!"* (Genesis 18:10-15).

Even when Sarah was not faithful, God remained faithful and brought to pass His will in her life. In Hebrews 11:11 we see an amazing transformation in Sarah's faith, *By faith Sarah herself also received strength to conceive seed, and she bore a child when she was past the age, because she judged Him faithful who had promised.*

Notice that Sarah received strength to conceive by faith. That faith was based upon her believing God's promise of a son. She had reached the same kind of faith that Hannah had as she judged God faithful to His promises. Thank God that He has not dealt with us according to our sins or rewarded us according to our iniquities. Sarah, who once waivered in faith and judged by sight, feelings, and the reality of her dead womb, was made to laugh in faith at God's faithful fulfillment of His promise, *And Sarah said, "God has made me laugh, and all who hear will laugh with me"* (Genesis 21:6).

Even though we see examples of God being patient with Gideon, Peter, and Sarah, we must not tempt God by our lack of faith. God also gives us illustrations of His expectation that we believe Him the first time He speaks to us. When the angel Gabriel announced the promised birth of John the Baptist, *Zacharias said to the angel, "How shall I know this? For I am an old man, and my wife is well advanced in years." And the angel answered and said to him, "I am Gabriel, who stands in the presence of God, and was sent to speak to you and bring you these glad tidings. But behold, you will be mute and not able to speak until the day these things take place, **because you did not believe my words which will be fulfilled in their own time**"* (Luke 1:18-20; emphasis mine). May we be believing – and not unbelieving – when the word of the Lord comes to us.

- What role does the Word of God have in your life in strengthening your faith when you are wavering? How does it encourage you to be faithful?

- Like Peter, have you ever stepped out in faith and then taken your eyes off of Jesus and His promise to you and allowed the circumstances to cause you sink?

- What is one lesson that you can apply to your life from Sarah's failure in faith and final victory in faith?

Hannah's experience proves that we can rejoice in the promised blessing before we received the blessing. Have you learned to thank God for the fulfillment of His promises before you see them with your eyes? Hannah did. In the next section, we want to learn how by faith we can rule over our emotions.

CHAPTER 16

Believing – Part 2

And she said, "Let your maidservant find favor in your sight. So the woman went her way and ate, and her face was no longer sad. Then they rose early in the morning and worshiped before the LORD, and returned" (1 Samuel 1:18-19).

THE SEVENTH TEST OF FAITH

The seventh test of faith asks,

> *Can we rejoice and thank God before the promise is fulfilled,*
> *and can we walk by faith and not by our feelings?*

In the previous chapter, we talked about trusting God by faith and rejoicing in the promised blessing before we actually received that blessing. Now let us address a second question.

2. HOW DO WE BY FAITH LEARN NOT TO ALLOW OUR FEELINGS TO ROB US OF THE JOY OF BELIEVING WITHOUT SEEING?

The moment Hannah seized the word of Eli as a personal promise from God, she had victory over her emotions. She had battled emotions of fear, anger, depression, worry, and sadness. But the moment those emotions were brought captive to the promise of God by faith, she was no longer sad. There were three immediate changes:

- There was a physical change: she ate. One of the results of depression is a loss of appetite. Hannah believed God … and her appetite returned.

- There was a spiritual change: she worshiped God. She knew she had heard from God … and she worshiped Him in thanksgiving.
- There was an emotional change: the most obvious and immediate change in Hannah was in her countenance. In the past, she could not hide her sad appearance but now she could not hide her joyful appearance.

In the New Testament we clearly see that there is a difference between our emotions and the fruits of the Spirit. Jesus noted this difference as He contrasted the disciple's emotions with His joy, His peace, and His love.

> *As the Father loved Me, I also have loved you; abide in My love. If you keep My commandments, you will abide in **My love**, just as I have kept My Father's commandments and abide in His love. These things I have spoken to you, that **My joy** may remain in you, and that **your joy** may be full.… Peace I leave with you, **My peace** I give to you; **not as the world gives** do I give to you. Let not your heart be troubled, neither let it be afraid (John 14:9-11, 27; emphasis mine).*

Our emotional love is limited but the love of God is boundless. With my emotional love it is easy to love those that bless me but difficult to love those that curse me. However, when the Holy Spirit manifests the love of God through me, it is a supernatural love that loves like Christ (Romans 5:5). When I have emotional peace, I do not worry until the circumstances become difficult; then my emotional peace is replaced with fear or fretting. But when I experience the peace of Christ as a fruit of the Holy Spirit, I am calm in the midst of the storm. When I experience emotional joy, I am happy; but that happiness vanishes when another emotion comes that robs me of my joy. However, when I experience the joy that comes from the Lord, then no circumstance, person, or competing emotion can take His joy from me.

I remember as a five year old waking up one morning happy about getting to go outside and play in our yard. But when I stood on our front porch and watched it rain, I lost my emotional joy and became sad. I began to irritate my mom by my constant questioning, *"When will it stop raining so I can play?"* (Looking back I could rephrase that statement as *"When will it stop raining so I can be happy again."*) Finally my mother taught me a rhyme to stop my whining. I stood on the front porch and spoke to my enemy the rain over and over again, *"Rain, rain, go away…Little Truman wants to play."* My emotional joy returned when I began the rhyme. However, after several minutes of vain repetition, the sadness returned. I could not change the rain and had become a prisoner of my emotions.

 ## FROM CHILDHOOD TO MATURITY

It was a great day in my walk with the Lord when He taught me the greater truth of who I was in Christ. When I learned that the fruits of the Spirit could overcome my changeable emotions, I was freed from the changing circumstances of life to rely on the power of God to give me victory over my circumstances.

In recognizing the difference between my emotions that are subject to my flesh, and the fruits of the Spirit that come as a result of my regenerated spirit in Christ, I have had the faith to claim that I am not what I feel I am, but what God's Word says I am. With that understanding, we, like Paul, can sing at midnight while in prison chains. Our *will* can begin to sing, *"Rain, rain, whether you go or stay…you will not rob me of my joy today…. For Christ's joy is mine and I will not sway…His will be done is what I prayed."* I cannot tell you how many times my emotions, like spoiled children, have cried to be heard but had to bow and submit to my will as I yielded to the Holy Spirit.

Hannah did not experience joy because her circumstances changed. She was not like a child in the candy store crying until she got what she wanted from her Father. She experienced such a deep assurance of faith that she had changed her behavior without getting a piece of candy to calm her emotions. God gave her His promise and she was standing so firmly on the promise that she saw by faith what God saw, that God had opened her barren womb. She saw her Samuel by faith. She experienced the ministry of the Holy Spirit in her life and the joy of the Lord became her strength.

Consider the following passages as we focus on our joy and the joy of the Lord as a fruit of the Spirit released in us by the Holy Spirit in every circumstance of life (emphasis mine).

- *But the fruit of the Spirit is love, **joy**, peace, longsuffering, kindness, goodness, faithfulness, gentleness, self-control* (Galatians 5:22-23).
- *Most assuredly, I say to you that you will weep and lament, but the world will rejoice; and you will be sorrowful, but your sorrow will be turned into **joy*** (John 16:20).
- *But now I come to You, and these things I speak in the world, that they may have My **joy** fulfilled in themselves* (John 17:13).
- *For the kingdom of God is not eating and drinking, but righteousness and peace and **joy** in the Holy Spirit* (Romans 14:17).
- *For this day is holy to our Lord. Do not sorrow, for the **joy** of the LORD is your strength* (Neh. 14:10).

I have often heard joy described in three facets: Joy as a fact, joy as a feeling and joy as an act of faith. [72]

- Joy as a fact:

  Many of the Scriptures above make it plain that every believer already has the joy of the Lord as a fact in his life. Consider the words of Jesus in John 14:10, *These things I have spoken to you, that **My joy** may remain in you, and that **your joy** may be full.* Everyday no matter how my emotions are influencing me, by faith I am to believe that I can choose the joy of Jesus over my variable emotions.

- Joy as a feeling:

---

[72]   My first exposure to this outline was through the writings of Warren Wiersbe, *Be Joyful: Even When Things Go Wrong, You Can Have Joy,* copyright © 1974 SP Publications.

The feeling of joy is a natural emotion, not our supernatural state. Each of us has our own unique personality that also influences how much our emotions influence our will and decision making process. It is often these normal emotions that define us to others as well as to ourselves.

People are often labeled by their emotions, *"You know they are easily depressed." "Be careful – they have a temper." "They are so happy go lucky and fun to be around." "They are so stable and seldom show their emotions."* Emotions do reflect our personality – but they should not dominate our spirituality. God does not want our emotions to rule over our will. Rather, our will ought to be enabled by the Holy Spirit to make our emotions bring glory to God.

How is that possible? Before we answer that question let us consider how emotional joy can hinder the will of God if we have not learned to control our emotions by faith.

Israel demonstrated unstable behavior under Moses' leadership. One day they worshiped God after Moses announced that he had come to deliver them from Pharaoh. However, when Pharaoh responded by increasing their burdens, they murmured against God. Their emotions were naturally high with good news and were naturally low with bad news (compare Exodus 4:31 with 5:21).

After God delivered Israel from Egypt, they went out with emotional joy, being free from their bondage. The day before, they were poor slaves, but now they were both free and rich, having taken the riches of Egypt with them. That joy only lasted for a few days. It vanished when they saw Pharaoh and his chariots prepared to war against them at the Red Sea. Once again their emotions ruled their wills and rather than embrace joy by faith, they murmured against God (see Exodus 14:12).

After God again delivered them, they believed their eyes and worshiped God with a song of praise. Once again, their emotions changed based upon sight and not faith. Those that let their emotions rule them will always walk by sight and not by faith.

Even after seeing God's power in Egypt and then again at the Red Sea, Israel's emotional joy lasted less than three days. When they grew thirsty on their walk from the Rea Sea, they lost their emotional joy and began to murmur against God. *And they went three days in the wilderness and found no water. Now when they came to Marah, they could not drink the waters of Marah, for they were bitter. Therefore the name of it was called Marah. And the people complained against Moses, saying, "What shall we drink?"* (Exodus 15:22-23).

Even though their circumstances were very difficult, God still expected them to walk by faith and not to be ruled by their emotions. God was expecting a supernatural response of faith in response to God even in difficult circumstances.

God expects the same of us as well. How then do we not allow our emotions to rule over our will?

- Joy as an act of faith:

The answer is to understand that we have joy as a fact in Christ as a gift from God. We are to know joy by faith as a reality in our daily walk with Him. We must acknowledge that joy is a command from God. If God commands joy, then He also gives joy and enables us to manifest joy. Since God commands joy, it is a matter of our will and not our emotions. Joy, then, is a choice. We choose to be joyful and we choose to be sad. God commands us to walk by faith and not by sight regardless of our circumstances *or emotional feelings*. Notice that principle in these passages:

- *Rejoice in the Lord always: and again I say, Rejoice* (Phil. 4:4).

- *My brethren, count it all joy when you fall into various trials, knowing that the testing of your faith produces patience. But let patience have its perfect work, that you may be perfect and complete, lacking nothing* (James 1:2-3).

- *Blessed are you when men hate you, and when they exclude you, and revile you, and cast out your name as evil, for the Son of Man's sake. Rejoice in that day and leap for joy! For indeed your reward is great in heaven, for in like manner their fathers did to the prophets* (Luke 6:22-23).

This is a critical fact that Christians *must* understand: *joy is a choice*. At this point some react in frustration and cry out, *"You do not how I feel. You have no right to tell me to be joyful when I am going through so much. My feelings are real. How could you be so insensitive?"* Sadly, I have heard this repeated by many Christians who have not discovered this amazing truth that *"you are not who you feel you are — but who God says you are."*

I could not tell a non-believer that joy is a choice for him. His emotions will only respond naturally to the circumstances of life without the indwelling Holy Spirit. But as Christians we are different; we indeed have joy as a fact in Christ and as the fruit of the Holy Spirit. Yet we will be no different from the lost world in our emotions if we do not learn this lesson of strength, fruitfulness, and fulfillment in the Lord.

A great liberation awaits those believers who will make the choice to experience joy by faith without feelings. The joy of the Lord is stronger than your emotional joy. When you learn this, your emotions will surrender to your will and the Holy Spirit and then your joy will be full.

APPLICATION QUESTIONS

- What is the difference between your natural emotions and the fruits of the Spirit? Are you able to distinguish them in your life?

- What part does your will have in making a choice by faith over your emotions in obedience to God?

- Write down a time when you did not want to obey God because of your feelings and how your obedience changed your emotions.

- Have you ever felt like a hypocrite because of your feelings?

- Is it better to obey God even when you do not feel like it, or not to obey God because you do not feel like it?

- If God commands you to obey in a certain area, can you make a choice to obey and leave the emotions to God?

ARE YOU WHO YOU FEEL YOU ARE – OR ARE YOU WHO GOD SAYS YOU ARE?

As a young Christian I thought my pastor was crazy when I said I felt one way and he said *"No you don't!"* He did not ask me *why* I felt a certain way; he did not care about the *why* of my feelings. I certainly thought it strange because everyone else I talked to would hear me justify why I felt a certain way. To me that was the caring and reasonable approach. However, to tell me that I did not know how I truly felt was presumptuous.

However, as I begin to understand who I had been in Adam and who I was now in Christ, I understood clearly the lesson he was trying to teach me. The main issue was not how I felt, but agreeing by faith with what was a reality in my new position in Christ, in my spirit, and not my former identity in Adam.

One of the first times I experienced this contrast was when I was ridiculed for sharing the Gospel with someone. Emotions immediately came to the surface: feelings of rejection, ridicule, embarrassment, followed by self-defense, anger, and a desire to verbally strike back. Then something amazing happened within me. I felt incredible fellowship with Jesus. Instead of the emotions of anger and rejection, I felt a love for the one who was cursing me. This was not "me" coming to the surface – it was the joy of the Lord springing up within my spirit through the Holy Spirit.

I experienced the difference between the emotions and feelings of my flesh and the life of Jesus and the fruits of the Spirit. My feelings came from my soul influenced by my flesh. However, deep in my spirit, in the inner man, had come the real me. The new man in Christ had surfaced in that situation to overcome my weak emotions. I learned that I could make a choice based on Scripture to rejoice when persecuted. From that lesson I began to recognize the truth behind my pastor's comment.

There is a refuge from the storms of life and the emotional roller coaster that many experience. You do not have to be in bondage to your fleshly emotions. There is a place of rest and fellowship with Jesus and His sufferings. Rather than escaping your troubles, trials, temptations and attacks, you can experience the very life of Jesus in the midst of them.

We all are emotional beings. And yet we're called to stand strong and firm in the face of the storms of life. How do we balance the very real emotions of life and yet stand strong?

 ## THE DIVISION OF SOUL AND SPIRIT

How do we really know ourselves? Can we be completely honest and correctly distinguish between our emotions, our flesh, our will, our spirit, and all the various thoughts that enter our mind? The Bible talks about the distinction between the body, soul and spirit (1 Thessalonians 5:23). We cannot know ourselves without the revelation of God's Word revealing the image of Adam in us and holding up the image of Christ before us. It is the Word of God that acts as a sharp sword to divide between our soul and spirit and helps us understand the difference between our soul, spirit, and body.

> *For the word of God is living and powerful, and sharper than any two-edged sword, piercing even to the division of soul and spirit, and of joints and marrow, and is a discerner of the thoughts and intents of the heart* (Hebrews 4:12).

Only as we allow God's Spirit to use the Word of God in our lives do we see ourselves from God's perspective.

Before salvation the natural man has a body and soul but his spirit is dead and filled with darkness, having no fellowship with God (Ephesians 2:1-4). But when we were saved by faith, the Holy Spirit regenerated us. The Holy Spirit came to live in our spirit and made us a new creation in Christ.

We have emotional love, but that is not the same as love as a fruit of the Spirit. We have joy as an emotion, but again it is not the same as the joy that Jesus deposited in us as a fruit of the Spirit.

After salvation we also began to discover that not every thought that came into our mind originated with us. It was the Word of God that began to reveal to us the true intents of our motives, thoughts, and heart.

I believe understanding the difference between our emotions and the fruit of the Spirit is one of the keys to experiencing strength, fruitfulness, and fulfillment.

QUESTIONS TO CONSIDER

- What is the nature of your flesh in Adam? What is the nature of your regenerated spirit in Christ?

- How do these two natures influence your emotions?

- What is the difference between emotional joy and joy as a fruit of the Spirit?

- Which nature is your will to daily yield to?

 ## VICTORY OVER OUR FEELINGS BY FAITH

It was a liberating day when I understood that the real truth about me was not found in my emotions, flesh, or my own appraisal of myself. It did not come from other's evaluation of me, nor was it the deceptive thoughts that entered my mind that led to self-condemnation. The real truth about me was what God said about me.

Let me share two experiences that were integral in helping me come to this conclusion.

 ## EXPERIENCE #1: HOW CAN YOU KNOW YOU ARE FORGIVEN?

As a young married man in college, I was just beginning to walk with God on a daily basis. One day I grieved over a particular sin that God had convicted me of. I asked God to forgive me. I was sincere and looked inside for a feeling of assurance that I was forgiven. But I did not feel anything. I prayed again, with more intensity, asking God for forgiveness. Still I felt nothing. I then began to beg God repeatedly for forgiveness, thinking the more I asked, the quicker I would find forgiveness. But the feelings of forgiveness still did not come. Now I felt desperate and pleaded with God to forgive me with promises that I would do better. In the midst of this pleading my emotions were released with tears. After the emotional release, I felt better and free of the guilt. I went to bed thinking that God had indeed forgiven me.

The next day, out of the blue, I remembered my sin and felt guilty all over again. My thought was, *"Lord, I thought you forgave me last night."* I walked around the campus that day with a cloud over my head, feeling condemned for my sin.

That night I got on my knees again and pleaded with God for forgiveness. Again I felt nothing. I tried to rationalize why I should feel forgiven, but still I felt guilty. It was not until I was able to have an emotional release of tears that I felt forgiven. I went to bed thinking surely the Lord has forgiven me now. However, the next day the memory and guilt of my sin returned and once again I questioned if God had really forgiven me. That up and down process continued every day and night that week.

On Sunday I was alone in the worship center when the pastor came in early. I asked, *"How do you know when God has forgiven you for a specific sin?"* Instead of giving me an answer, he asked me a question: *"What does God's Word say?"* Without hesitation I began to quote 1 John 1:9, *"If we confess our sins, He is faithful and just to forgive us of our sins and to cleanse us from all unrighteousness."* In the middle of quoting that verse, I had heard from God.

The way God spoke to me was simple but profound to me at that moment. The way that I had been quoting 1John 1:9 all week was by placing the emphasis on my confession, *If we **confess** our sins He is faithful and just to forgive.* However, that Sunday morning the emphasis shifted from **confess** to the truth of God's character, ***He is faithful and just to forgive.*** Then God opened my eyes to see the truth. I had been confessing my sin and then looking within to see if I felt forgiven, instead of looking to God and His promise and simply believing that I was forgiven by faith and not feelings.

I was forgiven the very first time I asked – nearly a week earlier. But I had been under condemnation from Satan because each time I remembered my sin I struggled with my feelings. The following Monday, I again had my sin come to my mind but this time I quoted 1 John 1:9 with the emphasis on God's faithfulness to forgive me because Christ had already paid the penalty for my sin once and for all at the cross. At that point the condemnation ceased.

LESSONS LEARNED

- The fact of God's Word is stronger than my feelings when I exercise faith in God's promises.
- Satan can use my feelings against me to question God's promises.
- I was looking inward to feel forgiven rather than looking upward to God and standing firmly on His promise by faith.
- Not every thought that enters my mind originates with me. Satan can put thoughts in my mind to tempt or deceive me.
- We are to filter all our thoughts through the truth of God's Word to discern their source, bringing every thought captive to the obedience of Christ.

Since learning this lesson about forgiveness, I have had many church members come to me who were repeating my same mistake. One of the questions I have learned to ask regarding discerning the difference between the sweet conviction of the Holy Spirit to His child and the condemnation of the world, the flesh, and the devil, *is "How many times have you confessed to God that particular one sin?"* Some have said they confessed the same sin not for a week, as in my case, but for months and even years. What liberty they found when they discovered the difference between the conviction of the Holy Spirit and the condemnation of the enemy!

Have you tried to pay for your sin before God when Jesus has already paid for it? Even though we were saved by faith and not by our works, our flesh is incurably religious and will still try to please God by the works of the flesh. We feel that little sins mean little confession and big sins required big confessions, promises, self-punishment, and even penitence. It makes us feel better if we can suffer a little for our sins to obtain forgiveness. However, that is not the Gospel. The Gospel says that Jesus paid it all. Just as we were saved from the penalty of sin once and for all at the cross, we are forgiven of individual sins in relationship to our fellowship with God by faith alone as well.

QUESTIONS TO CONSIDER

- Condemnation will drive you from the Word and conviction will draw you to the Word. It will isolate you from other believers and the church while conviction will draw you to the church. Have you experienced these in your life?

- Has Satan ever tried to condemn you for a sin that God has already forgiven?

- Is there a particular sin of your past that keeps coming back to your mind? Do you live in constant condemnation?

- Do you wait to feel forgiven before you accept God's forgiveness by faith?

- Do you feel that the greater your particular sin then the greater the confession of sin and the sorrow and misery you should feel?

EXPERIENCE #2: HOW DO YOU KNOW THE ORIGIN OF YOUR THOUGHTS?

In the first experience I stressed learning not to depend on my feelings and emotions but to stand firm by faith on the Word of God. In this experience I learned that not every thought that entered my mind was my thought.

One day I was walking across my college campus. I passed a student and a clear thought entered my mind to go share the Gospel with him. I had a Gospel tract with me and began to approach him when another thought entered my mind. It was a filthy thought followed by another thought; *"You are not ready to share Christ with him. Look at what you were just thinking about. If he could see your thoughts he would know that you are a hypocrite."* I agreed with myself and turned and walked away. A few days later again I seemed prompted by the Holy Spirit to witness to a student and as I approached him, again I had a filthy thought come to my mind followed by the same condemnation.

I began to attend a Saturday night prayer meeting where a few church members gathered to pray for the Sunday services. While I was listening to these mature believers pray, I had a dirty thought enter my mind followed by this rationalization: *"I am not ready to be part of this dedicated group of prayer warriors. If they knew the real me they would know what kind of a hypocrite I was."* I left that prayer meeting feeling like I did not belong and was not qualified to return.

Three times in one week I was prompted to obey God and each time I was defeated by my own unholy thoughts. I went to my pastor and told him of the three events. Again he asked me a question, *"Did you want to think on those thoughts?"* My answer was emphatic, *"No! I hate those thoughts."* He then asked a second eye-opening question, *"Who is the real you?"* I had never considered that I could be separate from all my thoughts. I had seen myself as all that I thought, felt, did, and willed. But in that moment a passage of Scripture again came to my mind:

> *For though we walk in the flesh, we do not war according to the flesh. For the weapons of our warfare are not carnal (of the flesh) but mighty in God for pulling down strongholds, casting down arguments (imaginations) and every high thing that exalts itself against the knowledge of God, bringing every* **thought** *into captivity to the obedience of Christ, and being ready to punish all disobedience when your obedience is fulfilled* (2 Corinthians 10:3-6; emphasis mine).

At that point I understood that Satan could put thoughts in my mind, using images of my past and temptations allied with my flesh. I was responsible for my will and the choices I made – not for every thought or temptation that entered my mind. I was to take an active part in the battle for my mind. I was to bring every thought captive to Christ and filter it through the Scripture. I was to think on pure thoughts and with my will reject any thought dishonoring to Christ.

For over a week Satan, manipulating my thought life, had deceived me. It was as if he held up a mirror and said, *"Take a good look at yourself and see just how big a hypocrite you are and that God cannot use you."* I was beginning to learn how to discern the thoughts that entered my mind.

The following week I again felt impressed to share Christ with a student. Once again an impure thought entered my mind followed quickly by the same type of condemnation as before. However, this time I did not attribute the thought to me but to Satan and my flesh. I immediately prayed, *"Dear Lord, this is not my thought. I did not will it; I did not desire it. In fact, I despise it. I bring this thought captive to You and reject it."* The condemnation was gone and I was then able look away from myself to Christ to share Jesus with someone. Once I learned that great lesson, the condemnation cycle of Satan was broken. Since that day as thoughts and temptations enter my mind, I know that the victory is won or lost by this battle for the mind.

WHO IS THE REAL YOU?

I want to ask you the same question my pastor asked me 43 years ago. *Who is the real you?* The truth about you is not what you feel, what you think, or even what you have experienced. The truest thing about you is what God says about you. And what does He say? He says …

- You are a new creation in Christ. (2 Corinthians 5:17). [73]
- You are called by God, justified through His Son, and guaranteed that the process will continue to ultimate glorification (Romans 8:30). [74]
- You are indwelt, sealed, and baptized with the Holy Spirit (1 Corinthians 3:16; 12:13; Ephesians 1:13).
- You are crucified with Christ, dead to the old man, and yet you live in newness of life (Galatians 2:20; Romans 6:1-6)
- You are seated with Christ in the heavens (Ephesians 2:6).
- You are being conformed to the image of Christ (Romans 8:29).
- You are accountable for your will and choices (Romans 7:14-20).
- You are still a sinner but saved by grace; you hate sin and are gaining victory over it (Romans 7:21-25).

Remember these truths:

- Your feelings and emotions change like the weather. They are not reflective of the real you, the *new you* in Jesus Christ.
- You do not initiate some thoughts. Satan places them in your mind and are his fiery darts designed to bring you down. However, you must take those thoughts captive to Christ.
- You are not what you are in the flesh. The flesh did not change at salvation and can never please God.

---

73   The phrase in Christ or in Him is used one hundred and sixty two times in the New Testament, emphasizing our union with Christ and our new identity with Him.

74   Paul is so certain of the completion of this salvation process that he uses the past tense for a future event to stress its certainty. He writes to the Romans as if their glorification is complete.

Do you exercise your will to make simple choices of faith – or do you let your feelings determine your choices? I have heard many Christians say, *"If I come to church when I do not feel like it, then I would be hypocritical. If I tithe when I do not feel like it, that would be hypocritical."*

My answer to those comments was, *"How do you know that you do not want to come to church? How do you know that you do not want to tithe? If you are truly saved does the inner man want to please God?"* Do we realize the difference from our old nature and our new nature? The flesh may be the source of one not wanting to come to church or tithe. Our feelings can be influenced by the flesh to side with it. However, every believer has the Holy Spirit indwelling his spirit and in the new man in Christ a believer desires to please and obey God. Our will is responsible to yield to the Holy Spirit and not to the flesh.

If we yield to the Spirit, our feelings will not keep us from obedience and deception. There have been many times where I have had my feelings try to hold me back from obedience to the Word of God. On several occasions I have been tired or busy and did not feel like going out witnessing on church-wide visitation night. Instead of giving in to my feelings, I exercised my will over my emotions and went out on a personal evangelism visit. Still feeling nothing, I began to share the Gospel and the Holy Spirit began to bring that individual under conviction and then to salvation. My feelings did not change until I was in the middle of presenting the Gospel. If I let my feelings rule me, then I would not have shared Christ that night. The enemy might try to whisper in my ear, *"You are hypocritical if you go out evangelizing when you do not feel like it."* However, the opposite is the truth. I would be hypocritical if I *didn't* go out witnessing, knowing that Christ saved me and has given me a testimony to share. The Holy Spirit who indwells me testifies of Jesus and I am called to bear witness. The Word of God commands me to go. The hypocrisy would be to believe my feelings over what God says are true of me in my spirit in the inner man.

I have preached for years, "You obey God whether you feel like it or not." You can change your feelings through faith and obedience. Never allow your feelings to change you.

- We are to go to church whether we feel like it or not.
- We are to tithe whether we feel like it or not.
- We are to witness whether we feel like it or not.
- We are to read God's Word whether we feel like it or not.
- We are to pray whether we feel like it or not.
- We are to love whether we feel like it or not.
- We are to sing and praise whether we feel like it or not.
- We are to serve whether we feel like it or not.
- We are to forgive whether we feel like it or not.

How can we justify disobedience to the commands of God because of our feelings? Can you honestly say to God, *"God I would be a hypocrite to love and forgive that person because I do not feel like it?"* Do you think that those feelings could be from your flesh and emotions? Do you think that in your regenerated spirit where the Holy Spirit dwells there is the grace and enabling power to obey God? The answer is yes!

We must exercise our will to yield to the Holy Spirit and obey the Word of God regardless of our emotions. The fruits of the Spirit will be manifest through our faith and obedience. Once we have learned that we must not yield to our emotions, but rather to the Spirit and the Word of God, we have taken a great step in learning to walk by faith and not by sight.

 ## STRONG FAITH IS REFLECTED IN OUR FACES

God gave Aaron the words of blessing for the sons of Israel: *The LORD bless you and keep you; the LORD make His face shine upon you, and be gracious to you;* **the LORD lift up His countenance upon you, and give you peace** (Numbers 6:24-26; emphasis mine). That last phrase describes how God changes our countenance when we faithfully walk with Him. We are filled with joy — and it shows.

The faith of Hannah's heart was reflected in her face. Her countenance showed her joy and trust in the promise of God. I have to wonder what it must have been like for Elkanah to see his dearly beloved wife smile with the radiance of God.

Evidence that you have believed God is when the shield of faith quenches all the fiery darts of the evil one (Ephesians 6:16). Often in battle a soldier would soak his shield in water. When the enemy shot an arrow that was on fire, his shield not only protected him from the piercing of the arrow but it quenched the fire as well. The smile of the face of Hannah in the presence of her adversary spoke loudly that her faith had triumphed in God.

APPLICATION QUESTIONS

- Has the life of Jesus ever manifested itself in you to the point where your emotions submitted to your will?

- Have you made the discovery that there is a vast difference between our emotional joy and joy as a fruit of the Spirit?

- Have you raised the shield of faith to quench the attacking arrows of the enemy? Has your faith triumphed even in the face of comments and criticisms from others?

Four Ifs

- If we do not rule over our emotions, then our emotions will rule over us.
- If we do not experience the fruits of the Spirit enabling our emotions and us to change, then our flesh and Satan will bring us into bondage to our emotions.
- If we do not exercise our will over our emotions, then we will continue to walk by sight and not by faith.
- If we are to discover the secret of strength, fruitfulness, and fulfillment then, we must believe what the Scripture says we are in Christ and not allow our emotions to define us.

CHAPTER 17

Bettered

*Then Elkanah her husband said to her, "Hannah, why do you weep? Why do you not eat? And why is your heart grieved? Am I not **better** to you than ten sons?"* (1 Samuel 1:8; emphasis mine).

THE EIGHTH TEST OF FAITH:

Will I walk with a new faith and dependence upon God in strength, fruitfulness, and fulfillment? (1 Samuel 2:1-10).

The reason Elkanah asked the question, *"Am I not better to you than ten sons"* was because his perspective of life was earthly and not heavenly. Had he seen what God saw, he would have been much more patient with Hannah and encouraged her faith.

IS IT WORTH IT?

Is the trial of faith worth it if we are made better from God's perspective? It was for Hannah. It was for Abraham, Joseph, David, Job, and all the examples of faith in Scripture. Left to ourselves, we would live for lesser things and not better things. And make no mistake: lesser things satisfy – but only for a moment. That's why we must live with an eternal perspective.

God has promised that He would complete the work that He began in us. Therefore He takes an active part in our refining to make us more like Christ and in our pruning that we might bear much fruit.

One of the great secrets to strength, fruitfulness and fulfillment is viewing life from God's perspective. Hannah was in the process of having her earthly view changed for the better to heaven's view of her life and purpose. Her prayer of praise reveals the paradox of life from God's perspective that the world does not understand. Elkanah viewed Hannah's burden through his own desires and perspective. He considered that his love was better than ten sons. Had he been brought into God's secret counsel as Hannah was, he would have seen things from God's perspective and not made such an insensitive evaluation of Hannah.

THE BENEFITS OF LIVING LIFE FROM GOD'S PERSPECTIVE

When we see life from God's perspective, we find the eternal values of God better than all this entire temporal world has to offer. We are free to seek first the kingdom of God and trust God for the "other things" that He provides (Matthew 6:33). Not only did Hannah receive the better things of a life transformed by grace and greater faith, but she received the *other things* of God's blessings as well, *And the* Lord *visited Hannah, so that she conceived and bore three sons and two daughters. Meanwhile the child Samuel grew before the* Lord (1 Samuel 2:21). Hannah became a better wife to her husband as a woman of faith. She became a better mother than Peninnah who reflected to her children her own strength, while Hannah reflected the strength of the Lord to Samuel and her other five children.

God's ways are higher than our ways and this is certainly seen in how He chooses to work His greater purpose in Christ through us. The men and women of faith that God illustrates in Scripture reveal God's ways with His children and help build our faith. None of us could fully understand God's master blueprint of His purpose for our lives. We are called to trust in God's eternal character and His love for us in all His dealings with us.

My guess is that Hannah would never have chosen to be barren but in God's greater purpose He chose to close her womb. In God's sovereignty, He knew this was a better plan than Hannah would have chosen. From hindsight we can see that God's intentions were to bless her and make her better as He fulfilled His amazing purpose that encompassed much more than Hannah could have ever imagined.

If Hannah had been given a magic "STOP" button, I am sure she would have pushed it several times in the years of suffering before she realized God's blessings. But through her sufferings, God's purpose for her, her child Samuel, and Israel was fulfilled. But such are the ways of God when He calls on us to just trust Him. We must trust Him even when we do not understand what we are going through or why we are going through it. God could have told Hannah how long she would have to wait for her Samuel, but He purposely did not. In wisdom, God calls us to trust Him. He not only accomplishes His purposes *through* His children, He accomplishes His purposes *in* His children as He conforms us more and more to the image of Christ. Part of God's wisdom was to make Hannah stronger in faith and fellowship with Him and thus better in the end. (God could have told us the exact time of the Second Coming of Christ, but He did not, in order that each generation would be preparing in their hearts for His imminent return.)

As those who possess the entire record of Scripture, we are able to look at the whole of Hannah's trial of faith and see that God did indeed work all things together for His glory and her good. In the end Hannah was bettered by the path that God chose which she would not have chosen for herself.

 ## SARAH'S CHOICE

If Sarah had been given the choice of having a son in the first year of her marriage, she probably would have chosen that path. After all, who would choose to be barren and wait until they were ninety to have the promised son? But if Sarah had her way, she would have marred God's greater purpose. Indeed, she did try to abort God's greater purpose by her lack of faith and Ishmael was the result. However, when God made her to laugh in faith with her Isaac, God received greater glory and Sarah was bettered.

 ## JOB'S PATH OF SUFFERING

I do not believe that Job would have chosen the path of suffering with the full knowledge of what he was about to endure. God chose Job to go through a trial of faith without explaining to Job the *why* of his sufferings. In the end, God was glorified, Christ was revealed, Job was bettered, and millions of believers were blessed throughout history. Let us consider Job for a moment and see how he was more than doubly blessed, he was bettered in his understanding of God.

There was no man as blameless and upright as Job. Like Abraham, he had both imputed righteousness by faith alone and he had practical righteousness in good works, which proved his faith. How could Job possibly be better? God allowed Satan to batter Job like no man in scripture. And through his great trial of faith, he was drawn closer to God.

> *There was a man in the land of Uz, whose name was Job; and that man was blameless and upright, and one who feared God and shunned evil. And seven sons and three daughters were born to him. Also, his possessions were seven thousand sheep, three thousand camels, five hundred yoke of oxen, five hundred female donkeys, and a very large household, so that this man was the greatest of all the people of the East.... Then the LORD said to Satan, "Have you considered My servant Job, that there is none like him on the earth, a blameless and upright man, one who fears God and shuns evil?" So Satan answered the LORD and said, "Does Job fear God for nothing? Have You not made a hedge around him, around his household, and around all that he has on every side? You have blessed the work of his hands, and his possessions have increased in the land. But now, stretch out Your hand and touch all that he has, and he will surely curse You to Your face!" (Job 1:1-3, 8-11).*

Satan began his attack against Job by destroying all his children and possessions. But Job's response was to remain faithful and continue trusting God.

> *Then the LORD said to Satan, "Have you considered My servant Job, that there is none like him on the earth, a blameless and upright man, one who fears God and shuns evil? And still he holds fast to his integrity, although you incited Me against him, to destroy him without*

cause." So Satan answered the LORD *and said, "Skin for skin! Yes, all that a man has he will give for his life. But stretch out Your hand now, and touch his bone and his flesh, and he will surely curse You to Your face. And the* LORD *said to Satan, "Behold, he is in your hand, but spare his life"* (Job 2:3-6).

Satan's second attack included an attack on Job's body that resulted in great suffering. After that, his friends, who accused him of hiding secret sin in his life, misunderstood him. Finally, Satan attacked the very character of God. After patiently enduring all of this suffering, Job began to question God. It was at that point that God Himself spoke clearly to Job. Through a series of questions, He reproved Job. Job saw the depths of his sin – that he was a greater sinner than he imagined. But he also saw the greatness of God – that He was wiser and greater than he had ever perceived. Job had spoken without knowledge and he repented before God. *I have heard of You by the hearing of the ear, But now my eye sees You. Therefore I abhor myself, and repent in dust and ashes* (Job 42:5-6).

Do you think it was worth what Job went through to come to know God in a much deeper way and in the process discover some of his own hidden self-righteousness? Elihu counseled Job to see himself from God's perspective, *Teach me what I do not see; if I have done iniquity, I will do no more'* (Job 34:32).

After his trials, God restored all that Job lost twofold – and in that way he was bettered. However, the greater way in which he was better was that he knew more of God. Job walked with God with a greater knowledge of Him and in greater humility for another 140 years.

> *And the* LORD *restored Job's losses when he prayed for his friends. Indeed the* LORD *gave Job twice as much as he had before.... Now the* LORD *blessed the latter days of Job more than his beginning; for he had fourteen thousand sheep, six thousand camels, one thousand yoke of oxen, and one thousand female donkeys. He also had seven sons and three daughters.... After this Job lived one hundred and forty years, and saw his children and grandchildren for four generations. So Job died, old and full of days* (Job 42:10, 12, 16).

Notice God blessed Job more in his latter days than he did earlier. You may feel comfortable in how God has blessed you, your family, your ministry, and your church. But what if God wanted to bless you even more? What if God wanted you to be even more fruitful? What if God wanted you to tap into the unlimited resources of heaven? Would you be willing for God to take you through a trial for a season in order to bless you in an even greater way? James tells us to remember the end of the Lord: *My brethren, take the prophets, who spoke in the name of the Lord, as an example of suffering and patience. Indeed we count them blessed who endure. You have heard of the perseverance of Job and seen the end intended by the Lord — that the Lord is very compassionate and merciful* (James 5:10-11).

- How do you view the trials you go through? Do you see them from an earthly or a heavenly perspective?

- In what ways do you feel that the trials you have gone through have strengthened you, made you more fruitful, and given you greater fulfillment?

- Have you considered that other Christians can be going through a testing period and you may not understand the deeper work that God is doing?

 ## How I Learned to Not Trust What The Doctor Said

I was diagnosed with shingles as a young boy. My mother told me the doctor would make me better. My biggest worry was that the doctor would give me a shot. I made my mother promise that the doctor would not do that. My godly mother did something that was unlike her – she lied to me. When we arrived at the doctor's office, I asked the receptionist *"Is the doctor going to give me a shot?"* She played along with my mother's conspiracy and told me no. When we were taken into the doctor's office, I asked the nurse the same question and she also told me no. When the doctor entered the room, I asked the one who was supposed to make me better, *"Are you going to give me a shot?"* He also lied to me as he left the room and said no. With this fourfold confirmation, I believed I would be made better without a shot. Then the doctor walked back into the room – holding a very big needle.

All the people that I should have been able to trust had conspired to deceive me into getting a shot. Catching them off guard, I jumped off the table, dodged the doctor and nurse and raced down the hall to the reception room. I'm sure it must have been a comical sight for those in the waiting room to see a young boy escaping the doctor's office with the doctor, nurse, and my mom in hot pursuit. I started running down the busy street until the doctor finally caught up to me and brought me back to his office.

Despite my best efforts to escape, he still gave me a shot that day – and for many days thereafter. My motivation for getting the rest of the series of shots came from another lie told by one of my older sisters. She said, *"You see all those scabs going around your chest and back. If they completely encircle your chest, you are going to die."* That lie filled me with worry. I often looked in the mirror to see how far the sores had gotten. I submitted to the doctor's shots so I wouldn't die. Eventually I got better … the doctor knew what I needed and treated me with the right prescription.

God made Hannah better through her trial of faith, and He never gave her a reason not to trust Him. God made Job better and He never lied to Job. The things that God has designed to strengthen us, make us fruitful, and bring us to fulfillment are often like the doctor's shot. It may cause a brief period of painful questioning, deafening silence, refining fire, and pruning, but if God is the one holding the needle, we do not need to run from the process. God will make us better through the trials He allows us to endure. Peter understood that trials have a redeeming purpose in our lives. He wrote to a group of Christians undergoing intense persecution. I'm sure they were questioning God and asking *"why?"* He told them to look at the bigger picture of what God is doing: *In this you greatly rejoice, though now for a little while, if need be, you have been grieved by various trials, that the genuineness of your faith, being much more precious than gold that perishes, though it is tested by fire, may be found to praise, honor, and glory at the revelation of Jesus Christ* (1 Peter1:7).

Neither Hannah nor Job knew the answers as to why they suffered in silence. Neither do we. In fact, not knowing all that God has planned requires us to trust and depend on the grace of God daily. There was only One who fully knew the sufferings He was to endure – and that was Jesus. He faced the cross knowing every detail of what He would endure for the glory of God and for our salvation.

The hiding of tomorrow makes us more dependent upon God in our journey of faith today. If we are to grow into Christ-like maturity, we must allow God to choose our path and walk faithfully with Him daily. It is better for God to lead us through dark trials in order that we would become so desperate for God and true fruitfulness that we will obtain by faith alone.

I began working on this book with my editor only a few weeks ago. During that time, Connie and I have been going to doctors and hospitals almost every other day. And now as we finish this last chapter, my wife has been diagnosed with a type of cancer called large cell lymphoma. The doctors are telling her the truth, as they know it regarding how difficult it will be for her to go through the chemo treatments. But I see in her a strength that I know that God has given her. She is not running from her shots. She is running to God.

My friend, God does not have to explain to us why He has chosen to lead us down a certain path. If we love and trust Him, we are to glorify Him by just taking His hand and walking with Him into greater fellowship, faith, and fruitfulness.

Are we afraid of full surrender to God because He might bring us through a great trial of faith to make us better? That is the thinking of an immature believer who has forgotten the principle of Romans 8:28 that God does indeed work all things together for His glory and our good.

FOR BETTER OR WORSE

On their wedding day, many young couples have looked into an unknown future and made a vow of marriage for better or worse, in sickness or in health till death do they part. It was their love for one another that enabled them to make a promise to walk into their unknown future together. Unfortunately, most couples break their promises and divorce when they encounter the unforeseen trials and difficulties of life.

With God, however, we can be sure that there is no worse – only better. Even those things that temporally appear to be bad, He turns for our good as we continue to walk with faith and patience. Hannah's prayer of praise revealed that the rest of her life will be better. She had a better knowledge of God, herself, and the way of faith and fruitfulness. The long night of trials was well worth what she received in exchange. The Apostle Paul understood God's purposes in trials and suffering. Notice what he considered better. *For I consider that the sufferings of this present time are not worthy to be compared with the glory which shall be revealed in us* (Romans 8:18).

> Notice the comparison of *"this present time"* to the future tense of *"the glory to be revealed."* Too many Christians look at life from the wrong end of the telescope as they try to view their present trouble without faith and vision. Jacob cried at the supposed death of Joseph, *All these things are against me* (Genesis 42:36). Had Jacob turned the telescope around and viewed the heavens as Joseph did, he could have said, *"God is working all things together for God's glory and my good."* If we are to be bettered by the trials of life, we must have a vision of God and of the way of faith by which He has chosen to work with His children.

Hannah's prayer in 1 Samuel 2:1-10 gives us insights about how God has brought about *"the better"* in her life:

- She experienced a lifestyle of rejoicing in the Lord (2:1).
- She gained greater strength in the Lord (2:1).
- She once wept at the words of Peninnah but now she laughed in victory (2:1).
- She rejoiced in the Lord's salvation (2:1).
- She knew the holiness of God as a reality in her life (2:2).
- She knew God as the only true God (2:2).
- She discovered that God was her rock and that no storm could destroy her (2:2).
- God preserved her while stumbling in weakness while the mighty were defeated (2:4).
- She hungered for God and His will and God filled her, while her adversary, who was full of this world's blessings, now lived in hunger (2:5).
- She was once barren but now had many children. She once had little faith and now had great faith and spiritual fruit (2:5).
- She was brought to death (or the desire not to live without God's purpose fulfilled in her life) and was raised up to experience living on a new level of faith and fellowship with God (2:6).
- She no longer lived like the wicked, on the way to their grave; she lived as one on her way to heaven (2:6).
- She previously had no fruit in her womb, but now was made rich in faith; she learned to draw upon the unlimited resources of God (2:7).
- She was brought low but now was lifted up by God (2:7).
- She once sat with the beggars on the ash heaps, but now was exalted by God to sit with God's princes (2:8).
- God preserved her and her feet did not slip (2:9).

- She learned the great secret that it is not by our strength but God's strength that we find victory (2:9).
- She understood the ultimate victory of God's anointed, Jesus Christ, who will ultimately put down all of God's enemies (2:10).

TIME TO REFLECT

- Do you remember a time as a child when you did not understand that the doctor's medicine was not to hurt you but to heal you and make you better?

- Knowing that God's purpose is not to hurt us but to heal us, how would you counsel a young Christian to trust God in the midst of trials?

 ## HANNAH'S PRAYER AND JESUS' SERMON ON THE MOUNT

Hannah ends her prayer with a prophecy of the coming King and Anointed One who will finally judge the ends of the earth in righteousness – the Lord Jesus Christ Himself. *The adversaries of the LORD shall be broken in pieces; From heaven He will thunder against them. The LORD will judge the ends of the earth. "He will give strength to His king, And exalt the horn of His anointed"* (1 Samuel 2:10).

Peter gives us insight that those who prophesied in the Old Testament were empowered to do so by the Spirit of Christ in them. *Of this salvation the prophets have inquired and searched carefully, who prophesied of the grace that would come to you, searching what, or what manner of time, the Spirit of Christ who was in them was indicating when He testified beforehand the sufferings of Christ and the glories that would follow* (1 Peter 1:10).

We can gain much insight by comparing Hannah's prayer with Jesus' Sermon on the Mount. Notice the universal principles of God that have always been true:

- Jesus: *Blessed are the poor in spirit, for theirs is the kingdom of heaven* (Matt. 5:3).

  Hannah: *The LORD makes poor and makes rich; He brings low and lifts up* (1 Sam. 2:7).

- Jesus: *Blessed are those who mourn, for they shall be comforted* (Matt.1:4).

  Hannah: *My heart rejoices in the LORD; my horn is exalted in the LORD. I smile at my enemies, because I rejoice in Your salvation* (1 Sam. 2:1).

- Jesus: *Blessed are the meek, for they shall inherit the earth* (Matt. 5:5).

   Hannah: *He raises the poor from the dust and lifts the beggar from the ash heap, to set them among princes and make them inherit the throne of glory* (1 Sam. 2:8).

- Jesus: *Blessed are those who hunger and thirst for righteousness, for they shall be filled* (Matt. 5:6).

   Hannah: *Those who were full have hired themselves out for bread, and the hungry have ceased to hunger* (1 Sam. 2:5).

- Jesus: *Blessed are the pure in heart, for they shall see God* (Matt. 5:8).

   Hannah: *No one is holy like the LORD, for there is none besides You, nor is there any rock like our God* (1 Sam. 2:2).

- Jesus said, *Blessed are those who are persecuted for righteousness' sake, for theirs is the kingdom of heaven* (Matt. 5:10).

   Hannah was indeed persecuted by Peninnah but God gave her grace to endure and to become even stronger. She said, *He will guard the feet of His saints, but the wicked shall be silent in darkness* (1 Sam. 1:8).

🌿 LIVING PARADOXICALLY

The ways of God are so different from the ways of the world. As you read Jesus' words from the Sermon on the Mount, perhaps you were struck, as I have been, with how we are called to live differently.

- Would it be better to be poor in spirit or to be rich?
- Would it be better to be reviled by this world or to be praised?
- Would it be better to hunger for God or to be full of this world's pleasures?

Jesus not only spoke to us regarding the better blessings of walking by His principles but He added *woes* to those who choose this temporal kingdom over His eternal kingdom, *But woe to you who are rich, for you have received your consolation. Woe to you who are full, for you shall hunger. Woe to you who laugh now, for you shall mourn and weep* (Luke 6:24-25).

How do you know if you have learned the lessons God has for you? How do you know if you have discovered this profound walk of grace that leads to strength, fruitfulness, and fulfillment? How do you know if the trials of faith have made you better? How do you know if God has made you spiritually fruitful?

The answer is both simple and deep. It is simple in that it begins with childlike faith and trust in a heavenly Father. We must learn to walk each day with Him. As the hymn writer said, *Trust and obey, for there is no other way to be happy in Jesus than to trust and obey.* It's that simple. And yet it is profoundly deep. We must learn that we cannot walk in our own natural strength. We must depend on God's supernatural strength and know the power of the Holy Spirit working in our lives. This takes time … year after year of walking with Jesus. We must learn the hard lessons of faith and come to the conclusion that life is not all about us, or what happens to us but it is about God, His glory and His kingdom. We have been called to build God's kingdom and change our world.

When I first seriously read through the Sermon on the Mount as a college student, it scared me. Surely the Lord did not intend for me to live this way. How is it even possible? Who walks like this? It was only natural to deal with people on the basis of what was fair and just. How could I go the extra mile or turn the other cheek to those who take advantage of me? Jesus truly talks about countercultural living:

> *But love your enemies, do good, and lend, hoping for nothing in return; and your reward will be great, and you will be sons of the Most High. For He is kind to the unthankful and evil. Therefore be merciful, just as your Father also is merciful. "Judge not, and you shall not be judged. Condemn not, and you shall not be condemned. Forgive, and you will be forgiven. Give, and it will be given to you: good measure, pressed down, shaken together, and running over will be put into your bosom. For with the same measure that you use, it will be measured back to you"* (Luke 6:35-38).

Are you ready to step out in faith and live as Jesus would have you live? It requires a supernatural dependence upon Him!

APPLICATION QUESTIONS

- How do you know if trials have made you better?

- Have you ever felt like the Sermon on the Mount was too high a standard for a Christian to live by?

- Could you live by the principles the Sermon on the Mount if Christ lived His life through you?

- Have you experienced the difference between dealing with people in your natural strength in contrast to walking in supernatural grace?

THE PARADOX OF BETTER

How we view life will determine how we value life. When I was around four years old I walked to our little farming town of Ida, Louisiana with my dad. [75] There was always a group of old timers who just sat outside of the general store and talked. One of the men loved to ask me my name. I learned that if I would add just one title to my name, he would give me a nickel. *"What's your name, son?"* Then I would parrot his desired response, *"My name is President Truman."* The men would laugh and I would take my nickel into the general store to buy a candy bar. I loved the special attention I got because of my name. Then one day expecting to cash in on having the same name as the President, he held out both hands to me and asked me to choose which coin I wanted. In one hand was a nickel and in the other was a dime. I did not hesitate to make my obvious choice. Anyone with a lick of sense knew that the nickel was the bigger coin and therefore of more value. With my distorted sense of value I chose the nickel. I knew I had done something wrong when the old timers got a great laugh at my expense. My dad also laughed but then used the experience to teach me the value of money.

I have found that I am not alone in the family of God when it comes to making poor choices. I see young Christians and carnal Christians choosing the shiny nickels that this world holds out to them. It may be a bigger house, fancier car or a new boat. It may be a second job to make more money to buy more things. Their choices often result in less time for family and serving in ministry. But the shiny nickel looks so appealing!

What will make you better? Some think it is a life with fewer problems and more leisure time. Some think it would be a long and healthy life. Some would choose wealth and influence. God gave Solomon an opportunity to choose from His hand. Solomon did not choose wealth, honor, power over his enemies, or a long life. Solomon made the right choice. He asked God for wisdom to do His will in order to lead God's people.

> *On that night God appeared to Solomon, and said to him, "Ask! What shall I give you?" And Solomon said to God: "You have shown great mercy to David my father, and have made me king in his place. Now, O Lord God, let Your promise to David my father be established, for You have made me king over a people like the dust of the earth in multitude.* **Now give me wisdom and knowledge,** *that I may go out and come in before this people; for who can judge this great people of Yours?" Then God said to Solomon: "Because this was in your heart, and you have not asked riches or wealth or honor or the life of your enemies, nor have you asked long life—but have asked wisdom and knowledge for yourself, that you may judge My people over whom I have made you king – wisdom and knowledge are granted to you; and I will give you riches and wealth and honor, such as none of the kings have had who were before you, nor shall any after you have the like"* (2 Chronicles 7:7-12; emphasis mine).

---

75   From this little town of about 500, God raised up a great evangelist and founder of Mid America Seminary, Dr. Grey Allison. Thirty four years later my second son, Jeremy, came to Christ when Dr. Allison preached in our church.

Solomon became the wisest man on earth. He recorded his wise thoughts in two books we now know as Proverbs and Ecclesiastes. Consider the contrast between man's worldview and God's eternal view of **better** (emphasis mine):

- Wisdom is better than gold and silver.

  *How much **better** to get wisdom than gold! And to get understanding is to be chosen rather than silver* (Proverbs 16:16).

- Humility is better than wealth with pride.

  *Pride goes before destruction, and a haughty spirit before a fall. **Better** to be of a humble spirit with the lowly, than to divide the spoil with the proud* (Proverbs 16:32).

- Patience and self-control is better than power and great accomplishments.

  *He who is slow to anger is **better** than the mighty, and he who rules his spirit than he who takes a city.* (Proverbs 16:32).

- Poverty with honesty is better than a one who gains through dishonesty.

  ***Better** is the poor who walks in his integrity than one who is perverse in his lips, and is a fool* (Proverbs 19:1). Consider how another translation renders this verse: ***Better** a poor man who walks in his integrity than he who is crooked in his ways and rich* (New American Bible).

- A good reputation is better than expensive gifts.

  *A good name is **better** than precious ointment* (Eccl. 7:1). The New Living Translation says, *A good reputation is more valuable than costly perfume.*

- The day of one's death is better than the day of one's birth.

  And the day of death than the day of one's birth (Eccl. 7:1). This could only be understood in light of those who are redeemed from their sins and at death are with the Lord in Heaven. Paul expressed this himself, *For I am hard-pressed between the two, having a desire to depart and be with Christ, which is far **better**. Nevertheless to remain in the flesh is more needful for you* (Philippians1: 23-24).

- It is better to consider eternity at a funeral than to escape reality at a party.

  ***Better** to go to the house of mourning than to go to the house of feasting, for that is the end of all men; and the living will take it to heart* (Eccl. 7:2).

- Godly sorrow that changes our heart is better than laughter that is only a passing emotion.

*Sorrow is **better** than laughter, for by a sad countenance the heart is made **better*** (Eccl. 7:3). Most of us would rather laugh with the prosperous than weep with those who are suffering. However, sometimes it takes sorrow to make us move from our shallow temporal thinking to mediate on the eternal values of God.

- Rebuke from the wise is better than the praise of fools.

    *It is **better** to hear the rebuke of the wise than for a man to hear the song of fools* (Eccl. 7:6).

Solomon made the better choice to ask God for wisdom. However, when he was older he departed from the wisdom that is found in the Word of God and allowed many wives to turn his heart to idols. He chose gold over the Word of God. Solomon is both an example and warning to us that the better choices that we made yesterday must be made daily or we can have our hearts go after other things.

I collected coins from the time I was young until I left home to plant our first church. In those days I could buy a one-ounce American gold coin for $37.50. Uncirculated Morgan Silver Dollars were $1.89. I sold my coin collection to move to our first mission assignment in 1970. Today each of the gold coins would sell for over $1,600 and each silver dollar would sell for over $60. Had I continued to invest in gold and silver coins, I would have made a wise investment. But I found a better and much more valuable investment than gold or silver. In that first year of ministry I was able to spend hours a day in the study of Scripture and I found its wisdom and truths to be life changing and faith building. The knowledge of the Word of God was better to me than gold and silver. So whatever it takes to get us into the Word daily is better than gold.

Consider how much better the wisdom of God's Word is over gold and silver (emphasis mine).

- *More to be desired are they than **gold**, yea, than much fine gold; sweeter also than honey and the honeycomb. Moreover by them Your servant is warned, and in keeping them there is great reward* (Psalm 19:10-11).
- *It is good for me that I have been afflicted, that I may learn Your statutes. The law of Your mouth is **better** to me than thousands of **coins of gold and silver*** (Psalm 119:71, 72).
- *Happy is the man who finds wisdom, and the man who gains understanding; for her proceeds are **better** than the profits of **silver**, and her gain than fine **gold**. She is more precious than rubies, and all the things you may desire cannot compare with her. Length of days is in her right hand, in her left hand riches and honor. Her ways are ways of pleasantness, and all her paths are peace. She is a tree of life to those who take hold of her, and happy are all who retain her* (Proverbs 3:13-18).
- *I love those who love me, and those who seek me diligently will find me. Riches and honor are with me, enduring riches and righteousness. My fruit is **better** than **gold**, yes, than fine gold, and my revenue than choice **silver*** (Proverbs 8:17).

The choices are set before us, which will you choose: the gold and silver of the world ... or the riches that are found in Christ alone?

- Take a moment and honestly pray this prayer to God:

  "Lord, I do not know how my choices fit into Your eternal purpose in Christ. I cannot see into the future. I cannot understand how my choices will impact my family, my church, and my world. Lord, I just want to surrender my life completely to You and ask that I might trust You and please You in all that I do. Give me wisdom beyond my years to choose wisely. Enable me to live with an eternal perspective."

- If God came to you and granted any request, what would you ask? Why?

- Of all the above Scripture verses describing what God calls *better*, which one do you feel that you struggle with the most?

 ## LEFT TO OURSELVES, WE WOULD CHOOSE …

I am too much like a sheep to make the right choices regarding God's greater purpose for my life. If left to myself, I would make the soft and comfortable choices. God loves us too much to leave some choices in our hands. If my mother had given me the choice of going to the doctor for shots, I would have not made the best choice. She took me to get a shot, and then the doctor ran me down and forced me to take the shot.

God brought Israel out of Egypt by His power. Unfortunately, the Israelites had made many compromises during their years in Egypt – and God had to begin a process of getting Egypt out of their hearts. As a loving Father, He lead them from place to place to humble, test, and wean them from this world in order to do them good in the latter end (Deut. 8:1-4, 16). Israel was carrying the gold and garments of Egypt as spoils of victory and did not know what was best for them. *Is this not the word that we told you in Egypt, saying, 'Let us alone that we may serve the Egyptians'? For it would have been **better** for us to serve the Egyptians than that we should die in the wilderness* (Exodus 14:12). *Why has the LORD brought us to this land to fall by the sword, that our wives and children should become victims? Would it not be **better** for us to return to Egypt?" So they said to one another, "Let us select a leader and return to Egypt"* (Numbers 14:3; emphasis mine).

Each time God tested Israel, they failed. They did not learn to trust that God's way was better than their own. Finally, God gave them their own way and they missed the Promised Land and died in the wilderness, still having Egypt in them. (*Egypt* in Scripture is often referenced as a type of this world.)

So often we quench the work of the Spirit of God in our lives because we misunderstand God's intentions in our lives. One of my church members kept putting off a medical procedure because they feared the process. After finally having the surgery he said, *"If I knew that I was going to feel this good, I would have done this years ago."* It is better not to waste years in unfruitful service to

God, but to go through the process of absolute surrender early in our walk with God so that the rest of our lives can be more fruitful. Peter writes,

Therefore, since Christ suffered for us in the flesh, arm yourselves also with the same mind, for he who has suffered in the flesh has ceased from sin, **that he no longer should live the rest of his time** *in the flesh for the lusts of men, but for the will of God. For we have spent enough of our past lifetime in doing the will of the Gentiles—when we walked in lewdness, lusts, drunkenness, revelries, drinking parties, and abominable idolatries* (1 Peter 4:1-3; emphasis mine).

The sooner we release the control of life over to the Lord, the more fulfilled and fruitful we will become.

Jesus used the word *better* in a context that illustrates a drastic action to save one's life from hell. *If your hand or foot causes you to sin, cut it off and cast it from you. It is* **better** *for you to enter into life lame or maimed, rather than having two hands or two feet, to be cast into the everlasting fire* (Matthew18:8-9; emphasis mine).

Jesus is not teaching us that our hand or foot is the cause of sin. It is not what goes in a man that causes him to sin but what comes out of the heart, *for out of the heart proceed evil thoughts, murders, adulteries, fornications, thefts, false witness, blasphemies* (Matthew 15:19). Jesus is teaching that we must take the most drastic measures not to allow our choices to keep us out of heaven.

DRASTIC MEASURES

In June 2010, Jonathan Metz had been working to replace the boiler fins on his furnace when his left arm became trapped. For three days the 31-year-old struggled to free himself. However, as the hours passed, he could smell the flesh of his crushed arm beginning to rot, the telltale sign of life-threatening infection. Floating in and out consciousness, and drinking water leaked from the furnace, Metz made a decision that doctors say saved his life: he placed a makeshift tourniquet near his left shoulder and, using the tools available to him, began to cut his arm off.

He was rescued after three days in his basement when worried friends called police. Firefighters cut the furnace apart to free him. Dr. David Shario, a trauma specialist, said Metz saved his own life by amputating his arm – the dying tissue would have caused a deadly infection that would have spread throughout his body. *In this 2006 family handout photo Jonathan Metz, 31, of West Hartford, Conn., left, stands with Melissa Mowder, 30, of Kinston, N.C., while attending a wedding in New Hampshire. Metz got his arm caught Sunday, June 6, 2010 while working on his furnace boiler in his West Hartford, Conn., home. He was rescued Wednesday, a day after he used his own tools and cut through most of his left arm.* **Close**

"People wonder how someone could go to that extent and remove his own extremity. But he saved his life by removing the non-viable part of the extremity. The wound released toxins that were circulating through the body. Cutting away that dead tissue saved his life." [76]

---

76   Sources: http://www.huffingtonpost.com/2010/06/10/jonathan-metz-tried-cutti_n_608124.html; ABC News article by Russell Goldman, June 11, 2010.

As I close this chapter, let me address two groups of people. First, there are those who have yet to enter into a saving relationship with Jesus Christ. Jonathan Metz took a drastic measure to save his life. However, you cannot go to heaven by cutting off a body part. Jesus suffered and died for you that you might be saved by faith alone. However, if you have not trusted the Lord Jesus as Savior and Lord, you must make the most drastic choice in your life. You must acknowledge that you are trapped in the furnace of sin and cannot free yourself. Only Jesus can. Realizing that Jesus has already died in order that you might be forgiven of all your sins, receive Christ now as your Lord and Savior. *For when we were still without strength, in due time Christ died for the ungodly* (Romans 5:6). *For whosoever shall call upon the name of the Lord shall be saved.* (Romans 10:13). There is no better time than today to trust Him!

Now let me say a word to those of you who know Christ as Savior and Lord. You need to invite the vinedresser to cut away or prune the unfruitful areas of your life so that you might bear much fruit. His plans for you are good … to bring you to a place of strength, fruitfulness and fulfillment. Do not let the wilderness of testing discourage you from following God fully. Don't let the treasures of Egypt entice you away from the better purpose that God has for your life. It is on to the Promised Land where the giants and the fortified walls of Jericho are no obstacle for great faith in Christ and His Word. Like Joshua, we are told to be strong. Every place the soles of our feet shall walk upon has been given to us. We are to be like Caleb who refused to be part of that generation that died in the wilderness. He laid claim to a vision and a mountain that God had given him many years before. It was this kind of faith that took drastic action not to be denied that inspired the daughter of Caleb to ask for more blessings than she had first been given. By faith, greater blessings were given her. These are some of the children of faith that inspired Hannah in a generation that was dominated by the wickedness of Eli's priesthood to believe God for a new demonstration of God in Israel.

Our generation needs those who are strong. I pray that God will raise up many by first bringing us to the end of our own strength to exchange it for the strength of the Lord.

CHAPTER 18
Conclusion

WHY DIDN'T YOU LET ME BLESS YOU LIKE I WANTED TO?

It was our second year of marriage. Going to school full time left us financially challenged each month. It was exam week and I really needed to study. Connie and I had made our normal weekly visit to mom and dad's house when dad asked me to cut the hedges that bordered the house. I had never directly told dad no for any task. However, this time was different. I had cut those hedges throughout my teenage years but now I did not live at home anymore. I was under pressure with many things to do – and this request was simply too much. I needed to prepare for finals and dad wanted his hedges cut. So for the first time in my life, I said, *"Dad, I just do not have the time right now."* I could see a look of disappointment on his face. Without saying a word, he turned and went to his bedroom. My mother followed me to the car and told me my dad's greater intentions. She said that dad had seen our financial struggle and had written a check for $100 to give to me after I cut the hedges. I felt terrible that my father had intended to bless me, and rather than be a servant, I chose to exercise my rights to independence.

I wonder how many times my heavenly Father has seen my needs, already written me a check – but before He gave it to me, He asked me to put aside my priorities and seek to build His kingdom first. A similar thought would come to me nearly five years later.

I was in my third year of ministry and a friend asked me a hypothetical question, *"Truman, what if God asks you when you get to heaven, 'Why didn't you let me bless you like I wanted to?'"* That one question made an impact on my life. As I drove home that night after preaching in his church, I asked myself that question over and over. What if I lived below the full potential that God desired for my life? The reality was that I was living far below what I knew was the potential not only for my life but also for all believers. I was experiencing fruitfulness but not to the potential that I knew was possible by a consistent walk of faith and the enabling of the Holy Spirit.

Many years later I would begin to pray, *"Lord, if I am left to myself I will waste much of my life that could have been invested in the Kingdom. Lord, please do what is necessary in my life that I might fulfill your purpose for me in Christ."*

I am so thankful that just as God put the burden of heaven in Hannah's heart to be fruitful, He has placed that burden in many Christians today. Do you have such a burden? Have you come to a point that you have a *"holy discontent"* with living below the possibility and potential that is available to any Christian who will come to a point of absolute surrender?

God desires to bless each of us and to make us strong, fruitful and fulfilled. In this final chapter, let's take each of those concepts and explore them one more time.

 ## GOD'S PROMISE OF STRENGTH

Isaiah 40 is one of the great chapters of the Bible. The prophet reveals both the greatness of God's character and the magnificence of His purposes. In verses 25-31 Isaiah records God's words to the nation of Israel:

> *To whom then will you liken Me, or to whom shall I be equal?" says the Holy One. Lift up your eyes on high, and see who has created these things, who brings out their host by number; He calls them all by name, by the greatness of His might and the strength of His power; not one is missing. Why do you say, O Jacob, and speak, O Israel: "My way is hidden from the LORD, and my just claim is passed over by my God"? Have you not known? Have you not heard? The everlasting God, the LORD, the Creator of the ends of the earth, neither faints nor is weary. His understanding is unsearchable. He gives power to the weak, and to those who have no might He increases strength. Even the youths shall faint and be weary, and the young men shall utterly fall, but those who wait on the LORD shall renew their strength; they shall mount up with wings like eagles, they shall run and not be weary, they shall walk and not faint.*

From these verses I see three principles relating to God's supernatural power:

- Our God is infinitely wise and all-powerful. He does not lack in strength, nor is His power ever diminished. As Isaiah states, *The everlasting God, the LORD, the Creator of the ends of the earth, neither faints nor is weary* (v. 28).

- We can personally experience God's supernatural power. When we quit trying in our self-effort to please Him and choose to simply trust Him, He infuses us with power. The Apostle Paul understood this when he wrote; *I can do all things through Christ who strengthens me* (Philippians 4:13).

- God's supernatural power comes when I wait patiently upon God to give me strength. All of God's power is available to me, as I simply trust Him. Isaiah says we *gain new strength* (v. 31). Strength comes as we wait upon the Lord. But don't misunderstand:

this *waiting* is never passive; it is not giving up in resignation; it is always active, looking to Jesus as our hope and the source of our strength.

Do you lack strength to face the trials before you? Look to Jesus. Focus on Him. To a group of first-century believers challenged by unbelievable adversity and persecution, God said, *Therefore we also, since we are surrounded by so great a cloud of witnesses, let us lay aside every weight, and the sin which so easily ensnares us, and let us run with endurance the race that is set before us, looking unto Jesus, the author and finisher of our faith, who for the joy that was set before Him endured the cross, despising the shame, and has sat down at the right hand of the throne of God* (Hebrews 12:1-2).

 ## GOD'S PROMISE OF FRUITFULNESS

The second concept to review is that of fruitfulness. Jesus taught that those who received the seed (the Word of God) in the good soil brought forth three levels of fruitfulness: *some a hundredfold, some sixty, and some thirty* (Matthew 13:8). Jesus desires that we grow to the point that we bear fruit in abundance, *For to everyone who has, more will be given, and he will have abundance* (Matthew 5:29). It is clear from Scripture that bearing fruit is one of the evidences of salvation as Jesus said, *"By their fruits you shall know them"* (Matthew 7:20). The great chapter in the Bible on bearing fruit is John 15. Jesus mentions three levels of bearing fruit in the first eight verses.

In verse 2 Jesus talks about those branches that bear fruit. That is the first level of fruit bearing.

- Those branches in verse 2 who *bear fruit* are pruned so they may bear more fruit.
- *More fruit* is the second level of fruit bearing. Pruning back the unnecessary things in our lives makes us more fruitful for the kingdom.
- Finally in verses 5 and 8, Jesus talks about the ultimate level of fruitfulness, where branches bear *much fruit*.

Fruitfulness fulfills the greater purpose of Jesus Christ for our lives. He said in verse 16 of the same chapter, *You did not choose Me, but I chose you and appointed you that you should go and bear fruit, and that your fruit should remain, that whatever you ask the Father in My name He may give to you.* We were designed for fruitfulness. We were destined for fruitfulness.

The Apostle Peter must have been taking good notes that night in the upper room, because he picked up on the concept of fruitfulness when he wrote,

To those who have obtained like precious faith with us by the righteousness of our God and Savior Jesus Christ: Grace and peace be multiplied to you in the knowledge of God and of Jesus our Lord, as His divine power has given to us all things that pertain to life and godliness, through the knowledge of Him who called us by glory and virtue, by which have been given to us exceedingly great and precious promises, that through these you may be partakers of the divine nature, having escaped the corruption that is in the world through lust.

But also for this very reason, giving all diligence, add to your faith virtue, to virtue knowledge, to knowledge self-control, to self-control perseverance, to perseverance godliness, to godliness brotherly

kindness, and to brotherly kindness love. For if these things are yours and abound, you will be neither barren nor unfruitful in the knowledge of our Lord Jesus Christ (2 Peter 1:1-8).

Are you experiencing fruitfulness in your Christian life? Would those around you say that you are *neither barren nor unfruitful in the knowledge of our Lord Jesus Christ?* Draw close to the One who is the source of all spiritual fruit. Abide in Him. Find your strength in Him. Allow Him to live His life in and through you by the power of the Holy Spirit – and look for the fruit He produces through your life!

 ## God's Promise of Fulfillment

Our third concept is fulfillment. A friend of mine says that fulfillment is the satisfaction of a life well lived. The Apostle Paul experienced that fulfillment. The last letter he ever wrote, to his disciple Timothy, includes this self-assessment:

> *For I am already being poured out as a drink offering, and the time of my departure is at hand. I have fought the good fight, I have finished the race, I have kept the faith. Finally, there is laid up for me the crown of righteousness, which the Lord, the righteous Judge, will give to me on that Day, and not to me only but also to all who have loved His appearing* (2 Timothy 4:6-8).

Paul knew the end of his life was near. And as he looked back on his life and ministry, he did so with complete fulfillment and satisfaction. His was a life well lived.

Years ago there was a statement that famously made its way around Christian circles. It expresses exactly what Paul was talking about: *Only one life will soon be past; only what's done for Christ will last.* Paul invested his life in those things that would outlive him. He preached the Gospel. He trained men. He planted churches. He loved his fellow believers well. And at the end of his life, he had no regrets.

Perhaps you are not at that point right now. If you were to die today, perhaps there would be regrets of lost opportunities and misplaced priorities. You cannot change the past. But you can change how you live in the future. What priorities are you currently living by? What is most important to you? If you were to stand before God today, would you be able to say with Paul, *I have fought the good fight, I have finished the race, I have kept the faith?*

APPLICATION QUESTIONS

- What are the 3 most significant lessons you have learned through this study?

- In what specific areas is your faith stronger as a result of this study?

- How are you seeing increased fruitfulness in your life?

- What promises has God given you during the course of this study?

- What lies or misconceptions did you believe about God? What truths have replaced those lies or misconceptions?

FINAL WORDS

This message has been in my heart for years, but only in the last few months have I worked with an editor to condense it into book form. While working on the next to last chapter we discovered that my wife had cancer. During the process of writing the conclusion, Connie had her first chemo treatment. Then two days later, at midnight, she woke up bleeding in the bed, losing a good amount of blood from her intestines. I walked her to the car to drive her to the emergency room. Before I could get Connie in the car she collapsed on the garage floor from blood loss. I immediately called 9-1-1. Lying on the garage floor and waiting for ambulance, Connie was growing weaker. We prayed together and then she asked me a question that was very hard to answer: *"Am I dying?"* I was amazed as I looked into her eyes and saw no fear. Her question was not from panic but was peaceful and calm. I could tell that Connie was prepared to die if this was death. I answered Connie with a calm and positive answer, *"No! You are not dying."* Within a few minutes, the ambulance had her at the emergency room where they gave her the first of two units of blood. Then she was given two more units of blood over the next three days. After five days in the hospital I brought Connie home. We still are praying that God will heal her and draw us both closer to Him during this time.

Connie had faced what she thought could have been her death and was at peace with God. Her faith in that moment encouraged my faith a great deal. But I have gone over that question several times in my mind, *"Am I dying?"* I want to answer that question differently now. *"Yes, I am dying!"* I am dying. My days are numbered. I only have a few days to serve God and then my journey of faith is over and I will see Jesus face to face and spend eternity in heaven.

Knowing that I only have a limited time to impact eternity fills me with the utmost humility and zeal to serve God to the fullest. My friend let us not waste our lives but invest it in God's eternal kingdom. May we join with the many in Scripture who, like Hannah, learned the secret of fruitfulness, *"for by strength shall no man prevail."*

Read again, the words of Hannah's praise song:

> *The bows of the **mighty** men are broken,*
> *And those who <u>stumbled</u> are girded with strength.*
> *Those who were **full** have hired themselves out for bread,*
> *And the <u>hungry</u> have ceased to hunger.*
> *Even the <u>barren</u> has borne seven,*
> *And **she who has many children** has become feeble.*
> *The LORD **kills** and <u>makes alive</u>;*
> *He **brings down** to the grave and <u>brings up</u>.*
> *The LORD **makes poor** and <u>makes rich</u>;*
> *He **brings low** and <u>lifts up.</u>*
> *He <u>raises the poor</u> from the dust*
> *And <u>lifts the beggar</u> from the ash heap,*
> *To <u>set them among princes</u>*
> *And <u>make them inherit</u> the throne of glory.*
> *For the pillars of the earth are the LORD's,*
> *And He has set the world upon them.*
> *He will <u>guard the feet</u> of His saints,*
> *But the wicked shall be **silent in darkness**.*
> *For by strength no man shall prevail* (1 Samuel 2:4-9, emphasis mine).

Notice the verse: *The Lord kills and makes alive; He brings down to the grave and brings up.* I held the MRI report in my left hand that reported cancer in several lymph nodes of Connie's body. In just five weeks, I held a new MRI report that showed that the cancer was gone after only two chemotherapy treatments. I asked our cancer doctor how often he had seen such a case? He said, "Only once or twice." I then asked the doctor how he explained the quick healing. He said, "It must be your prayers and my chemo."

Connie and I both felt it was the Lord who "*brings down to the grave and brings up,*" had brought Connie up.

Seeing the First and Last Adam
E. Truman Herring

My conscience bore witness against me
A sinner yes, but still some good
Then called by God's Law to a Higher Court
At the Bar of His Holy Word I stood.

I saw myself in Adam
I saw the fig leaves that I made
Trying to cover my own sins
Not knowing the price that Jesus paid.

Then I saw myself in Cain
He was his father's son
There I substituted my own works
For the blood of God's Holy One.

I saw myself in Noah's day
Only evil filled my thoughts
I should have drowned a thousand times
For the love I refused and fought.

Then I saw myself in Esau
And a birthright I despised
Sin and a mess of pottage
Was more important than God's eternal prize.

I saw myself in Pharoah
Who hardened his heart to the Light
I too grieved God's Spirit
And chose darkness instead of Sight.

As I read another chapter
And turned the pages of God's Book
I read it, but it read me
And showed me the God that I forsook.

There I was in Aaron
Bowing before a golden calf
There I was in Korah
As the earth swallowed me in God's wrath.

In Ahab and in Jezebel
I found my common root
Their sins were just like my sins
For we bore a common fruit.

I saw myself in many faces
As I turned from page to page
I was Pilate and I was Judas
As I condemned Jesus to human rage.

I was Paul who stoned Stephen
I was the rich young ruler who turned away
I was the soldier who spat upon Jesus
I was the Pharisee who mocked Him on that day

Then I was guilty Barabbas who was pardoned
As Jesus took my rugged cross
There I saw He died my death
And there He paid my sins' final cost.

Then I was the thief on the cross beside Him
Condemned justly for my crimes
Then! I saw the Lamb of God
Dying for The Sin and sins of all times.

The Law had done its condemning work
And I saw what my sin had done
The Schoolmaster left me at the cross of Jesus
And I confessed Jesus as God's Son.

Enlightened, I turned again the pages of the mirror
Of God's own Holy Book
There Grace abounded everywhere
Then I saw Jesus everywhere I looked.

Again I saw myself in Adam
But with a covering that God had made
I, like Abel, was the other son
Who by faith was fully saved.

Again, I saw myself as Noah
Who found Grace in God's sight
Then I was like subtle Jacob
Saved but not by human might.

I walked with Abraham up the mountain
As Isaac was marked to die
Jesus was my sin offering Ram
Jehovah-Jirah did provide.

I saw Him at the burning bush
And took my shoes from off my feet
I saw Him in the Passover Lamb
Where a sinner and Holy God did meet.

I stood at Marah and complained
Its bitter waters I could not drink
And I saw Jesus as my tree cast in
And my bitter water was made sweet.

Then I saw Him in the manna
And in the Rock from which the water flowed
And I, like Moses, esteemed Him greater
Than Egypt's treasures and its gold.

Christ was there in symbols and in shadows
On every page I could read
The Ark, the Veil and the Atonement
And the Brazen Serpent lifted up for me.

At Jericho I was marked for judgment
But like Rahab saved by Grace
My proud heart broke in two
As I looked in Jesus' face.

At the temple on Atonement Day
I too laid my hands upon the goat's head
And said, "You now bear my sins"
See Jesus your Scapegoat, the Spirit said.

Everything I read pointed to the Cross
So there I watched Him die
"It is finished!" was His triumphant shout
And became my victor's cry.

Grace had made me see
I was the Prodigal who came home
The lost coin that was found
And the Harlot whose sins were gone.

I was once condemned in Adam
And in my wretched sin I pined
But now complete in Jesus Christ
His Righteousness is mine.

Thank God, no longer in Adam
For in Christ I died with Him
And raised to a new position
I am freed from the power of sin.

In Him, I am righteous and I am holy
I am blameless and undefiled
I am washed in the Blood of Jesus
Counted as God's very own child.

I am fore-known and predestined
To be conformed to His plan
Called, Redeemed and Sanctified
In the Righteousness of Christ I stand.

Now you too, look long in God's Mirror
And see the path that sinners trod
And humbly bow and say before Him
"There go I, but for the Grace of God."